Sarah Whitman, Francis Marion Crawford

A Roman Singer

Sarah Whitman, Francis Marion Crawford

A Roman Singer

ISBN/EAN: 9783744673778

Printed in Europe, USA, Canada, Australia, Japan

Cover: Foto ©Thomas Meinert / pixelio.de

More available books at **www.hansebooks.com**

A ROMAN SINGER

BY

F. MARION CRAWFORD

AUTHOR OF "MR. ISAACS," "DOCTOR CLAUDIUS," "TO LEEWARD"

BOSTON
HOUGHTON, MIFFLIN AND COMPANY
New York: 11 East Seventeenth Street
The Riverside Press, Cambridge
1884

A ROMAN SINGER.

I.

I, CORNELIO GRANDI, who tell you these things, have a story of my own, of which some of you are not ignorant. You know, for one thing, that I was not always poor, nor always a professor of philosophy, nor a scribbler of pedantic articles for a living. Many of you can remember why I was driven to sell my patrimony, the dear castello in the Sabines, with the good corn-land and the vineyards in the valley, and the olives, too. For I am not old yet; at least, Mariuccia is older, as I often tell her. These are queer times. It was not any fault of mine. But now that Nino is growing to be a famous man in the world, and people are saying good things and bad about him, and many say that he did wrong in this matter, I think it best to tell you all the whole truth and what I think of it. For Nino is just like a son to me; I brought him up from a little child, and taught him Latin, and would have made a philosopher of him. What could I do? He had so much voice that he did not know what to do with it.

His mother used to sing. What a piece of a
woman she was! She had a voice like a man's,
and when De Pretis brought his singers to the
festa once upon a time, when I was young, he heard
her far down below, as we walked on the terrace
of the palazzo, and asked me if I would not let him
educate that young tenor. And when I told him it
was one of the contadine, the wife of a tenant of
mine, he would not believe it. But I never heard
her sing after Serafino — that was her husband —
was killed at the fair in Genazzano. And one day
the fevers took her, and so she died, leaving Nino a
little baby. Then you know what happened to me,
about that time, and how I sold Castel Serveti and
came to live here in Rome. Nino was brought to
me here. One day in the autumn, a carrettiere
from Serveti, who would sometimes stop at my
door and leave me a basket of grapes in the vin-
tage, or a pitcher of fresh oil in winter, because he
never used to pay his house-rent when I was his
landlord — but he is a good fellow, Gigi — and so
he tries to make amends now; well, as I was saying, he came one day and gave me a great basket
of fine grapes, and he brought Nino with him, a little boy of scarce six years — just to show him to
me, he said.

He was an ugly little boy, with a hat of no particular shape and a dirty face. He had great black
eyes, with ink-saucers under them, *calamai*, as we
say, just as he has now. Only the eyes are bigger
now, and the circles deeper. But he is still suffi-

ciently ugly. If it were not for his figure, which is
pretty good, he could never have made a fortune
with his voice. De Pretis says he could, but I do
not believe it.

Well, I made Gigi come in with Nino, and
Mariuccia made them each a great slice of toasted
bread and spread it with oil, and gave Gigi a glass
of the Serveti wine, and little Nino had some with
water. And Mariuccia begged to have the child
left with her till Gigi went back the next day; for
she is fond of children and comes from Serveti
herself. And that is how Nino came to live with
us. That old woman has no principles of economy,
and she likes children.

"What does a little creature like that eat?"
said she. "A bit of bread, a little soup — macchè!
You will never notice it, I tell you. And the poor
thing has been living on charity. Just imagine
whether you are not quite as able to feed him as
Gigi is!" So she persuaded me. But at first I did
it to please her, for I told her our proverb, which
says there can be nothing so untidy about a house
as children and chickens. He was such a dirty
little boy, with only one shoe and a battered hat,
and he was always singing at the top of his voice
and throwing things into the well in the cortile.

Mariuccia can read a little, though I never believed it until I found her one day teaching Nino
his letters out of the Vite dei Santi. That was
probably the first time that her reading was ever of
any use to her. and the last, for I think she knows

the Lives of the Saints by heart, and she will certainly not venture to read a new book at her age.
However, Nino very soon learned to know as much
as she, and she will always be able to say that she
laid the foundation of his education. He soon
forgot to throw handfuls of mud into the well, and
Mariuccia washed him, and I bought him a pair of
shoes, and we made him look very decent. After
a time he did not even remember to pull the cat's
tail in the morning, so as to make her sing with
him, as he said. When Mariuccia went to church
she would take him with her, and he seemed very
fond of going, so that I asked him one day if he
would like to be a priest when he grew up, and
wear beautiful robes and have pretty little boys to
wait on him with censers in their hands.

"No," said the little urchin, stoutly, "I won't
be a priest." He found in his pocket a roast
chestnut Mariuccia had given him, and began to
shell it.

"Why are you always so fond of going to church,
then?" I asked.

"If I were a big man," quoth he, "but really
big, I would sing in church, like · Maestro de
Pretis."

"What would you sing, Nino?" said I, laughing.
He looked very grave and got a piece of brown
paper and folded it up. Then he began to beat
time on my knees and sang out boldly, *Cornu ejus
exaltabitur.*

It was enough to make one laugh, for he was

only seven years old, and ugly too. But Mariuccia, who was knitting in the hall-way, called out that it was just what Maestro Ercole had sung the day before at vespers, every syllable.

I have an old piano in my sitting-room. It is a masterpiece of an instrument, I can tell you; for one of the legs is gone and I propped it up with two empty boxes, and the keys are all black except those that have lost the ivory, — and those are green. It has also five pedals, disposed as a harp underneath; but none of them make any impression on the sound, except the middle one, which rings a bell. The sound-board has a crack in it somewhere, Nino says, and two of the notes are dumb since the great German maestro came home with my boy one night, and insisted on playing an accompaniment after supper. We had stewed chickens and a flask of Cesanese, I remember, and I knew something would happen to the piano. But Nino would never have any other, for De Pretis has a very good one; and Nino studies without anything — just a common tuning fork that he carries in his pocket. But the old piano was the beginning of his fame. He got into the sitting-room one day, by himself, and found out that he could make a noise by striking the keys, and then he discovered that he could make tunes, and pick out the ones that were always ringing in his head. After that he could hardly be dragged away from it, so that I sent him to school to have some quiet in the house.

He was a clever boy, and I taught him Latin and
gave him our poets to read; and as he grew up I
would have made a scholar of him, but he would
not.   At least, he was always willing to learn and
to read; but he was always singing, too.   Once I
caught him declaiming " Arma virumque cano " to
an air from the Trovatore, and knew he could
never be a scholar then, though he might know a
great deal.   Besides, he always preferred Dante to
Virgil, and Leopardi to Horace.

One day, when he was sixteen or thereabouts, he
was making a noise, as usual, shouting some motive
or other to Mariuccia and the cat, while I was
laboring to collect my senses over a lecture I had to
prepare.   Suddenly his voice cracked horribly and
his singing ended in a sort of groan.   It happened again once or twice, the next day, and then
the house was quiet.   I found him at night asleep
over the old piano, his eyes all wet with tears.

"What is the matter, Nino?" I asked.   "It is
time for youngsters like you to be in bed."

"Ah, Messer Cornelio," he said, when he was
awake, "I had better go to bed, as you say.   I shall
never sing again, for my voice is all broken to
pieces;" and he sobbed bitterly.

"The saints be praised," thought I; "I shall
make a philosopher of you yet!"

But he would not be comforted, and for several
months he went about as if he were trying to find
the moon, as we say; and though he read his books
and made progress, he was always sad and wretched,

and grew much thinner, so that Mariuccia said he was consuming himself, and I thought he must be in love. But the house was very quiet.

I thought as he did, that he would never sing again, but I never talked to him about it, lest he should try, now that he was as quiet as a nightingale with its tongue cut out. But nature meant differently, I suppose. One day De Pretis came to see me; it must have been near the new year, for he never came often at that time. It was only a friendly recollection of the days when I had a castello and a church of my own at Serveti, and used to have him come from Rome to sing at the festa, and he came every year to see me; and his head grew bald as mine grew gray, so that at last he wears a black skull cap everywhere, like a priest, and only takes it off when he sings the Gloria Patri, or at the Elevation. However, he came to see me, and Nino sat mutely by, as we smoked a little and drank the syrup of violets with water that Mariuccia brought us. It was one of her external extravagances, but somehow, though she never understood the value of economy, my professorship brought in more than enough for us, and it was not long after this that I began to buy the bit of vineyard out of Porta Sâlara, by installments from my savings. And since then, we have our own wine.

De Pretis was talking to me about a new opera that he had heard. He never sang except in church, of course, but he used to go to the theatre of an evening; so it was quite natural that he should go

to the piano and begin to sing a snatch of the tenor
air to me, explaining the situation as he went along,
between his singing.

Nino could not sit still, and went and leaned over
Sor Ercole, as we call the maestro, hanging on the
notes, not daring to try and sing, for he had lost his
voice, but making the words with his lips.

"Dio mio!" he cried at last, "how I wish I could
sing that!"

"Try it," said De Pretis, laughing and half interested by the boy's earnest look. "Try it — I
will sing it again." But Nino's face fell.

"It is no use," he said. "My voice is all broken
to pieces now, because I sang too much before."

"Perhaps it will come back," said the musician
kindly, seeing the tears in the young fellow's eyes.
"See, we will try a scale." He struck a chord.
"Now, open your mouth — so — Do-o-o-o!" He
sang a long note. Nino could not resist any longer,
whether he had any voice or not. He blushed red
and turned away, but he opened his mouth and
made a sound.

"Do-o-o-o!" He sang like the master, but much
weaker.

"Not so bad; now the next, Re-e-e!" Nino followed him. And so on, up the scale.

After a few more notes, De Pretis ceased to smile,
and cried, "Go on, go on!" after every note, authoritatively, and in quite a different manner from
his first kindly encouragement. Nino, who had not
sung for months, took courage and a long breath,

and went on as he was bid, his voice gaining volume and clearness as he sang higher. Then De Pretis stopped and looked at him earnestly.

"You are mad," he said. "You have not lost your voice at all."

- "It was quite different when I used to sing before," said the boy.

"Per Bacco, I should think so," said the maestro. "Your voice has changed. Sing something, can't you?"

Nino sang a church air he had caught somewhere. I never heard such a voice, but it gave me a queer sensation that I liked — it was so true, and young, and clear. De Pretis sat open-mouthed with astonishment and admiration. When the boy had finished, he stood looking at the maestro, blushing very scarlet, and altogether ashamed of himself. The other did not speak.

"Excuse me," said Nino, "I cannot sing. I have not sung for a long time. I know it is not worth anything." De Pretis recovered himself.

"You do not sing," said he, "because you have not learned. But you can. If you will let me teach you, I will do it for nothing."

"Me!" screamed Nino, "you teach *me!* Ah, if it were any use — if you only would!"

"Any use?" repeated De Pretis half aloud, as he bit his long black cigar half through in his excitement. "Any use? My dear boy, do you know that you have a very good voice? A remarkable voice," he continued, carried away by his admiration, "such a voice as I have never heard. You can be the first tenor of your age, if you please — in three years you will sing anything you like, and go to London and Paris, and be a great man. Leave it to me."

I protested that it was all nonsense, that Nino was meant for a scholar and not for the stage, and I was quite angry with De Pretis for putting such ideas into the boy's head. But it was of no use. You cannot argue with women and singers, and they always get their own way in the end. And whether I liked it or not, Nino began to go to Sor Ercole's house once or twice a week, and sang scales and exercises very patiently, and copied music in the evening, because he said he would not be dependent on me, since he could not follow my wishes in choosing a profession. De Pretis did not praise him much to his face after they had begun to study, but he felt sure he would succeed.

"Caro Conte," — he often calls me Count, though I am only plain Professore, now — "he has a voice like a trumpet, and the patience of all the angels. He will be a great singer."

"Well, it is not my fault," I used to answer; for what could I do?

When you see Nino now, you cannot imagine that he was ever a dirty little boy from the mountains, with one shoe, and that infamous little hat. I think he is ugly still, though you do not think so when he is singing, and he has good strong limbs and broad shoulders, and carries himself like a soldier. Besides, he is always very well dressed, though he has no affectations. He does not wear his hair plastered into a love lock on his forehead, like some of our dandies, nor is he eternally pulling a pair of monstrous white cuffs over his hands. Everything is very neat about him, and very quiet, so that you would hardly think he was an artist' after all; and he talks but little, though he can talk very well when he likes, for he has not forgotten his Dante nor his Leopardi. De Pretis says the reason he sings so well is because he has a mouth like the slit in an organ pipe, as wide as a letter-box at the post-office. But I think he has succeeded because he has great square jaws like Napoleon. People like that always succeed. My jaw is small, and my chin is pointed under my beard — but then, with the beard no one can see it. But Mariuccia knows.

Nino is a thoroughly good boy, and until a year ago he never cared for anything but his art; and now he cares for something, I think, a great deal better than art, even than art like his. But he is a singer still, and always will be, for he has an iron throat, and never was hoarse in his life. All those years when he was growing up, he never had a love-scrape, or owed money, or wasted his time in the caffè.

"Take care," Mariuccia used to say to me, "if he ever takes a fancy to some girl with blue eyes and fair hair, he will be perfectly crazy. Ah, Sor Conte, *she* had blue eyes, and her hair was like the

corn-silk.   How many years is that, Sor Conte
mio?"   Mariuccia is an old witch.

I am writing this story to tell you why Mariuccia is a witch, and why my Nino, who never so much
as looked at the beauties of the generone, as they
came with their fathers and brothers and mothers
to eat ice-cream in the Piazza Colonna, and listen
to the music of a summer's evening, — Nino, who
stared absently at the great ladies as they rolled
over the Pincio in their carriages, and was whist-
ling airs to himself for practice when he strolled
along the Corso, instead of looking out for pretty
faces, — Nino, the cold in all things save in music, why he fulfilled Mariuccia's prophecy, little by
little, and became perfectly crazy about blue eyes
and fair hair.   That is what I am going to tell
you, if you have the leisure to listen.   And you
ought to know it, because evil tongues are more
plentiful than good voices in Rome, as elsewhere,
and people are saying many spiteful things about
him, — though they clap loudly enough at the theatre when he sings.

He is like a son to me, and perhaps I am recon-
ciled, after all, to his not having become a philosopher.   He would never have been so famous as he
is now, and he really knows so much more than
Maestro De Pretis — in other ways than music —
that he is very presentable indeed.   What is blood,
nowadays?   What difference does it make to society whether Nino Cardegna, the tenor, was the
son of a vine-dresser?   Or what does the University

care for the fact that I, Cornelio Grandi, am the
last of a race as old as the Colonnas, and quite as
honorable? What does Mariuccia care? What
does anybody care? Corpo di Bacco! if we begin
talking of race we shall waste as much time as
would make us all great celebrities! I am not a
celebrity — I never shall be now, for a man must
begin at that trade young. It is a profession — being celebrated — and it has its signal advantages.
Nino will tell you so, and he has tried it. But one
must begin young, very young! I cannot begin
again.

And then, as you all know, I never began at all.
I took up life in the middle, and am trying hard to
twist a rope of which I never held the other end.
I feel sometimes as though it must be the life of
another that I have taken, leaving my own unfin-
ished, for I was never meant to be a professor.
That is the way of it; and if I am sad and inclined
to melancholy humors, it is because I miss my old
self, and he seems to have left me without even a
kindly word at parting. I was fond of my old self.
But I did not respect him much. And my present
self I respect, without fondness. Is that meta-
physics? Who knows? It is vanity in either
case, and the vanity of self-respect is perhaps a
more dangerous thing than the vanity of self-love,
though you may call it pride if you like, or give it
any other high-sounding title. But the heart of
the vain man is lighter than the heart of the proud.
Probably Nino has always had much self-respect,

but I doubt if it has made him very happy — until lately. True, he has genius, and does what he must by nature do or die, whereas I have not even talent, and I make myself do for a living what I can never do well. What does it serve, to make comparisons? I could never have been like Nino, though I believe half my pleasure of late has been in fancying how I should feel in his place, and living through his triumphs by my imagination. Nino began at the very beginning, and when all his capital was one shoe and a ragged hat, and certainly not more than a third of a shirt, he said he would be a great singer; and he is, though he is scarcely of age yet. I wish it had been something else than a singer, but since he is the first already, it was worth while. He would have been great in anything, though, for he has such a square jaw, and he looks so fierce when anything needs to be overcome. Our forefathers must have looked like that, with their broad eagle noses and iron mouths. They began at the beginning, too, and they went to the very end. I wish Nino had been a general, or a statesman, or a cardinal, or all three, like Richelieu.

But you want to hear of Nino, and you can pass on your ways, all of you, without hearing my reflections and small-talk about goodness, and success, and the like. Moreover, since I respect myself now, I must not find so much fault with my own doings, or you will say that I am in my dotage. And, truly, Nino Cardegna is a better man, for all his peasant blood, than I ever was; a better lover, and perhaps a better hater. There is his guitar, that he always leaves here, and it reminds me of him and his ways. Fourteen years he lived here with me, from child to boy and from boy to man, and now he is gone, never to live here any more. The end of it will be that I shall go and live with him, and Mariuccia will take her cat and her knitting, and her Lives of the Saints back to Serveti, to end her life in peace, where there are no professors and no singers. For Mariuccia is older than I am, and she will die before me. At all events, she will take her tongue with her, and ruin herself at her convenience without ruining me. I wonder what life would be, without Mariuccia? Would anybody darn my stockings, or save the peel of the mandarins to make cordial? I certainly would not have the mandarins, if she were gone — it is a luxury. No, I would not have them. But then, there would be no cordial, and I should have to buy new stockings every year or two. No, the mandarins cost less than the stockings — and — well, I suppose I am fond of Mariuccia.

2

II.

IT was really not so long ago — only one year. The scirocco was blowing up and down the streets, and about the corners, with its sickening blast, making us all feel like dead people, and hiding away the sun from us. It is no use trying to do anything when it blows scirocco, at least for us who are born here. But I had been persuaded to go with Nino to the house of Sor Ercole to hear my boy sing the opera he had last studied, and so I put my cloak over my shoulders, and wrapped its folds over my breast, and covered my mouth, and we went out. For it was a cold scirocco, bringing showers of tepid rain from the south, and the drops seemed to chill themselves as they fell. One moment you are in danger of being too cold, and the next minute the perspiration stands on your forehead, and you are oppressed with a moist heat. Like the prophet, when it blows a real scirocco you feel as if you were poured out like water, and all your bones were out of joint. Foreigners do not feel it until they have lived with us a few years, but Romans are like dead men when the wind is in that quarter.

I went to the maestro's house and sat for two hours listening to the singing. Nino sang very creditably, I thought, but I allow that I was not as

attentive as I might have been, for I was chilled
and uncomfortable. Nevertheless, I tried to be very
appreciative, and I complimented the boy on the
great progress he had made. When I thought of it,
it struck me that I had never heard anybody sing
like that before, but still there was something lacking; I thought it sounded a little unreal, and I said
to myself that he would get admiration, but never
any sympathy. So clear, so true, so rich it was,
but wanting a ring to it, the little thrill that goes
to the heart. He sings very differently now.

Maestro Ercole de Pretis lives in the Via Paola,
close to the Ponte Sant' Angelo, in a most decent
little house — that is, of course, on a floor of a
house, as we all do. But De Pretis is well to do,
and he has a marble door-plate, engraved in black
with his name, and two sitting-rooms. They are
not very large rooms, it is true, but in one of them
he gives his lessons, and the grand piano fills it up
entirely, so that you can only sit on the little black
horsehair sofa at the end, and it is very hard to
get past the piano on either side. Ercole is as
broad as he is long, and takes snuff when he is not
smoking. But it never hurts his voice.

It was Sunday, I remember, for he had to sing
in St. Peter's in the afternoon; and it was so near,
we walked over with him. Nino had never lost his
love for church music, though he had made up his
mind that it was a much finer thing to be a primo
tenore assoluto at the Apollo Theatre than to sing
in the Pope's choir for thirty scudi a month. We

walked along over the bridge, and through the
Borgo Nuovo, and across the Piazza Rusticucci, and
then we skirted the colonnade on the left, and entered the church by the sacristy, leaving De Pretis
there to put on his purple cassock and his white
cotta. Then we went into the Capella del Coro to
wait for the vespers.

All sorts of people go to St. Peter's on Sunday
afternoon, but they are mostly foreigners, and bring
strange little folding chairs, and arrange themselves
to listen to the music as though it were a concert.
Now and then one of the young gentlemen-in-wait-
ing from the Vatican strolls in and says his prayers,
and there is an old woman, very ragged and miserable, who has haunted the chapel of the choir for
many years, and sits with perfect unconcern, telling her beads at the foot of the great reading-desk
that stands out in the middle and is never used.
Great ladies crowd in through the gate when Rai-
mondi's hymn is to be sung, and disreputable artists make sketches surreptitiously during the benediction without the slightest pretense at any de-
votion that I can see. The lights shine out more
brightly as the day wanes, and the incense curls up
as the little boys swing the censers, and the priests
and canons chant, and the choir answers from the
organ loft; and the crowd looks on, some saying
their prayers, some pretending to, and some looking about for the friend or lover they have come to
meet.

That evening when we went over together, I

found myself pushed against a tall man with an immense gray mustache standing out across his face like the horns of a beetle. He looked down on me from time to time, and when I apologized for crowding him his face flushed a little, and he tried to bow as well as he could in the press, and said something with a German accent which seemed to be courteous. But I was separated from Nino by him. Maestro Ercole sang, and all the others, turn and turn about, and so at last it came to the benediction. The tall old foreigner stood erect and unbending, but most of the people around him kneeled. As the crowd sank down, I saw that on the other side of him sat a lady on a small folding stool, her feet crossed one over the other, and her hands folded on her knees. She was dressed entirely in black, and her fair face stood out wonderfully clear and bright against the darkness. Truly she looked more like an angel than a woman, though perhaps you will think she is not so beautiful after all, for she is so unlike our Roman ladies. She has a delicate nose, full of sentiment, and pointed a little downward for pride ; she has deep blue eyes, wide apart and dreamy, and a little shaded by brows that are quite level and even, with a straight penciling over them, that looks really as if it were painted. Her lips are very red and gentle, and her face is very white, so that the little ringlet that has escaped control looks like a gold tracery on a white marble ground.

And there she sat, with the last light from the

tall windows and the first from the great wax candles shining on her, while all around seemed dark by contrast. She looked like an angel; and quite as cold, perhaps most of you would say. Diamonds are cold things, too, but they shine in the dark; whereas a bit of glass just lets the light through it, even if it is colored red and green and put in a church window, and looks ever so much warmer than the diamond.

But though I saw her beauty and the light of her face, all in a moment, as though it had been a dream, I saw Nino too; for I had missed him, and had supposed he had gone to the organ loft with De Pretis. But now, as the people kneeled to the benediction, imagine a little what he did! he just dropped on his knees with his face to the white lady, and his back to the procession; it was really disgraceful, and if it had been lighter I am sure every one would have noticed it. At all events, there he knelt, not three feet from the lady, looking at her as if his heart would break. But I do not believe she saw him, for she never looked his way. Afterwards everybody got up again, and we hurried to get out of the chapel; but I noticed that the tall old foreigner gave his arm to the beautiful lady, and when they had pushed their way through the gate that leads into the body of the church, they did not go away, but stood aside for the crowd to pass. Nino said he would wait for De Pretis, and immediately turned his whole attention to the foreign girl, hiding himself in the shadow and never taking his eyes from her.

I never saw Nino look at a woman before as
though she interested him in the least, or I would
not have been surprised now to see him lost in admiration of the fair girl. I was close to him and
could see his face, and it had a new expression on
it that I did not know. The people were almost
gone, and the lights were being extinguished when
De Pretis came round the corner, looking for us.
But I was astonished to see him bow low to the
foreigner and the young lady, and then stop and
enter into conversation with them. They spoke
quite audibly, and it was about a lesson that the
young lady had missed. She spoke like a Roman,
but the old gentleman made himself understood in
a series of stiff phrases, which he fired out of his
mouth like discharges of musketry.

" Who are they ? " whispered Nino to me, breathless with excitement, and trembling from head to
foot. " Who are they, and how does the maestro
know them ? "

" Eh, caro mio, what am I to know ? " I answered, indifferently. " They are some foreigners,
some pupil of De Pretis, and her father. How
should I know ? "

" She is a Roman," said Nino between his teeth.
" I have heard foreigners talk. The old man is a
foreigner, but she — she is Roman," he repeated
with certainty.

" Eh," said I, " for my part she may be Chinese.
The stars will not fall on that account." You see,
I thought he had seen her before, and I wanted to

exasperate him by my indifference so that he should
tell me; but he would not, and indeed I found
out afterwards that he had really never seen her
before.

Presently the lady and gentleman went away,
and we called De Pretis, for he could not see us
in the gloom. Nino became very confidential, and
linked an arm in his as we went away.

"Who are they, caro maestro, these enchanting
people?" inquired the boy when they had gone a
few steps, and I was walking by Nino's side, and
we were all three nearing the door.

"Foreigners, — my foreigners," returned the
singer, proudly, as he took a colossal pinch of
snuff. He seemed to say that he in his profession was constantly thrown with people like that,
whereas I — oh, I, of course, was always occupied
with students and poor devils who had no voice,
nothing but brains.

"But she," objected Nino, — "she is Roman, I
am sure of it."

"Eh," said Ercole, "you know how it is. These
foreigners marry and come here and live, and their
children are born here; and they grow up and
call themselves Romans, as proudly as you please.
But they are not really Italians, any more than the
Shah of Persia." The maestro smiled a pitying
smile. He is a Roman of Rome, and his great
nose scorns pretenders. In his view Piedmontese,
Tuscans, and Neapolitans are as much foreigners as
the Germans or the English. More so, for he likes

the Germans and tolerates the English, but he can
call an enemy by no worse name than " Napole-
tano " or " Piemontese."

" Then they live here?" cried Nino in delight.

" Surely."

" In fine, maestro mio, who are they?"

" What a diavolo of a boy! Dio mio!" and
Ercole laughed under his big mustache, which is
black still. But he is bald, all the same, and wears
a skull-cap.

" Diavolo as much as you please, but I will
know," said Nino sullenly.

" Oh bene! Now do not disquiet yourself, Nino
— I will tell you all about them. She is a pupil
of mine, and I go to their house in the Corso and
give her lessons."

" And then?" asked Nino impatiently.

" Who goes slowly goes surely," said the maestro
sententiously; and he stopped to light a cigar as
black and twisted as his mustache. Then he continued, standing still in the middle of the piazza to
talk at his ease, for it had stopped raining and the
air was moist and sultry, " They are Prussians, you
must know. The old man is a colonel, retired, pen-
sioned, everything you like, wounded at Königgratz
by the Austrians. His wife was delicate, and he
brought her to live here long before he left the service, and the signorina was born here. He has told
me about it, and he taught me to pronounce the
name Königgratz, so — Conigherazzo," said the
maestro proudly, " and that is how I know."

"Capperi! What a mouthful!" said I.

"You may well say that, Sor Conte, but singing teaches us all languages. You would have found it of great use in your studies." I pictured to myself a quarter of an hour of Schopenhauer, with a piano accompaniment and some one beating time.

"But their name, their name I want to know," objected Nino, as he stepped aside and flattened himself against the pillar to let a carriage pass. As luck would have it, the old officer and his daughter were in that very cab, and Nino could just make them out by the evening twilight. He took off his hat, of course, but I am quite sure they did not see him.

"Well, their name is prettier than Conigherazzo," said Ercole. "It is Lira — Erre Gheraffe fonne Lira." (Herr Graf von Lira, I suppose he meant. And he has the impudence to assert that singing has taught him to pronounce German.) "And that means," he continued, "Il Conte di Lira, as we should say."

"Ah! what a divine appellation!" exclaimed Nino enthusiastically, pulling his hat over his eyes to meditate upon the name at his leisure.

"And her name is Edvigia," volunteered the maestro. That is the Italian for Hedwig, or Hadwig, you know. But we should shorten it and call her Gigia, just as though she were Luisa. Nino does not think it so pretty. Nino was silent. Perhaps he was already shy of repeating the familiar name of the first woman he had ever

loved. Imagine! At twenty he had never been
in love! It is incredible to me, — and one of
our own people, too, born at Serveti.

Meanwhile the maestro's cigar had gone out,
and he lit it with a blazing sulphur match, before
he continued; and we all walked on again. I remember it all very distinctly, because it was the
beginning of Nino's madness. Especially I call to
mind his expression of indifference when Ercole
began to descant upon the worldly possessions of
the Lira household. It seemed to me that if Nino
so seriously cast his eyes on the Contessina Edvigia
he might at least have looked pleased to hear she
was so rich ; or he might have looked disappointed,
if he thought that her position was an obstacle in
his way. But he did not care about it at all, and
walked straight on, humming a little tune through
his nose with his mouth shut, for he does everything to a tune.

"They are certainly gran' signori," Ercole said.
"They live on the first floor of the Palazzo Carmandola, — you know, in the Corso, — and they
have a carriage, and keep two men in livery, just
like a Roman prince. Besides, the count once sent
me a bottle of wine at Christmas. It was as weak
as water, and tasted like the solfatara of Tivoli,
but it came from his own vineyard in Germany,
and was at least fifty years old. If he has a vineyard, he has a castello, of course. And if he has a
castello, he is a gran' signore, — eh ? what do you
think, Sor Conte ? You know about such things."

"I did once, maestro mio. It is very likely."

"And as for the wine being sour, it was because it was so old. I am sure the Germans cannot make wine well. They are not used to drinking it good, or they would not drink so much when they come here." We were crossing the bridge, and nearing Ercole's house..

"Maestro," said Nino, suddenly. He had not spoken for some time, and he had finished his tune.

"Well?"

"Is not to-morrow our day for studying?"

"Diavolo! I gave you two hours to-day. Have you forgotten?"

"Ah, — it is true. But give me a lesson to-morrow, like a good maestro as you are. I will sing like an angel, if you will give me a lesson to-morrow."

"Well, if you like to come at seven in the morning, and if you promise to sing nothing but solfeggi of Bordogni for an hour, and not to strain your voice, or put too much vinegar in your salad at supper, I will think about it. Does that please you? Conte, don't let him eat too much vinegar."

"I will do all that, if I may come," said Nino, readily, though he would rather not sing at all, at most times, than sing Bordogni, De Pretis tells me.

"Meglio cosi, — so much the better. Good-night, Sor Conte. Good-night. Nino." And so he turned down the Via Paola, and Nino and I went our way. I stopped to buy a cigar at the little tobacco shop just opposite the Tordinona Theatre. They used

to be only a baiocco apiece, and I could get one at
a time. But now they are two for three baiocchi;
and so I have to get two always, because there
are no half baiocchi any more — nothing but cen-
times. That is one of the sources of my extravagance. Mariuccia says I am miserly; she was born
poor, and never had to learn the principles of economy.

"Nino mio," I said, as we went along, "you
really make me laugh."

"Which is to say" — He was humming a tune
again, and was cross because I interrupted him.

"You are in love. Do not deny it. You are
already planning how you can make the acquaintance of the foreign contessa. You are a fool. Go
home, and get Mariuccia to give you some syrup
of tamarind to cool your blood."

"Well? Now tell me, were you never in love
with any one yourself?" he asked, by way of answer; and I could see the fierce look come into his
eyes in the dark, as he said it.

"Altro, — that is why I laugh at you. When
I was your age I had been in love twenty times.
But I never fell in love at first sight — and with
a doll; really a wax doll, you know, like the Ma-
donna in the prescpio that they set up at the Ara
Cœli, at Epiphany."

"A doll!" he cried. "Who is a doll, if you
please?" We stopped at the corner of the street
to argue it out.

"Do you think she is really alive?" I asked,

laughing. Nino disdained to answer me, but he looked savagely from under the brim of his hat. " Look here," I continued, " women like that are only made to be looked at. They never love, for they have no hearts. It is lucky if they have souls, like Christians."

" I will tell you what I think," said he stoutly ; " she is an angel."

" Oh! is that all? Did you ever hear of an angel being married ? "

" You shall hear of it, Sor Cornelio, and before long. I swear to you, here, that I will marry the Contessina di Lira — if that is her name — before two years are out. Ah, you do not believe me. Very well. I have nothing more to say."

" My dear son," said I, — for he is a son to me, — " you are talking nonsense. How can anybody in your position hope to marry a great lady, who is an heiress? Is it not true that it is all stuff and nonsense ? "

" No, it is not true," cried Nino, setting his square jaw like a bit and speaking through his teeth. " I am ugly, you say; I am dark, and I have no position, or wealth, or anything of the kind. I am the son of a peasant and of a peasant's wife. I am anything you please, but I will marry her if I say I will. Do you think it is for nothing that you have taught me the language of Dante, of Petrarca, of Silvio Pellico? Do you think it is for nothing that Heaven has given me my voice? Do not the angels love music, and cannot I make

as good songs as they? Or do you think that because I am bred a singer my hand is not as strong
as a fine gentleman's — contadino as I am? I will
— I will and I will, Basta!"

I never saw him look like that before. He had
folded his arms, and he nodded his head a little at
each repetition of the word, looking at me so hard,
as we stood under the gas lamp in the street, that
I was obliged to turn my eyes away. He stared
me out of countenance — he, a peasant boy! Then
we walked on.

"And as for her being a wax doll, as you call
her," he continued, after a little time, "that is nonsense, if you want the word to be used. Truly, a
doll! And the next minute you compare her to
the Madonna! I am sure she has a heart as big as
this," and he stretched out his hands into the air.
"I can see it in her eyes. Ah, what eyes!"

I saw it was no use arguing on that tack, and I
felt quite sure that he would forget all about it,
though he looked so determined, and talked so
grandly about his will.

"Nino," I said, "I am older than you." I said
this to impress him, of course, for I am not really
so very old.

"Diamini!" he cried impertinently, "I believe
it!"

"Well, well, do not be impatient. I have seen
something in my time, and I tell you those foreign
women are not like ours, a whit. I fell in love,
once, with a northern fairy, — she was not German,

but she came from Lombardy, you see, — and that
is the reason why I lost Serveti and all the rest."

"But I have no Serveti to lose," objected Nino.

"You have a career as a musician to lose. It is
not much of a career, to be stamping about with
a lot of figuranti and scene-shifters, and screaming yourself hoarse every night." I was angry, because he laughed at my age. "But it is a career,
after all, that you have chosen for yourself. If you
get mixed up in an intrigue now, you may ruin
yourself. I hope you will."

"Grazie! And then?"

"Eh, it might not be such a bad thing, after
all. For if you could be induced to give up the
stage" —

"I — *I* give up singing?" he cried, indignantly.

"Oh, such things happen, you know. If you
were to give it up, as I was saying, you might then
possibly use your mind. A mind is a much better
thing than a throat, after all."

"Ebbene! talk as much as you please, for, of
course, you have the right, for you have brought
me up, and you have certainly opposed my singing
enough to quiet your conscience. But, dear professor, I will do all that I say, and if you will give
me a little help in this matter you will not repent
it."

"Help? Dio mio! What do you take me for?
As if I could help you, or would! I suppose you
want money to make yourself a dandy, a paino, to
go and stand at the corner of the Piazza Colonna

and ogle her as she goes by! In truth! You have fine projects."

"No," said Nino, quietly, "I do not want any money, or anything else, at present, thank you. And do not be angry, but come into the caffè and drink some lemonade; and I will invite you to it, for I have been paid for my last copying, that I sent in yesterday." He put his arm in mine, and we went in. There is no resisting Nino, when he is affectionate. But I would not let him pay for the lemonade. I paid for it myself. What extravagance!

3

III.

Now I ought to tell you that many things in this story were only told me quite lately; for at first I would not help Nino at all, thinking it was but a foolish fancy of his boy's heart and would soon pass. I have tried to gather and to order all the different incidents into one harmonious whole, so that you can follow the story; and you must not wonder that I can describe some things that I did not see, and that I know how some of the people felt; for Nino and I have talked over the whole matter very often, and the baroness came here and told me her share, though I wonder how she could talk so plainly of what must have given her so much pain. But it was very kind of her to come; and she sat over there in the old green arm-chair, by the glass case that has the artificial flowers under it, and the sugar lamb that the padre curato gave Nino when he made his first communion at Easter. However, it is not time to speak of the baroness yet, but I cannot forget her.

Nino was very amusing when he began to love the young countess, and the very first morning — the day after we had been to St. Peter's — he went out at half past six, though it was only just sunrise, for we were in October. I knew very well

that he was going for his extra lesson with De
Pretis, but I had nothing to say about it, and I
only recommended him to cover himself well, for
the scirocco had passed and it was a bright morning, with a clear tramontana wind blowing fresh
from the north. I can always tell when it is a tramontana wind, before I open my window, for Mariuccia makes such a clattering with the coffee-pot
in the kitchen, and the goldfinch in the sitting-room
sings very loud ; which he never does if it is
cloudy. Nino, then, went off to Maestro Ercole's
house for his singing, and this is what happened
there.

De Pretis knew perfectly well that Nino had
only asked for the extra lesson in order to get a
chance of talking about the Contessina di Lira, and
so, to tease him, as soon as he appeared the maestro made a great bustle about singing scales, and
insisted upon beginning at once. Moreover, he
pretended to be in a bad humor ; and that is always
pretense with him.

" Ah, my little tenor," he began ; " you want a
lesson at seven in the morning, do you ? That is
the time when all the washerwomen sing at the
fountain ! Well, you shall have a lesson, and by
the body of Bacchus it shall be a real lesson !
Now, then ! Andiamo — Do-o-o ! " and he roared
out a great note that made the room shake, and a
man who was selling cabbage in the street stopped
his hand-cart and mimicked him for five minutes.

" But I am out of breath, maestro," protested
Nino, who wanted to talk.

" Out of breath ? A singer is never out of
breath. Absurd ! What would you do if you got
out of breath, say, in the last act of Lucia, so —
Bell' alma ado— Then your breath ends, eh ?
Will you stay with the ' adored soul ' between your
teeth ? A fine singer you will make ! Andiamo !
Do-o-o ! "

Nino saw he must begin, and he set up a shout,
much against his will, so that the cabbage-vender
chimed in, making so much noise that the old
woman who lives opposite opened her window
and emptied a great dustpan full of potato peel-
ings and refuse leaves of lettuce right on his
head. And then there was a great noise. But the
maestro paid no attention, and went on with the
scale, hardly giving Nino time to breathe. Nino,
who stood behind De Pretis while he sang, saw the
copy of Bordogni's solfeggi lying on a chair, and
managed to slip it under a pile of music near by,
singing so lustily all the while that the maestro
never looked round.

When he got to the end of the scale, Ercole began hunting for the music, and as he could not find
it Nino asked him questions.

" Can she sing, — this contessina of yours, maestro ? " De Pretis was overturning everything in
his search.

" An apoplexy on those solfeggi and on the man
who made them ! " he cried. " Sing, did you say ?
Yes, a great deal better than you ever will. Why
can you not look for your music, instead of chat-

tering?" Nino began to look where he knew it
was not.

"By the bye, do you give her lessons every
day?" asked the boy.

"Every day? Am I crazy, to ruin people's voices
like that?"

"Caro maestro, what is the matter with you,
this morning? You have forgotten to say your
prayers!"

"You are a donkey, Nino; here he is, this blessed
Bordogni, — now, come."

"Sor Ercole mio," said Nino in despair, "I must
really know something about this angel, before I
sing at all." Ercole sat down on the piano stool,
and puffed up his cheeks, and heaved a tremendous
sigh, to show how utterly bored he was by his pupil. Then he took a large pinch of snuff, and
sighed again.

"What demon have you got into your head?"
he asked, at length.

"What angel, you mean," answered Nino, delighted at having forced the maestro to a parley.
"I am in love with her — crazy about her," he
cried, running his fingers through his curly hair,
"and you must help me to see her. You can easily
take me to her house to sing duets, as part of her
lesson. I tell you I have not slept a wink all night
for thinking of her, and unless I see her I shall
never sleep again as long as I live. Ah!" he cried,
putting his hands on Ercole's shoulders, "you do
not know what it is to be in love! How every-

thing one touches is fire, and the sky is like lead,
and one minute you are cold and one minute you
are hot, and you may turn and turn on your pillow all night, and never sleep, and you want to
curse everybody you see, or to embrace them, it
makes no difference — anything to express the " —

" Devil! and may he carry you off! " interrupted Ercole, laughing. But his manner changed.
" Poor fellow," he said presently, " it appears to
me you are in love."

" It appears to you, does it? 'Appears' — a
beautiful word, in faith. I can tell you it appears
to me so, too. Ah! it 'appears' to you — very
good indeed! " and Nino waxed wroth.

" I will give you some advice, Ninetto mio. Do
not fall in love with any one. It always ends badly."

" You come late with your counsel, Sor Ercole.
In truth, a very good piece of advice, when a man
is fifty, and married, and wears a skull-cap. When
I wear a skull-cap and take snuff, I will follow
your instructions." He walked up and down the
room, grinding his teeth and clapping his hands together. Ercole rose and stopped him.

" Let us talk seriously," he said.

" With all my heart; as seriously as you please."

" You have only seen this signorina once."

" Once! " cried Nino, — " as if once were not " —

" Diavolo! let me speak. You have only seen
her once. She is noble, an heiress, a great lady —
worse than all, a foreigner; as beautiful as a statue,
if you please, but twice as cold. She has a father

who knows the proprieties, a piece of iron, I tell
you, who would kill you just as he would drink a
glass of wine, with the greatest indifference, if he
suspected you lifted your eyes to his daughter."

"I do not believe your calumnies," said Nino,
still hotly. "She is not cold, and if I can see her
she will listen to me. I am sure of it."

"We will speak of that by and by. You —
what are you? Nothing but a singer, who has not
even appeared before the public, without a baiocco
in the world, or anything else but your voice. You
are not even handsome."

"What difference does that make to a woman of
heart?" retorted Nino angrily. "Let me only
speak to her" —

"A thousand devils!" exclaimed De Pretis, impatiently; "what good will you do by speaking to
her? Are you Dante, or Petrarca, or a preacher —
what are you? Do you think you can have a great
lady's hand for the asking? Do you flatter yourself that you are so eloquent that nobody can with-
stand you?"

"Yes," said Nino boldly. "If I could only speak
to her" —

"Then, in Heaven's name, go and speak to her.
Get a new hat and a pair of lavender gloves, and
walk about the Villa Borghese until you meet her,
and then throw yourself on your knees and kiss her
feet, and the dust from her shoes; and say you are
dying for her, and will she be good enough to walk
as far as Santa Maria del Popolo and be married to

you! That is all; you see it is nothing you ask — a
mere politeness on her part — oh, nothing, nothing."
And De Pretis rubbed his hands and smiled, and
seeing that Nino did not answer, he blew his nose
with his great blue cotton handkerchief.

"You have no heart at all, maestro," said Nino
at last. "Let us sing."

They worked hard at Bordogni for half an hour,
and Nino did not open his mouth except to produce
the notes. But as his blood was up from the pre-
ceding interview he took great pains, and Ercole,
who makes him sing all the solfeggi he can from
a sense of duty, himself wearied of the ridiculous
old-fashioned runs and intervals.

"Bene," he said; "let us sing a piece now, and
then you will have done enough." He put an opera
on the piano, and Nino lifted up his voice and sang,
only too glad to give his heart passage to his lips.
Ercole screwed up his eyes with a queer smile he
has when he is pleased.

"Capperi!" he ejaculated, when Nino had done.

"What has happened?" asked the latter.

"I cannot tell you what has happened," said Ercole, "but I will tell you that you had better always
sing like that, and you will be applauded. Why
have you never sung that piece in that way before?"

"I do not know. Perhaps it is because I am unhappy."

"Very well, never dare to be happy again, if you
mean to succeed. You can make a statue shed tears
if you please." Ercole took a pinch of snuff, and

turned round to look out of the window. Nino
leaned on the piano, drumming with his fingers and
looking at the back of the maestro's head. The
first rays of the sun just fell into the room and
gilded the red brick floor.

"Then instead of buying lavender kid gloves,"
said Nino at last, his face relaxing a little, "and going to the Villa Borghese, you advise me to borrow
a guitar and sing to my statue?   Is that it?"

" Che Diana! I did not say that!" said Ercole,
still facing the window and finishing his pinch of
snuff with a certain satisfaction. "But if you want
the guitar, take it, — there it lies. I will not answer
for what you do with it." His voice sounded kindly, for he was so much pleased. Then he made Nino
sing again, a little love song of Tosti, who writes
for the heart and sings so much better without a
voice than all your stage tenors put together. And
the maestro looked long at Nino when he had done,
but he did not say anything. Nino put on his hat,
gloomily enough, and prepared to go.

"I will take the guitar, if you will lend it to me,"
he said.

"Yes, if you like, and I will give you a handkerchief to wrap it up with," said De Pretis, absently, but he did not get up from his seat. He
was watching Nino, and he seemed to be thinking.
Just as the boy was going with the instrument
under his arm, he called him back.

" Ebbene?" said Nino, with his hand on the lock
of the door.

" I will make you a song to sing to your guitar,"
said Ercole.

" You ? "

" Yes — but without music. Look here, Nino —
sit down. What a hurry you are in! I was young
myself, once upon a time."

" Once upon a time ! Fairy stories — once upon
a time there was a king, and so on." Nino was not
to be easily pacified.

" Well, perhaps it is a fairy tale, but it is in the
future. I have an idea."

" Oh, is that all? But it is perhaps the first
time. I understand."

" Listen. Have you read Dante ? "

" I know the Vita Nuova by heart, and some of
the Commedia. But how the diavolo does Dante
enter into this question ? "

" And Silvio Pellico, and a little literature ? "
continued Ercole, not heeding the comment.

" Yes, after a fashion. And you? Do you
know them ? "

" Che c'entro io ? " cried Ercole impatiently ;
" what do I want to know such things for? But I
have heard of them."

" I congratulate you," replied Nino ironically.

" Have patience. You are no longer an artist.
You are a professor of literature."

" I — a professor of literature ? What nonsense
are you talking ? "

" You are a great stupid donkey, Nino. Supposing I obtain for you an engagement to read lit-

erature with the Contessina di Lira, will you not
be a professor? If you prefer singing" — But
Nino comprehended in a flash the whole scope of the
proposal, and threw his arms round Ercole's neck
and embraced him.

"What a mind! Oh, maestro mio, I will die for
you! Command me, and I will do anything for
you; I will run errands for you, black your boots,
anything" — he cried in the ecstasy of delight that
overmastered him.

"Piano, piano," objected the maestro, disengaging himself from his pupil's embrace. "It is not
done yet. There is much, much to think of first."

Nino retreated, a little disconcerted at not finding his enthusiasm returned, but radiant still.

"Calm yourself," said Ercole, smiling. "If you
do this thing, you must act a part. You must
manage to conceal your occupation entirely. You
must look as solemn as an undertaker and be a real
professor. They will ultimately find you out, and
throw you out of the window, and dismiss me for
recommending you. But that is nothing."

"No," said Nino, "that is of no importance."
And he ran his fingers through his hair, and looked
delighted.

"You shall know all about it this evening, or
to-morrow" —

"This evening, Sor Ercole, this evening, or I
shall die. Stay, let me go to the house with you,
when you give your lesson, and wait for you at the
door."

"Pumpkin-head! I will have nothing to do with you," said De Pretis.

"Ah, I will be as quiet as you please. I will be like a lamb, and wait until this evening."

· "If you will really be quiet, I will do what you wish. Come to me this evening, about the Ave Maria — or a little earlier. Yes, come at twenty-three hours." In October that is about five o'clock, by French time.

"And I may take the guitar?" said Nino, as he rose to go.

"With all my heart. But do not spoil everything by singing to her, and betraying yourself."

So Nino thanked the maestro enthusiastically and went away, humming a tune, as he now and again struck the strings of the guitar that he carried under his arm, to be sure it was there.

Do not think that because De Pretis suddenly changed his mind, and even proposed to Nino a plan for making the acquaintance of the young countess, he is a man to veer about like a weather-cock, nor yet a bad man, willing to help a boy to do mischief. That is not at all like Ercole de Pretis. He has since told me he was much astonished at the way Nino sang the love song at his lesson; and he was instantly convinced that in order to be a great artist Nino must be in love always. Besides, the maestro is as liberal in his views of life as he is conservative in his ideas about government. Nino is everything the most strait-laced father could wish him to be, and as he was then

within a few months of making his first appearance
on the stage, De Pretis, who understands those
things, could very well foresee the success he has
had. Now De Pretis is essentially a man of the
people, and I am not; therefore he saw no objec-
tion in the way of a match between a great singer
and a noble damigella. But had I known what
was going on, I would have stopped the whole affair
at that point, for I am not so weak as Mariuccia
seems to think. I do not mean that now everything
is settled I would wish it undone. Heaven forbid!
But I would have stopped it then, for it is a most
incongruous thing, a peasant boy making love to a
countess.

Nino, however, has one great fault, and that is
his reticence. It is true, he never does anything
he would not like me, or all the world, to know.
But I would like to know, all the same. It is a
habit I have fallen into, from having to watch that
old woman, for fear she should be too extravagant.
All that time he never said anything, and I supposed he had forgotten all about the contessina, for
I did not chance to see De Pretis; and when I did,
he talked of nothing but Nino's *début* and the arrangements that were to be made. So that I knew
nothing about it, though I was pleased to see him
reading so much. He took a sudden fancy for literature, and read when he was not singing, and
even made me borrow Ambrosoli, in several volumes, from a friend. He read every word of it,
and talked very intelligently about it, too. I never
thought there was any reason.

But De Pretis thinks differently. He believes that a man may be the son of a ciociaro — a fellow who ties his legs up in rags and thongs, and lives on goats' milk in the mountains — and that if he has brains enough, or talent enough, he may marry any woman he likes without ever thinking whether she is noble or not. De Pretis must be old-fashioned, for I am sure I do not think in that way, and I know a hundred times as much as he — a hundred times.

I suppose it must have been the very day when Nino had been to De Pretis in the morning, that he had instructions to go to the house of Count von Lira on the morrow; for I remember very well that Nino acted strangely in the evening, singing and making a noise for a few minutes, and then burying himself in a book. However that may be, it was very soon afterwards that he went to the Palazzo Carmandola, dressed in his best clothes, he tells me, in order to make a favorable impression on the count. The latter had spoken to De Pretis about the lessons in literature, to which he attached great importance, and the maestro had turned the idea to account for his pupil. But Nino did not expect to see the young contessa on this first day, or at least he did not hope he would be able to speak to her. And so it turned out.

The footman, who had a red waistcoat and opened the door with authority, as if ready to close it again on the smallest provocation, did not frighten Nino at all, though he eyed him suspiciously enough, and after ascertaining his business departed to announce him to the count. Meanwhile Nino, who was very much excited at the idea of being under the same roof with the object of his adoration, sat himself down on one of the carved chests that surrounded the hall. The green baize door at the other end swung noiselessly on its hinges, closing itself behind the servant, and the boy was left alone. He might well be frightened, if not at the imposing appearance of the footman, at least at the task he had undertaken. But a boy like Nino is afraid of nothing, when he is in love, and he simply looked about him, realizing that he was without doubt in the house of a gran' signore, and from time to time brushing a particle of dust from his clothes, or trying to smooth his curly black hair, which he had caused to be clipped a little for the occasion; a very needless expense, for he looks better with his hair long.

Before many moments the servant returned, and with some condescension said that the count awaited him. Nino would rather have faced the mayor, or the king himself, than Graf von Lira, though he was not at all frightened — he was only very much excited, and he strove to calm himself, as he was ushered through the apartments to the small sitting-room, where he was expected.

Graf von Lira, as I have already told you, is a foreigner of rank, who had been a Prussian colonel, and was wounded in the war of 1866. He is very tall, very thin, and very gray, with wooden features and a huge mustache that stands out like the beaks on the colonna rostrata. His eyes are small and very far apart, and fix themselves with terrible severity when he speaks, even if he is only saying "good - morning." His nails are very long and most carefully kept, and though he is so lame that he could not move a step without the help of his stick, he is still an upright and military figure. I remember well how he looked, for he came to see me under peculiar circumstances, many months after the time of which I am now speaking; and besides, I had stood next to him for an hour in the chapel of the choir in St. Peter's.

He speaks Italian intelligibly, but with the strangest German constructions, and he rolls the letter *r* curiously in his throat. But he is an intelligent man for a soldier, though he thinks talent is a matter of education, and education a matter of drill. He is the most ceremonious man I ever saw; and Nino says he rose from his chair to meet him, and would not sit down again until Nino was seated.

"The signore is the professor of Italian literature recommended to me by Signor De Pretis?" inquired the colonel in iron tones, as he scrutinized Nino.

"Yes, Signor Conte," was the answer.

"You are a singularly young man to be a professor." Nino trembled. "And how have you the education obtained in order the obligations and not-to-be-avoided responsibilities of this worthy-of-all honor career to meet?"

"I went to school here, Signor Conte, and the Professor Grandi, in whose house I always have lived, has taught me everything else I know."

"What do you know?" inquired the count, so suddenly that Nino was taken off his guard. He did not know what to answer. The count looked very stern and pulled his mustaches. "You have not come here," he continued, seeing that Nino made no answer, "without knowing something. Evident it is, that, although a man young be, if he nothing knows, he cannot a professor be."

"You speak justly, Signor Conte," Nino answered at last, "and I do know some things. I know the Commedia of Alighieri, and Petrarca, and I have read the Gerusalemme Liberata, with Professor Grandi, and I can repeat all of the Vita Nuova by heart, and some of the"—

"For the present that is enough," said the count. "If you nothing better to do have, will you so kind be as to begin?"

"Begin?"—said Nino, not understanding.

"Yes, signore; it would unsuitable be if I my daughter to the hands of a man committed unacquainted with the matter he to teach her proposes. I desire to be satisfied that you all these things really know."

"Do I understand, Signor Conte, that you wish me to repeat to you some of the things I know by heart?"

"You have me understood," said the count severely. "I have all the books bought, of which you

4

speak. You will repeat, and I will in the book follow. Then shall we know each other much better.

Nino was not a little astonished at this mode of procedure, and wondered how far his memory would serve him in such an unexpected examination.

"It will take a long time to ascertain in this way " — he began.

" This," said the count coldly, as he opened a volume of Dante, " is the celestial play by Signor Alighieri. If you anything know, you will it repeat."

Nino resigned himself, and began repeating the first canto of the Inferno. When he had finished it he paused.

"Forwards," said the count, without any change of manner.

" More ? " inquired Nino.

" March ! " said the old gentleman in military tone, and the boy went on with the second canto.

" Apparently know you the beginning." The count opened the book at random in another place. " The thirtieth canto of Purgatory. You will now it repeat."

" Ah ! " cried Nino, " that is where Dante meets Beatrice."

" My hitherto not-by-any-means-extensive, but always from - the - conscience - undertaken, reading reaches not so far. You will it repeat. So shall we know." Nino passed his hand inside his collar as though to free his throat, and began again, losing all consciousness of his tormentor in his own enjoyment of the verse.

"When was the Signore Alighieri born?" inquired Graf von Lira, very suddenly, as though to catch him.

"May, 1265, in Florence," answered the other as quickly.

"I said when, not where. I know he was in Florence born. When *and* where died he?" The question was asked fiercely.

"Fourteenth of September, 1321, at Ravenna."

"I think really you something of Signore Alighieri know," said the count, and shut up the volume of the poet, and the dictionary of dates he had been obliged to consult to verify Nino's answers. "We will proceed."

Nino is fortunately one of those people whose faculties serve them best at their utmost need, and during the three hours — three blessed hours — that Graf von Lira kept him under his eye, asking questions and forcing him to repeat all manner of things, he acquitted himself fairly well.

"I have now myself satisfied that you something know," said the count, in his snappish military fashion, and he shut the last book, and never from that day referred in any manner to Nino's extent of knowledge, taking it for granted that he had made an exhaustive investigation. "And now," he continued, "I desire you to engage for the reading of literature with my daughter, upon the usual terms." Nino was so much pleased that he almost lost his self-control, but a moment restored his reflection.

"I am honored " — he began.

"You are not honored at all," interrupted the count coldly. "What are the usual terms?"

"Three or four francs a lesson " — suggested Nino.

"Three or four francs are not the usual terms. I have inquiries made. Five francs are the usual terms. Three times in the week, at eleven. You will on the morrow begin. Allow me to offer you some cigars." And he ended the interview.

IV.

In a sunny room overlooking the great courtyard of the Palazzo Carmandola, Nino sat down to give Hedwig von Lira her first lesson in Italian literature. He had not the remotest idea what the lesson would be like, for in spite of the tolerably wide acquaintance with the subject which he owed to my care and my efforts to make a scholar of him, he knew nothing about teaching. Nevertheless, as his pupil spoke the language fluently, though with the occasional use of words of low origin, like all foreigners who have grown up in Rome and have learned to speak from their servants, he anticipated little difficulty. He felt quite sure of being able to interpret the hard places, and he had learnt from me to know the best and finest passages in a number of authors.

But imagine the feelings of a boy of twenty, perfectly in love, without having the smallest right to be so, suddenly placed by the side of the object of his adoration, and told to teach her all he knows — with her father in the next room and the door open between! I have always thought it was a proof of Nino's determined character, that he should have got over this first lesson without accident.

Hedwig von Lira, the contessina, as we always

call her, is just Nino's age, but she seemed much younger, as the children of the North always do. I have told you what she was like to look at, and you will not wonder that I called her a statue. She looked as cold as a statue, just as I said, and so I should hardly describe her as beautiful. But then I am not a sculptor, nor do I know anything about those arts, though I can tell a good work when I see it. I do not wish to appear prejudiced, and so I will not say anything more about it. I like life in living things, and sculptors may, if it please them, adore straight noses, and level brows, and mouths that no one could possibly eat with. I do not care in the least, and if you say that I once thought differently I answer that I do not wish to change your opinion, but that I will change my own as often as I please. Moreover, if you say that the contessina did not act like a statue in the sequel, I will argue that if you put marble in the fire it will take longer to heat and longer to cool than clay; only clay is made to be put into the fire, and marble is not. Is not that a cunning answer?

The contessina is a foreigner in every way, although she was born under our sun. They have all sorts of talents, these people, but so little ingenuity in using them that they never accomplish anything. It seems to amuse them to learn to do a great many things, although they must know from the beginning that they can never excel in any one of them. I dare say the contessina plays on the piano very creditably, for even Nino says she plays well; but is it of any use to her?

Nino very soon found out that she meant to read literature very seriously, and, what is more, she meant to read it in her own way. She was as different from her father as possible in everything else, but in a despotic determination to do exactly as she liked she resembled him. Nino was glad that he was not called upon to use his own judgment, and there he sat, content to look at her, twisting his hands together below the table to concentrate his attention, and master himself; and he read just what she told him to read, expounding the words and phrases she could not understand. I dare say that with his hair well brushed, and his best coat, and his eyes on the book, he looked as proper as you please. But if the high-born young lady had returned the glances he could not refrain from bending upon her now and then, she would have seen a lover, if she could see at all.

She did not see. The haughty Prussian damsel hardly noticed the man, for she was absorbed by the professor. Her small ears were all attention, and her slender fingers made notes with a common pencil, so that Nino wondered at the contrast between the dazzling white hand and the smooth, black, varnished instrument of writing. He took no account of time that day, and was startled by the sound of the midday gun and the angry clashing of the bells. The contessina looked up suddenly and met his eyes, but it was the boy that blushed.

"Would you mind finishing the canto?" she

asked. " There are only ten lines more "— Mind!
Nino flushed with pleasure.

" Anzi — by all means," he cried. " My time is
yours, signorina."

When they had done, he rose, and his face was
sad and pale again. He hated to go, but he was
only a teacher, and at his first lesson, too. She
also rose, and waited for him to leave 'the room.
He could not hold his tongue.

"Signorina "— he stammered, and checked himself. She looked at him, to listen, but his heart
smote him when he had thus arrested her attention.
What could he say, as he stood bowing? It was
sufficiently stupid, what he said.

" I shall have the honor of returning to-morrow
— the day after to-morrow, I would say."

" Yes," said she, " I believe that is the arrangement. Good-morning, Signor Professore." The
title of professor rang strangely in his ear. Was
there the slightest tinge of irony in her voice?
Was she laughing at his boyish looks? Ugh! the
thought tingled. He bowed himself out.

That was the first lesson, and the second was
like it, I suppose, and a great many others about
which I knew nothing, for I was always occupied
in the middle of the day, and did not ask where he
went. It seemed to me that he was becoming a
great dandy, but as he never asked me for any
money from the day he learned to copy music I
never put any questions. He certainly had a new
coat before Christmas, and gloves, and very nice

boots, that made me smile when I thought of the
day when he arrived, with only one shoe — and it
had a hole in it as big as half his foot. But now
he grew to be so careful of his appearance that
Mariuccia began to call him the " signorino." De
Pretis said he was making great progress, and so I
was contented, though I always thought it was a
sacrifice for him to be a singer.

Of course, as he went three times a week to the
Palazzo Carmandola, he began to be used to the
society of the contessina. I never understood how
he succeeded in keeping up the comedy of being a
professor. A real Roman would have discovered
him in a week. But foreigners are different. If
they are satisfied, they pay their money and ask no
questions. Besides, he studied all the time, saying
that if he ever lost his voice he would turn man
of letters — which sounded so prudent that I had
nothing to say. Once, we were walking in the
Corso, and the contessina with her father passed in
the carriage. Nino raised his hat, but they did not
see him, for there is always a crowd in the Corso.

" Tell me," he cried excitedly as they went by,
" is it not true that she is beautiful?"

" A piece of marble, my son," said I, suspecting
nothing; and I turned into a tobacconist's to buy a
cigar.

One day — Nino says it was in November — the
contessina began asking him questions about the
Pantheon. It was in the middle of the lesson, and
he wondered at her stopping to talk. But you may

imagine whether he was glad or not to have an opportunity of speaking about something besides Dante.

" Yes, signorina," he answered, " Professor Grandi says it was built for public baths; but, of course, we all think it was a temple."

" Were you ever there at night ? " asked she, indifferently, and the sun ·through the window so played with her golden hair that Nino wondered how she could ever think of night at all.

" At night, signorina ? No indeed ! What should I go there at night to do, in the dark ! I was never there at night."

" I will go there at night," she said briefly.

" Ah — you would have it lit up with torches, as they do the Coliseum ? "

" No. Is there no moon in Italy, professore ? "

" The moon there is. But there is such a little hole in the top of the Rotonda " — that is our Roman name for the Pantheon — " that it would be very dark."

" Precisely," said she. " I will go there at night, and see the moon shining through the hole in the dome."

" Eh," cried Nino laughing, " you will see the moon better outside in the piazza. Why should you go inside, where you can see so little of it ? "

" I will go," replied the contessina. " The Italians have no sense of the beautiful — the mysterious." Her eyes grew dreamy as she tried to call up the picture she had never seen.

" Perhaps," said Nino, humbly. " But," he
added, suddenly brightening at the thought, " it is
very easy, if you would like to go. I will arrange
it. Will you allow me ? "

" Yes, arrange it. Let us go on with our lesson."

I would like to tell you all about it ; how Nino
saw the sacristan of the Pantheon that evening, and
ascertained from his little almanach — which has
all kinds of wonderful astrological predictions, as
well as the calendar — when it would be full moon.
And perhaps what Nino said to the sacristan, and
what the sacristan said to Nino, might be amusing.
I am very fond of these little things, and fond of
talking too. For since it is talking that distinguishes us from other animals, I do not see why I
should not make the most of it. But you who
are listening to me have seen very little of the Contessina Hedwig as yet, and unless I quickly tell you
more you will wonder how all the curious things
that happened to her could possibly have grown out
of the attempt of a little singer like Nino to make
her acquaintance. Well, Nino is a great singer
now, of course, but he was little once ; and when he
palmed himself off on the old count for an Italian
master without my knowledge, nobody had heard
of him at all.

Therefore since I must satisfy your curiosity before anything else, and not dwell too long on the
details — the dear, commonplace details — I will
simply say that Nino succeeded without difficulty
in arranging with the sacristan of the Pantheon to

allow a party of foreigners to visit the building at
the full moon, at midnight. I have no doubt he
even expended a franc with the little man, who is
very old and dirty, and keeps chickens in the vesti-
bule — but no details !

/   On the appointed night Nino, wrapped in that
old cloak of mine (which is very warm, though it
is threadbare), accompanied the party to the temple, or church, or whatever you like to call it. The
party were simply the count and his daughter, an
Austrian gentleman of their acquaintance, and the
dear baroness — that sympathetic woman who broke
so many hearts and cared not at all for the chatter
of the people. Every one has seen her, with her
slim, graceful ways, and her face that was like a
mulatto peach for darkness and fineness, and her
dark eyes and tiger-lily look. They say she lived
entirely on sweetmeats and coffee, and it is no
wonder she was so sweet and so dark. She called
me " count " — which is very foolish now, but if
I were going to fall in love I would have loved
her. I would not love a statue. As for the Austrian gentleman, it is not of any importance to describe him.

These four people Nino conducted to the little
entrance at the back of the Pantheon, and the sacristan struck a light to show them the way to the
door of the church. Then he put out his taper, and
let them do as they pleased.

Conceive if you can the darkness of Egypt, the
darkness that can be felt, impaled and stabbed

through its whole thickness by one mighty moon-beam, clear and clean and cold, from the top to the bottom. All around, in the circle of the outer black, lie the great dead in their tombs, whispering to each other of deeds that shook the world; whispering in a language all their own as yet — the language of the life to come — the language of a stillness so dread and deep that the very silence clashes against it, and makes dull, muffled beatings in ears that strain to catch the dead men's talk: the shadow of immortality falling through the shadow of death, and bursting back upon its heavenward course from the depth of the abyss; climbing again upon its silver self to the sky above, leaving behind the horror of the deep.

So in that lonely place at midnight falls the moon upon the floor, and through the mystic shaft of rays ascend and descend the souls of the dead. Hedwig stood out alone upon the white circle on the pavement beneath the dome, and looked up as though she could see the angels coming and going. And, as she looked, the heavy lace veil that covered her head fell back softly, as though a spirit wooed her and would fain look on something fairer than he, and purer. The whiteness clung to her face, and each separate wave of hair was like spun silver. And she looked steadfastly up. For a moment she stood, and the hushed air trembled about her. Then the silence caught the tremor, and quivered, and a thrill of sound hovered and spread its wings, and sailed forth from the night.

"Spirto gentil dei sogni miei" —

Ah, Signorina Edvigia, you know that voice now, but you did not know it then. How your heart stopped, and beat, and stopped again, when you first heard that man sing out his whole heartful — you in the light and he in the dark! And his soul shot out to you upon the sounds, and died fitfully, as the magic notes dashed their soft wings against the vaulted roof above you, and took new life again and throbbed heavenward in broad, passionate waves, till your breath came thick and your blood ran fiercely — ay, even your cold northern blood — in very triumph that a voice could so move you. A voice in the dark. For a full minute after it ceased you stood there, and the others, wherever they might be in the shadow, scarcely breathed.

That was how Hedwig first heard Nino sing. When at last she recovered herself enough to ask aloud the name of the singer, Nino had moved quite close to her.

"It is a relation of mine, signorina, a young fellow who is going to be an artist. I asked him as a favor to come here and sing to you to-night. I thought it might please you."

"A relation of yours!" exclaimed the contessina. And the others approached so that they all made a group in the disc of moonlight. "Just think, my dear baroness, this wonderful voice is a relation of Signor Cardegna, my excellent Italian master!" There was a little murmur of admiration; then the old count spoke.

"Signore," said he, rolling in his gutturals, "it is my duty to very much thank you. You will now, if you please, me the honor do, me to your all-the-talents-possible-possessing relation to present." Nino had foreseen the contingency, and disappeared into the dark. Presently he returned.

"I am so sorry, Signor Conte," he said. "The sacristan tells me that when my cousin had finished he hurried away, saying he was afraid of taking some ill if he remained here where it is so damp. I will tell him how much you appreciated him."

"Curious is it," remarked the count. "I heard him not going off."

"He stood in the doorway of the sacristy, by the high altar, Signor Conte."

"In that case is it different."

"I am sorry," said Nino. "The signorina was so unkind as to say, lately, that we Italians have no sense of the beautiful, the mysterious" —

"I take it back," said Hedwig gravely, still standing in the moonlight. "Your cousin has a very great power over the beautiful."

"And the mysterious," added the baroness, who had not spoken, "for his departure without showing himself has left me the impression of a sweet dream. Give me your arm, Professore Cardegna. I will not stay here any longer, now that the dream is over." Nino sprang to her side politely, though to tell the truth she did not attract him at first sight. He freed one arm from the old cloak, and reflected that she could not tell in the dark how very shabby it was.

"You give lessons to the Signorina di Lira?" she asked, leading him quickly away from the party.

"Yes — in Italian literature, signora."

"Ah — she tells me great things of you. Could you not spare me an hour or two in the week, professore?"

Here was a new complication. Nino had certainly not contemplated setting up for an Italian teacher to all the world, when he undertook to give lessons to Hedwig.

"Signora" — he began, in a protesting voice.

"You will do it to oblige me, I am sure," she said eagerly, and her slight hand just pressed upon his arm a little. Nino had found time to reflect that this lady was intimate with Hedwig, and that he might possibly gain an opportunity of seeing the girl he loved if he accepted the offer.

"Whenever it pleases you, signora," he said at length.

"Can you come to me to-morrow at eleven?" she asked.

"At twelve, if you please, signora, or half past. Eleven is the contessina's hour to-morrow."

"At half past twelve, then, to-morrow," said she, and she gave him her address, as they went out into the street. "Stop," she added, "where do you live?"

"Number twenty-seven, Santa Catarina dei Funari," he answered, wondering why she asked. The rest of the party came out, and Nino bowed to the ground, as he bid the contessina good-night.

He was glad to be free of that pressure on his arm, and he was glad to be alone, to wander through the streets under the moonlight and to think over what he had done.

"There is no risk of .my being discovered," he said to himself, confidently. "The story of the near relation was well imagined, and, besides, it is true. Am I not my own nearest relation? I certainly have no others that I know of. And this baroness — what can she want of me? She speaks Italian like a Spanish cow, and indeed she needs a professor badly enough. But why should she take a fancy for me as a teacher? Ah! those eyes! Not the baroness's. Edvigia — Edvigia di Lira — Edvigia Ca— Cardegna! Why not?" He stopped to think, and looked long at the moonbeams playing on the waters of the fountain. "Why not? But the baroness — may the diavolo fly away with her! What should I do — I indeed! with a pack of baronesses? I will go to bed and dream — not of a baroness! Macchè, never a baroness in my dreams, with eyes like a snake and who cannot speak three words properly in the only language under the sun worth speaking! Not I — I will dream of Edvigia di Lira — she is the spirit of my dreams. Spirto gentil" — and away he went, humming the air from the Favorita in the top of his head, as is his wont.

The next day the contessina could talk of nothing during her lesson but the unknown singer who had made the night so beautiful for her, and Nino flushed red under his dark skin and ran his fingers wildly through his curly hair, with pleasure. But he set his square jaw, that means so much, and explained to his pupil how hard it would be for her to hear him again. For his friend, he said, was soon to make his appearance on the stage, and of course he could not be heard singing before that. And as the young lady insisted, Nino grew silent, and remarked that the lesson was not progressing. Thereupon Hedwig blushed — the first time he had ever seen her blush — and did not approach the subject again.

After that he went to the house of the baroness, where he was evidently expected, for the servant asked his name and immediately ushered him into her presence. She was one of those lithe, dark women of good race, that are to be met with all over the world, and she has broken many hearts. But she was not like a snake at all, as Nino had thought at first. She was simply a very fine lady who did exactly what she pleased; and if she did not always act rightly, yet I think she rarely acted unkindly. After all, the buon Dio has not made us all paragons of domestic virtue. Men break their hearts for so very little, and, unless they are ruined, they melt the pieces at the next flame and join them together again like bits of sealing wax.

The baroness sat before a piano in a boudoir,

where there was not very much light. Every part
of the room was crowded with fans, ferns, palms,
Oriental carpets and cushions, books, porcelain,
majolica, and pictures. You could hardly move
without touching some ornament, and the heavy
curtains softened the sunshine, and a small open
fire of wood helped the warmth. There was also
an odor of Russian tobacco. The baroness smiled
and turned on the piano seat.

"Ah, professore! You come just in time," said
she. "I am trying to sing such a pretty song to
myself, and I cannot pronounce the words. Come
and teach me." Nino contrasted the whole air of
this luxurious retreat with the prim, soldierly order
that reigned in the count's establishment.

"Indeed, signora, I come to teach you whatever
I can. Here I am. I cannot sing, but I will stand
beside you and prompt the words."

Nino is not a shy boy at all, and he assumed the
duties required of him immediately. He stood by
her side, and she just nodded and began to sing a
little song that stood on the desk of the piano.
She did not sing out of tune, but she made wrong
notes and pronounced horribly.

"Pronounce the words for me," she repeated
every now and then.

"But pronouncing in singing is different from
speaking," he objected at last, and fairly forgetting
himself, and losing patience, he began softly to sing
the words over. Little by little, as the song pleased
him, he lost all memory of where he was, and stood

beside her singing just as he would have done to
De Pretis, from the sheet, with all the accuracy and
skill that were in him. At the end, he suddenly
remembered how foolish he was. But, after all, he
had not sung to the power of his voice, and she
might not recognize in him the singer of last night.
The baroness looked up with a light laugh.

"I have found you out," she cried, clapping her
hands. "I have found you out."

"What, signora?"

"You are the tenor of the Pantheon — that is
all. I knew it. Are you so sorry that I have
found you out?" she asked, for Nino turned very
white, and his eyes flashed at the thought of the
folly he had committed.

V.

NINO was thoroughly frightened, for he knew that discovery portended the loss of everything most dear to him. No more lessons with Hedwig, no more parties to the Pantheon — no more peace, no more anything. He wrung his fingers together and breathed hard.

"Ah, signora!" he found voice to exclaim, "I am sure you cannot believe it possible" —

"Why not, Signor Cardegna?" asked the baroness, looking up at him from under her half-closed lids with a mocking glance. "Why not? Did you not tell me where you lived? And does not the whole neighborhood know that you are no other than Giovanni Cardegna, commonly called Nino, who is to make his début in the Carnival season?"

"Dio mio!" ejaculated Nino in a hoarse voice, realizing that he was entirely found out, and that nothing could save him. He paced the room in an agony of despair, and his square face was as white as a sheet. The baroness sat watching him with a smile on her lips, amused at the tempest she had created, and pretending to know much more than she did. She thought it not impossible that Nino, who was certainly poor, might be supporting himself by teaching Italian while studying for the stage, and she inwardly admired his sense and two-fold talent, if that were really the case. But she was willing to torment him a little, seeing that she had the power.

"Signor Cardegna " — she called him in her soft voice. He turned quickly, and stood facing her, his arms crossed.

"You look like Napoleon at Waterloo, when you stand like that," she laughed. He made no answer, waiting to see what she would do with her victory. "It seems that you are sorry I have discovered you," she added presently, looking down at her hands.

"Is that all! " he said, with a bitter sneer on his pale young face.

"Then, since you are sorry, you must have a reason for concealment," she went on, as though reflecting on the situation. It was deftly done, and Nino took heart.

"Signora," he said in a trembling voice, "it is natural that a man should wish to live. I give lessons now, until I have appeared in public, to support myself."

"Ah — I begin to understand," said the baroness. In reality, she began to doubt, reflecting that if this were the whole truth Nino would be too proud — or any other Italian — to say it so plainly. She was subtle, the baroness!

"And do you suppose," he continued, "that if once the Conte di Lira had an idea that I was to be a public singer he would employ me as a teacher for his daughter? "

"No, but others might," she objected.

"But not the count,"— Nino bit his lip, fearing he had betrayed himself.

"Nor the contessina," laughed the baroness, completing the sentence. He saw at a glance what she suspected, and instead of keeping cool grew angry.

"I came here, Signora Baronessa, not to be cross-examined, but to teach you Italian. Since you do not desire to study, I will say good-morning." He took his hat, and moved proudly to the door.

"Come here," she said, not raising her voice, but still commanding. He turned, hesitated, and came back. He thought her voice was changed. She rose, and swept her silken morning-gown between the chairs and tables, till she reached a deep divan on the other side of the room. There she sat down.

"Come and sit beside me," she said kindly, and he obeyed in silence.

"Do you know what would have happened," she continued, when he was seated, "if you had left me just now? I would have gone to the Graf von Lira and told him that you were not a fit person to teach his daughter; that you are a singer, and not a professor at all; and that you have assumed this disguise for the sake of seeing his daughter." But I do not believe that she would have done it.

"That would have been a betrayal," said Nino fiercely, looking away from her. She laughed lightly.

"Is it not natural," she asked, "that I should make inquiries about my Italian teacher, before I begin lessons with him? And if I find he is not what he pretends to be, should I not warn my intimate friends?" She spoke so reasonably that he was fain to acknowledge that she was right.

"It is just," he said sullenly. "But you have been very quick to make your inquiries, as you call them."

"The time was short, since you were to come this morning."

"That is true," he answered. He moved uneasily. "And now, signora, will you be kind enough to tell me what you intend to do with me?"

"Certainly, since you are more reasonable. You see I treat you altogether as an artist, and not at all as an Italian master. A great artist may idle away a morning in a woman's boudoir; a simple teacher of languages must be more industrious."

"But I am not a great artist," said Nino, whose vanity — we all have it — began to flutter a little.

"You will be one before long, and one of the greatest. You are a boy yet, my little tenor," said she, looking at him with her dark eyes, "and I might almost be your mother. How old are you, Signor Nino?"

"I was twenty on my last birthday," he answered, blushing.

"You see! I am thirty — at least," she added, with a short laugh.

"Well, signora, what of that?" asked Nino, half amused. "I wish I were thirty myself."

"I am glad you are not," said she. "Now listen.

You are completely in my power, do you understand? Yes. And you are apparently very much in love with my young friend, the Contessina di Lira " — Nino sprang to his feet, his face white again, but with rage this time.

" Signora," he cried, " this is too much! It is insufferable! Good-morning," and he made as though he would go.

" Very well," said the baroness; " then I will go to the Graf and explain who you are. Ah — you are calm again in a moment? Sit down. Now I have discovered you, and I have a right to you, do you see? It is fortunate for you that I like you."

" You! You like me? In truth, you act as though you did! Besides, you are a stranger, Signora Baronessa, and a great lady. I never saw you till yesterday." But he resumed his seat.

" Good," said she. " Is not the Signorina Edvigia a great lady, and was there never a day when she was a stranger too? "

" I do not understand your caprices, signora. In fine, what do you want of me? "

" It is not necessary that you should understand me," answered the dark-eyed baroness. " Do you think I would hurt you — or rather your voice? "

" I do not know."

" You know very well that I would not; and as for my caprices, as you call them, do you think it is a caprice to love music? No, of course not. And who loves music loves musicians; at least," she added, with a most enchanting smile, " enough

to wish to have them near one. That is all. I
want you to come here often and sing to me. Will
you come and sing to me, my little tenor?"

Nino would not have been human had he not felt
the flattery through the sting. And I always say
that singers are the vainest kind of people.

"It is very like singing in a cage," he said, in
protest. Nevertheless, he knew he must submit;
for, however narrow his experience might be, this
woman's smile and winning grace, even when she
said the hardest things, told him that she would
have her own way. He had the sense to understand, too, that whatever her plans might be, their
object was to bring him near to herself, a reflection
which was extremely soothing to his vanity.

"If you will come and sing to me, — only to me,
of course, for I would not ask you to compromise
your début, — but if you will come and sing to me,
we shall be very good friends. Does it seem to you
such a terrible penance to sing to me in my solitude?"

"It is never a penance to sing," said Nino simply. A shade of annoyance crossed the baroness's
face.

"Provided," she said, "it entails nothing. Well,
we will not talk about the terms."

They say women sometimes fall in love with a
voice : *vox et præterea nihil*, as the poet has it. I
do not know whether that is what happened to the
baroness at first, but it has always seemed strange
to me that she should have given herself so much

trouble to secure Nino, unless she had a very strong
fancy for him. I, for my part, think that when a
lady of her condition takes such a sudden caprice
into her head, she thinks it necessary to maltreat
the poor man a little at first, just to satisfy her conscience, and to be able to say later that she did not
encourage him. I have had some experience, as
everybody is aware, and so I may speak boldly.
On the other hand, a man like Nino, when he is in
love, is absolutely blind to other women. There
is only one idea in his soul that has any life, and
every one outside that idea is only so much landscape; they are no better for him — the other women — than a museum of wax dolls.

The baroness, as you have seen, had Nino in her
power, and there was nothing for it but submission; he came and went at her bidding, and often
she would send for him when he least expected it.
He would do as she commanded, somewhat sullenly
and with a bad grace, but obediently, for all that;
she had his destiny in her hands, and could in a
moment frustrate all his hopes. But, of course, she
knew that if she betrayed him to the count, Nino
would be lost to her also, since he came to her only
in order to maintain his relations with Hedwig.

Meanwhile, the blue-eyed maiden of the North
waxed fitful. Sometimes two or three lessons
would pass in severe study. Nino, who always took
care to know the passages they were reading, so
that he might look at her instead of at his book,
had instituted an arrangement by which they sat

opposite each other at a small table. He would watch her every movement and look, and carry away a series of photographs of her, — a whole row, like the little books of Roman views they sell in the streets, strung together on a strip of paper, — and these views of her lasted with him for two whole days, until he saw her again. But sometimes he would catch a glimpse of her in the interval, driving with her father.

There were other days when Hedwig could not be induced to study, but would overwhelm Nino with questions about his wonderful cousin who sang; so that he longed with his whole soul to tell her it was he himself who had sung. She saw his reluctance to speak about it, and she blushed when she mentioned the night at the Pantheon; but for her life she could not help talking of the pleasure she had had. Her blushes seemed like the promise of spring roses to her lover, who drank of the air of her presence till that subtle ether ran like fire through his veins. He was nothing to her, he could see; but the singer of the Pantheon engrossed her thoughts and brought the hot blood to her cheek. The beam of moonlight had pierced the soft virgin darkness of her sleeping soul, and found a heart so cold and spotless that even a moon ray was warm by comparison. And the voice that sang "Spirto gentil dei sogni miei" had itself become by memory the gentle spirit of her own dreams. She is so full of imagination, this statue of Nino's, that she heard the notes echoing after

her by day and night, till she thought she must go
mad unless she could hear the reality again. As
the great solemn statue of Egyptian Memnon murmurs sweet, soft sounds to its mighty self at sunrise, a musical whisper in the desert, so the pure
white marble of Nino's living statue vibrated with
strange harmonies all the day long.

One night, as Nino walked homeward with De
Pretis, who had come to supper with us, he induced
the maestro to go out of his way at least half a
mile, to pass the Palazzo Carmandola. It was a
still night, not over-cold for December, and there
were neither stars nor moon. As they passed the
great house Nino saw a light in Hedwig's sitting-
room — the room where he gave her the lessons.
It was late, and she must be alone. On a sudden
he stopped.

"What is the matter?" asked De Pretis.

For all answer, Nino, standing in the dark street
below, lifted up his voice and sang the first notes
of the air he always associated with his beautiful
contessina. Before he had sung a dozen bars, the
window opened, and the girl's figure could be seen,
black against the light within. He went on for a
few notes, and then ceased suddenly.

"Let us go," he said in a low voice to Ercole;
and they went away, leaving the contessina listening in the stillness to the echo of their feet. A
Roman girl would not have done that; she would
have sat quietly inside, and never have shown herself. But foreigners are so impulsive!

Nino never heard the last of those few notes, any
more than the contessina, literally speaking, ever
heard the end of the song.

"Your cousin, about whom you make so much
mystery, passed under my window last night," said
the young lady the next day, with the usual display of carnation in her cheeks at the mention of
him.

"Indeed, signorina?" said Nino calmly, for he
expected the remark. "And since you have never
seen him, pray how did you know it was he?"

"How should one know?" she asked scornfully.
"There are not two such voices as his in Italy.
He sang."

"He sang?" cried Nino, with an affectation of
alarm. "I must tell the maestro not to let him
sing in the open air; he will lose his voice."

"Who is his master?" asked Hedwig, suddenly.

"I cannot remember the name just now," said
Nino, looking away. "But I will find out, if you
wish." He was afraid of putting De Pretis to any
inconvenience by saying that the young singer was
his pupil. "However," he continued, "you will
hear him sing as often as you please, after he makes
his début next month." He sighed when he thought
that it would all so soon be over. For how could
he disguise himself any longer, when he should be
singing in public every night? But Hedwig clapped
her hands.

"So soon?" she cried. "Then there will be an
end of the mystery."

" Yes," said Nino gravely, " there will be an end of the mystery."

"At least you can tell me his name, now that we shall all know it ? "

" Oh, his name — his name is Cardegna, like mine. He is my cousin, you know." And they went on with the lesson. But something of the kind occurred almost every time he came, so that he felt quite sure that, however indifferent he might be in her eyes, the singer, the Nino of whom she knew nothing, interested her deeply.

Meanwhile he was obliged to go very often to the baroness's scented boudoir, which smelled of incense and other Eastern perfumes, whenever it did not smell of cigarettes; and there he sang little songs, and submitted patiently to her demands for more and more music. She would sit by the piano and watch him as he sang, wondering whether he were handsome or ugly, with his square face and broad throat and the black circles round his eyes. He had a fascination for her, as being something utterly new to her.

One day she stood and looked over the music as he sang, almost touching him, and his hair was so curly and soft to look at that she was seized with a desire to stroke it, as Mariuccia strokes the old gray cat for hours together. The action was quite involuntary, and her fingers rested only a moment on his head.

" It is so curly," she said, half playfully, half apologetically. But Nino started as though he had been stung, and his dark face grew pale. A girl could not have seemed more hurt at a strange man's touch.

"Signora!" he cried, springing to his feet. The baroness, who is as dark as he, blushed almost red, partly because she was angry, and partly because she was ashamed.

"What a boy you are!" she said, carelessly enough, and turned away to the window, pushing back one heavy curtain with her delicate hand, as if she would look out.

"Pardon me, signora, I am not a boy," said Nino, speaking to the back of her head as he stood behind her. "It is time we understood each other better. I love like a man and I hate like a man. I love some one very much."

"Fortunate contessina!" laughed the baroness, mockingly, without turning round.

"It does not concern you, signora, to know whom I love, nor, if you know, to speak of her. I ask you a simple question. If you loved a man with your whole soul and heart, would you allow another man to stand beside you and stroke your hair, and say it was curly?" The baroness burst out laughing. "Do not laugh," he continued. "Remember that I am in your power only so long as it pleases me to submit to you. Do not abuse your advantage, or I will be capable of creating for myself situations quite as satisfactory as that of Italian master to the Signorina di Lira."

"What do you mean?" she asked, turning suddenly upon him. "I suppose you would tell me that you will make advautages for yourself which you will abuse, against me? What do you mean?"

"I do not mean that. I mean only that I may not wish to give lessons to the contessina much longer." By this time the baroness had recovered her equanimity; and as she would have been sorry to lose Nino, who was a source of infinite pleasure and amusement to her, she decided to pacify him, instead of teasing him any more.

"Is it not very foolish for us to quarrel about your curly hair?" said she. "We have been such good friends, always." It might have been three weeks, her "always."

"I think it is," answered Nino gravely. "But do not stroke my hair again, Signora Baronessa, or I shall be angry." He was quite serious, if you believe it, though he was only twenty. He forthwith sat down to the piano again and sang on. The baroness sat very silent and scarcely looked at him; but she held her hands clasped on her knee, and seemed to be thinking. After a time Nino stopped singing, and sat silent also, absently turning over the sheets of music. It was warm in the room, and the sounds from the street were muffled and far away.

"Signor Nino," said the lady at last, in a different voice, "I am married."

"Yes, signora," he replied, wondering what would come next.

"It would be very foolish of me to care for you."

6

"It would also be very wicked," he said calmly; for he is well grounded in religion. The baroness stared at him in some surprise; but seeing he was perfectly serious, she went on.

"Precisely, as you say, very wicked. That being the case, I have decided not to care for you any more — I mean, not to care for you at all. I have made up my mind to be your friend."

"I am much obliged to your ladyship," he answered, without moving a muscle. For you see, he did not believe her.

"Now tell me, then, Signor Nino, are you in earnest in what you are doing? Do you really set your heart on doing this thing?"

"What?" asked Nino, annoyed at the persistence of the woman.

"Why need you be afraid to understand me? Can you not forgive me? Can you not believe in me, that I will be your friend? I have always dreamed of being the friend of a great artist. Let me be yours, and believe me, the thing you have in your heart shall be done."

"I would like to hope so," he said. But he smiled incredulously. "I can only say that if you can accomplish what it is in my heart to do, I will go through fire and water at your bidding; and if you are not mocking me, I am very grateful for the offer. But if you please, signora, we will not speak any more of this at present. I may be a great artist, some day. Sometimes I feel sure that I shall. But now I am simply Giovanni Cardegna, teacher

of literature ; and the highest favor you can confer
on me is not to deprive me of my means of support,
by revealing to the Conte di Lira my other occupation. I may fail hopelessly at the outset of my
artistic career, and in that case I shall certainly
remain a teacher of language."

"Very well," said the baroness, in a subdued
voice ; for, in spite of her will and willfulness, this
square-faced boy of mine was more than a match
for her. "Very well, you will believe me another
day, and now I will ask you to go, for I am tired."

I cannot be interrupted by your silly questions
about the exact way in which things happened. I
must tell this story in my own way, or not at all ;
and I am sacrificing a great deal to your taste in
cutting out all the little things that I really most
enjoy telling. Whether you are astonished at the
conduct of the baroness, after a three weeks' acquaintance, or not, I care not a fig. It is just the
way it happened, and I dare say she was really
madly in love with Nino. If I had been Nino, I
should have been in love with her. But I would
like you to admire my boy's audacity, and to review
the situation, before I go on to speak of that important event in his life, his first appearance on the
boards of the opera. At the time of his début he
was still disguised as a teacher of Italian to the
young contessina. She thought him interesting
and intelligent, but that was all. Her thoughts
were entirely, though secretly, engrossed by the
mysterious singer, whom she had heard twice, but

had not seen, as far as she knew. Nino, on the
other hand, loved her to desperation, and would
have acted like a madman had he been deprived of
his privilege of speaking to her three times a week.
He loved her with the same earnest determination
to win her that he had shown for years in the study
of his art, and with all the rest of his nature besides, which is saying much — not to mention his
soul, of which he thinks a great deal more than
I do.

Besides this, the baroness had apparently fallen
in love with him, had made him her intimate, and
flattered him in a way to turn his head. Then she
seemed to have thought better of her passion, and
had promised him her friendship, — a promise
which he himself considered of no importance
whatever. As for the old Conte di Lira, he read
the German newspapers, and cared for none of
these things. De Pretis took an extra pinch of his
good snuff, when he thought that his liberal ideas
might yet be realized, and a man from the people
marry a great lady by fairly winning her. Do not,
after this, complain that I have left you in the
dark, or that you do not know how it happened.
It is as clear as water, and it was about four
months from the time Nino saw Hedwig in St. Peter's to the time when he first sang in public.

Christmas passed by, — thank Heaven, the mu-
nicipality has driven away those most detestable
pifferari, who played on their discordant bagpipes
at every corner for a fortnight, and nearly drove

me crazy, — and the Befana, as we call the Epiphany in Rome, was gone, with its gay racket, and the night fair in the Piazza Navona, and the days for Nino's first appearance drew near. I never knew anything about the business arrangements for the début, since De Pretis settled all that with Jacovacci, the impresario; but I know that there were many rehearsals, and that I was obliged to stand security to the theatrical tailor, together with De Pretis, in order that Nino might have his dress made. As for the cowl in the last act, De Pretis has a brother who is a monk, and between them they put together a very decent friar's costume; and Mariuccia had a good piece of rope, which Nino used for a girdle.

"What does it matter?" he said, with much good sense. "For if I sing well, they will not look at my monk's hood; and if I sing badly, I may be dressed like the Holy Father, and they will hiss me just the same. But in the beginning I must look like a courtier, and be dressed like one."

"I suppose so," said I; "but I wish you had taken to philosophy."

VI.

I SHALL never forget the day of Nino's first appearance. You may imagine whether we were in a state of excitement or not, after all these years of study and waiting. There was much more trouble and worry than if he had written a great book, and was just to publish it, and receive the homage of all the learning and talent in Europe; which is the kind of début I had hoped he would make in life, instead of putting on a foolish dress, and stamping about on a stage, and squalling love songs to a packed house, making pantomime with his hands, and altogether behaving like an idiot, — a crowd of people ready to hiss him at the slightest indication of weakness, or to carry him on their shoulders if they fancied his voice to their taste.

No wonder Nino was sad and depressed all day, and when he tried his voice in the afternoon thought it was less clear than usual, and stared at himself in the looking-glass, wondering whether he were not too ugly altogether, as I always told him. To tell the truth, he was not so ugly as he had been; for the months with the contessina had refined him singularly, and perhaps he had caught a certain grace of manner from the baroness. He had grown more silent, too, and seemed always preoccupied, as well he might be; but he had concealed his affair with the Lira family from me until that day, and I supposed him anxious about his appearance.

Early in the morning came De Pretis, and suggested that it would be better for Nino to take a walk and breathe the fresh air a little; so I bade him go, and I did not see him again until the afternoon. De Pretis said that the only cause for anxiety was from stage fright, and went away taking snuff and flourishing his immense cotton handkerchief. I thought a man must be a fool to work for years in order to sing, and then, when he had learned to do it quite well, to be afraid of showing what he knew. I did not think Nino would be frightened.

Of course, there was a final rehearsal at eleven, and Nino put off the hour of the lesson with the contessina to three in the afternoon, by some excuse or other. He must have felt very much pressed for time, having to give her a lesson on the very day of his coming out; and besides, he knew very well that it might be the last of his days with her, and that a great deal would depend on the way he bore himself at his trial. He sang badly, or thought he did, at the rehearsal, and grew more and more depressed and grave as the day advanced. He came out of the little stage door of the Apollo theatre at Tordinona, and his eyes fell upon the broad bills and posters announcing the first appearance of "Giovanni Cardegna, the most distinguished pupil of the Maestro Ercole De Pretis, in

Verdi's opera the Favorita." His heart sank at
the sight of his own name, and he turned towards
the Bridge of Sant' Angelo to get away from it.
He was the last to leave the theatre, and De Pretis
was with him.

At that moment he saw Hedwig von Lira sitting
in an open carriage, in front of the box office. De
Pretis bowed low; she smiled; and Nino took off
his hat, but would not go near her, escaping in the
opposite direction. He thought she looked somewhat surprised, but his only idea was to get away,
lest she should call him and put some awkward
question.

An hour and a half later he entered her sitting-
room. There she sat, as usual, with her books,
awaiting him perhaps for the last time, a fair, girl-
ish figure with gold hair, but oh, so cold! — it
makes me shiver to think of how she used to look.
Possibly there was a dreaminess about her blue
eyes that made up for her manner; but how Nino
could love her, I cannot understand. It must have
been like making love to a pillar of ice.

" I am much indebted to you for allowing me to
come at this hour, signorina," he said, as he bowed.

"Ah, professore, it looks almost as though it
were you yourself who were to make your début,"
said she, laughing and leaning back in her chair.
"Your name is on every corner in Rome, and I
saw you coming out of a side door of the theatre
this morning." Nino trembled, but reflected that
if she had suspected anything she would not have
made so light of it.

" The fact is, signorina, my cousin is so nervous that he begged me earnestly to be present at the rehearsal this morning; and as it is the great event of his life, I could not easily refuse him. I presume you are going to hear him, since I saw your carriage at the theatre."

" Yes. At the last minute, my father wanted to change our box for one nearer the stage, and so we went ourselves. The baroness — you know, the lady who went with us to the Pantheon — is going with us to-night." It was the first time Hedwig had mentioned her, and it was evident that Nino's intimacy with the baroness had been kept a secret. How long would it be so ? Mechanically he proceeded with the lesson, thinking mournfully that he should never give her another. But Hedwig was more animated than he had ever seen her, and often stopped to ask questions about the coming performance. It was evident that she was entirely absorbed with the thought of at last hearing to its fullest extent the voice that had haunted her dreams; most of all, with the anticipation of what this wonderful singer would be like. Dwelling on the echo of his singing for months had roused her interest and curiosity to such a pitch that she could hardly be quiet a moment, or think calmly of what she was to enjoy; and yet she looked so very cold and indifferent at most times. But Nino had noticed all this, and rejoiced at it; young as he was, however, he understood that the discovery she was about to make would be a shock that would certainly produce some palpable result, when she should see him from her box in the theatre. He trembled for the consequences.

The lesson was over all too soon, and Nino lingered a moment to see whether the very last drops of his cup of happiness might not still be sweet. He did not know when he should see her again, to speak with her; and though he determined it should not be long, the future seemed very uncertain, and he would look on her loveliness while he might.

"I hope you will like my cousin's singing," he said, rather timidly.

"If he sings as he has sung before he is the greatest artist living," she said calmly, as though no one would dispute it. "But I am curious to see him, as well as to hear him."

"He is not handsome," said Nino, smiling a little. "In fact, there is a family resemblance; he is said to look like me."

"Why did you not tell me that before?" she asked quickly, and fixed her blue eyes on Nino's face, as though she wished to photograph the features in her mind.

"I did not suppose the signorina would think twice about a singer's appearance," said Nino quietly. Hedwig blushed and turned away, busying herself with her books. At that moment Graf von Lira entered from the next room. Nino bowed.

"Curious is it," said the count, "that you and

the about-to-make-his-appearance tenor should the
same name have."

"He is a near relation, Signor Conte, — the same
whom you heard sing in the Pantheon. I hope
you will like his voice."

"That is what we shall see, Signor Professore,"
answered the other severely. He had a curious
way of bowing, as though he were made only in
two pieces, from his waist to his heels, and from
his waist to the crown of his head. Nino went his
way sadly, and wondering how Hedwig would look
when she should recognize him from her box in the
theatre, that very evening.

It is a terrible and a heart-tearing thing to part
from the woman one loves. That is nothing new,
you say. Every one knows that. Perhaps so,
though I think not. Only those can know it who
have experienced it, and for them no explanations
are in any way at all necessary. The mere word
"parting" calls up such an infinity of sorrow that
it is better to draw a veil over the sad thing and
bury it out of sight, and put upon it the seal on
which is graven "No Hope."

Moreover, when a man only supposes, as Nino
did, that he is leaving the woman he loves, or is
about to leave her, until he can devise some new
plan for seeing her, the case is not so very serious.
Nevertheless, Nino, who is of a very tender con-
stitution of the affections, suffered certain pangs
which are always hard to bear, and as he walked
slowly down the street he hung his head low, and

did not look like a man who could possibly be successful in anything he might undertake that day.
Yet it was the most important day of his life, and
had it not been that he had left Hedwig with little
hope of ever giving her another lesson, he would
have been so happy that the whole air would have
seemed dancing with sunbeams and angels and
flowers. I think that when a man loves he cares
very little for what he does. The greatest success
is indifferent to him, and he cares not at all for
failure, in the ordinary undertakings of life. These
are my reflections, and they are worth something,
because I once loved very much myself, and was
parted from her I loved many times, before the last
parting.

It was on this day that Nino came to me and
told me all the history of the past months, of which
I knew nothing; but, as you know all about it, I
need not tell you what the conversation was like,
until he had finished. Then I told him he was
the prince and chief of donkeys, which was no more
than the truth, as everybody will allow. He only
spread out his palms and shrugged his shoulders,
putting his head on one side, as though to say he
could not help it.

" Is it perhaps my fault that you are a little donkey? " I asked; for you may imagine whether I
was angry or not.

" Certainly not, Sor Cornelio," he said. " It is
entirely my own doing; but I do not see that I am
a donkey."

"Blood of Bacchus!" I ejaculated, holding up my hands. "He does not believe he is a great stupid!" But Nino was not angry at all. He busied himself a little with his costume, which was laid out on the piano, with the sword and the tinsel collar, and all the rest of it.

"I am in love," he said. "What would you have?"

"I would have you put a little giudizio, just a grain of judgment and common sense, into your love affairs. Why, you go about it as though it were the most innocent thing in the world to disguise yourself, and present yourself as a professor in a nobleman's house, in order to make love to his daughter! You, to make love to a noble damigella, a young countess, with a fortune! Go back to Serveti, and marry the first contadina girl you meet; it is much more fitting, if you must needs marry at all. I repeat it, you are an ignorant donkey!"

"Eh!" cried Nino, perfectly unmoved, "if I am ignorant, it is not for lack of your teaching; and as for being the beast of burden to which you refer, I have heard it said that you were once in love yourself. Meanwhile, I have told you this, because there will perhaps be trouble, and I did not intend you to be surprised."

"Surprised?" said I. "I would not be surprised at anything you might fancy doing, now. No, I would not dream of being surprised!"

"So much the better," answered Nino impertur-

bably. He looked sad and weary, though, and as I
am a prudent man I put my anger away to cool for
a little while, and indulged in a cigar until it should
be time to go to the theatre; for of course I went
with him, and Mariuccia too, to help him with his
dress. Poor old Mariuccia! she had dressed him
when he was a ragged little boy, and she was determined to put the finishing touches to his appearance now that he was about to be a great man, she
said. His dressing-room was a narrow little place,
sufficiently ill lighted, and there was barely space
to turn round. Mariuccia, who had brought the cat
and had her pocket full of roasted chestnuts, sat
outside on a chair until he was ready for her; and
I am sure that if she had spent her life in the profession of adorning players she could not have used
her fingers more deftly in the arrangement of the
collar and sword. Nino had a fancy to wear a
mustache and a pointed beard through the first part
of the opera; saying that a courtier always had
hair on his face, but that he would naturally shave
if he turned monk. I represented to him that it
was needless expense, since he must deposit the
value of the false beard with the theatre barber,
who lives opposite; and it was twenty-three francs.
Besides, he would look like a different man — two
separate characters.

"I do not care a cabbage for that," said Nino.
"If they cannot recognize me with their ears, they
need not trouble themselves to recognize me at all."

"It is a fact that their ears are quite long
enough," said Mariuccia.

" Hush, Mariuccia! " I said. " The Roman public is the most intelligent public in the world." And at this she grumbled.

But I knew well enough why he wanted to wear the beard. He had a fancy to put off the evil moment as long as possible, so that Hedwig might not recognize him till the last act, — a foolish fancy, in truth, for a woman's eyes are not like a man's; and though Hedwig had never thought twice about Nino's personality, she had not sat opposite him three times a week for nearly four months without knowing all his looks and gestures. It is an absurd idea, too, to attempt to fence with time, when a thing must come in the course of an hour or two. What is it, after all, the small delay you can produce? The click of a few more seconds in the clock-work, before the hammer smites its angry warning on the bell, and leaves echoes of pain writhing through the poor bronze, — that is Time. As for Eternity, it is a question of the calculus, and does not enter into a singer's first appearance, nor into the recognition of a lover. If it did, I would give you an eloquent dissertation upon it, so that you would yawn and take snuff, and wish me carried off by the diavolo to some place where I might lecture on the infinite without fear of being interrupted, or of keeping sinners like you unnecessarily long awake. There will be no hurry then. Poor old diavolo! he must have a dull time of it among all those heretics. Perhaps he has a little variety, for they say he has written up on his door, " Ici l'on

parle français," since Monsieur de Voltaire died.
But I must go on, or you will never be any wiser
than you are now, which is not saying overmuch.

I am not going to give you a description of the
Favorita, which you may hear a dozen times a year
at the theatre, for more or less money — but it is
only a franc if you stand; quite enough, too. I
went upon the stage before it began, and peeped
through the curtain to see what kind of an audience
there was. It is an old curtain, and there is a hole
in it on the right-hand side, which De Pretis says
was made by a foreign tenor, some years ago, between the acts; and Jacovacci, the impresario, tried
to make him pay five francs to have it repaired, but
did not get the money. It is a better hole than the
one in the middle, which is so far from both sides
of the house that you cannot see the people well.
So I looked through, and there, sure enough, in a
box very near to the stage, sat the Contessina di
Lira and the baroness, whom I had never seen before, but recognized from Nino's description; and
behind them sat the count himself, with his great
gray mustaches and a white cravat. They made me
think of the time when I used to go to the theatre
myself and sit in a box, and applaud or hiss, just
as I pleased. Dio mio! what changes in this
world!

I recognized also a great many of our noble
ladies, with jewels and other ornaments, and it
seemed to me that some of them were much more
beautiful than the German contessina whom Nino

had elected to worship, though she was well enough, to be sure, in white silk and white fur, with her little gold cross at her throat. To think that a statue like that, brought up with all the proprieties, should have such a strange chapter of life! But my eye began to smart from peering through the little hole, and just then a rough-looking fellow connected with the stage reminded me that, whatever relation I might be to the primo tenore, I was not dressed to appear in the first act; then the audience began to stamp and groan because the performance did not begin, and I went away again to tell Nino that he had a packed house. I found De Pretis giving him blackberry syrup, which he had brought in a bottle, and entreating him to have courage. Indeed, it seemed to me that Nino had the more courage of the two; for De Pretis laughed and cried and blew his nose, and took snuff with his great fat fingers, and acted altogether like a poor fool; while Nino sat on a rush-bottomed chair and watched Mariuccia, who was stroking the old cat and nibbling roasted chestnuts, declaring all the while that Nino was the most beautiful object she had ever seen. Then the bass and the baritone came, together, and spoke cheering words to Nino, and invited him to supper afterwards; but he thanked them kindly, and told them that he was expected at home, and would go with them after the next performance — if there ever were a "next." He thought he might fail at the last minute.

Nino had judged more rightly than I, when he

7

supposed that his beard and mustaches would disguise him from Hedwig during the first two acts.
She recognized the wondrous voice, and she saw the
strong resemblance he had spoken of.   Once or
twice, as he looked toward her, it seemed indeed
that the eyes must be his, with their deep circles
and serious gaze.   But it was absurd to suppose it
anything more than a resemblance.   As the opera
advanced, it became evident that Nino was making
a success.   Then in the second act it was clear that
the success was growing to be an ovation, and the
ovation a furore, in which the house became entirely
demoralized, and vouchsafed to listen only so long
as Nino was singing — screaming with delight before he had finished what he had to sing in each
scene.   People sent their servants away in hot
haste to buy flowers wherever they could, and he
came back to his dressing-room, from the second
act, carrying bouquets by the dozen, small bunches
and big, such as people had been able to get, or had
brought with them.   His eyes shone like the coals
in Mariuccia's scaldino, as he entered, and he was
pale through his paint.   He could hardly speak
for joy; but, as old habits return unconsciously at
great moments in a man's life, he took the cat on
his knee and pulled its tail.

"Sing thou also, little beast," he said gravely;
and he pulled the tail till the cat squeaked a little,
and he was satisfied.

"Bene!" he cried; "and now for the tonsure
and frock.   So Mariuccia was turned out into the

passage while he changed his dress. De Pretis came back a moment later, and tried to help him; but he was so much overcome that he could only shed tears and give a last word of advice for the next act.

"You must not sing it too loud, Nino mio," he said.

"Diavolo!" said Nino. "I should think not!"

"But you must not squeak it out in a little wee false voice, as small as this;" the maestro held up his thumb and finger, with a pinch of snuff between them.

"Bah! Sor Ercole, do you take me for a soprano?" cried the boy, laughing, as he washed off the paint and the gum, where the beard had stuck. Presently he got into his frock, which, as I told you, was a real one, provided by Ercole's brother, the Franciscan — quite quietly, of course, for it would seem a dreadful thing to use a real monk's frock in an opera. Then we fastened the rope round his waist, and smoothed his curly hair a little to give him a more pious aspect. He looked as white as a pillow when the paint was gone.

"Tell me a little, my father," said old Mariuccia, mocking him, "do you fast on Sundays, that you look so pale?" Whereat Nino struck an attitude, and began singing a love song to the ancient woman. Indeed, she was joking about the fast, for she had expended my substance, of late, in fattening Nino, as she called it, for his appearance, and there was to be broiled chickens for supper that very night. He was only pale because he was in love. As for me, I made up my mind to stand in the slides, so that I could see the contessina; for Nino had whispered to me that she had not yet recognized him, though she stared hard across the footlights. Therefore I took up a good position on the left of the stage, facing the Lira box, which was on the right.

The curtain went up, and Nino stood there, looking like a real monk, with a book in his hand and his eyes cast down, as he began to walk slowly along. I saw Hedwig von Lira's gaze rest on his square, pale face at least one whole minute. Then she gave a strange little cry, so that many people in the house looked toward her ; and she leaned far back in the shadow of the deep box, while the reflected glare of the footlights just shone faintly on her features, making them look more like marble than ever. The baroness was smiling to herself, amused at her companion's surprise, and the old count stared stolidly for a moment or two, and then turned suddenly to his daughter.

" Very curious is it," he was probably saying, " that this tenor should so much your Italian professor resemble." I could almost see his gray eyes sparkle angrily across the theatre. But as I looked, a sound rose on the heated air, the like of which I have never known. To tell the truth, I had not heard the first two acts, for I did not suppose there was any great difference between Nino's singing on the stage and his singing at home, and I still wished he might have chosen some other profession. But when I heard this, I yielded, at least for the time, and I am not sure that my eyes were as clear as usual.

" Spirto gentil dei sogni miei " — the long sweet notes sighed themselves to death on his lips, falling and rising magically like a mystic angel song, and swaying their melody out into the world of lights and listeners ; so pathetic, so heart-breaking, so laden with death and with love, that it was as though all the sorrowing souls in our poor Rome breathed in one soft sigh together. Only a poor monk dying of love in a monastery, tenderly and truly loving to the bitter end. Dio mio ! there are perhaps many such. But a monk like this, with a face like a conqueror, set square in its whiteness, and yet so wretched to see in his poor patched frock and his bare feet ; a monk, too, not acting love, but really and truly ready to die for a beautiful woman not thirty feet from him, in the house ; above all, a monk with a voice that speaks like the clarion call of the day of judgment in its wrath, and murmurs more plaintively and sadly in sorrow than ever the poor Peri sighed at the gates of Paradise — such a monk, what could he not make people feel ?

The great crowd of men and women sat utterly stilled and intent till he had sung the very last note. Not a sound was heard to offend the sorrow that spoke from the boy's lips. Then all those people seemed to draw three long breaths of wonder — a pause, a thrilling tremor in the air, and then there

burst to the roof such a roar of cries, such a huge
thunder of hands and voices, that the whole house
seemed to rock with it, and even in the street outside they say the noise was deafening.

Alone on the stage stood Nino, his eyes fixed on
Hedwig von Lira in her box. I think that she
alone of all that multitude made no sound, but only
gripped the edge of the balcony hard in her white
hands, and leaned far forward with straining eyes
and beating heart to satisfy her wonder. She knew
well enough, now, that there was no mistake. The
humble little Professor Cardegna, who had patiently explained Dante and Leopardi to her for
months, bowing to the ground in her presence, and
apologizing when he corrected her mistakes, as
though his whole life was to be devoted to teaching
foreigners his language; the decently clad young
man, who was always pale, and sometimes pathetic
when he spoke of himself, was no other than Giovanni Cardegna the tenor, singing aloud to earth
and heaven with his glorious great voice — a man
on the threshold of a European fame, such as falls
only to the lot of a singer or a conqueror. More,
he was the singer of her dreams, who had for
months filled her thoughts with music and her
heart with a strange longing, being until now a
voice only. There he stood looking straight at her,
— she was not mistaken, — as though to say, " I
have done it for you, and for you only." A woman
must be more than marble to feel no pride in the
intimate knowledge that a great public triumph has

been gained solely for her sake. She must be colder than ice if she cannot see her power when a conqueror loves her.

The marble had felt the fire, and the ice was in the flame at last. Nino, with his determination to be loved, had put his statue into a very fiery furnace, and in the young innocence of his heart had prepared such a surprise for his lady as might have turned the head of a hardened woman of the world, let alone an imaginative German girl, with a taste for romance — or without; it matters little. All Germans are full of imagination, and that is the reason they know so much. For they not only know all that is known by other people, but also all that they themselves imagine, which nobody else can possibly know. And if you do not believe this, you had better read the works of one Fichte, a philosopher.

I need not tell you any more about Nino's first appearance. It was one of those really phenomenal successes that seem to cling to certain people through life. He was very happy and very silent when it was over; and we were the last to leave the theatre, for we feared the enthusiasm of the crowd. So we waited till every one had gone, and then marched home together, for it was a fine night. I walked on one side of Nino, and De Pretis on the other, all of us carrying as many flowers as we could; Mariuccia came behind, with the cat under her shawl. I did not discover until we reached home why she had brought the beast. Then she explained that, as there was so much food in the kitchen, in anticipation of our supper, she had been afraid to leave the cat alone in the house, lest we should find nothing left to eat when we returned. This was sufficiently prudent, for a scatter-brained old spendthrift like Mariuccia.

That was a merry supper, and De Pretis became highly dramatic when we got to the second flask.

VII.

ON the day following Nino's début, Maestro Ercole de Pretis found himself in hot water, and the choristers at St. Peter's noticed that his skull-cap was awry, and that he sang out of tune; and once he tried to take a pinch of snuff when there was only three bars' rest in the music, so that instead of singing C sharp he sneezed very loud. Then all the other singers giggled, and said " Salute! " — which we always say to a person who sneezes — quite audibly.

It was not that Ercole had heard anything from the Graf von Lira as yet; but he expected to hear, and did not relish the prospect. Indeed, how could the Prussian gentleman fail to resent what the maestro had done, in introducing to him a singer disguised as a teacher? It chanced, also, that the contessina took a singing lesson that very day in the afternoon, and it was clear that the reaping of his evil deeds was not far off. His conscience did not trouble him at all, it is true, for I have told you that he has liberal ideas about the right of marriage; but his vanity was sorely afflicted at the idea of abandoning such a very noble and creditable pupil as the Contessina di Lira. He applauded himself for furthering Nino's wild schemes, and he blamed himself for being so reckless about his own interests. Every moment he expected a formal notice from the count to discontinue the lessons. But still it did not come, and at the appointed hour Ercole's wife helped him to put on his thick winter coat, and wrapped his comforter about his neck, and pulled his big hat over his eyes, — for the weather was threatening, — and sent him trudging off to the Palazzo Carmandola.

Though Ercole is stout of heart, and has broad shoulders to bear such burdens as fall to his lot, he lingered long on the way, for his presentiments were gloomy; and at the great door of the palazzo he even stopped to inquire of the porter whether the contessina had been seen to go out yet, half hoping that she would thus save him the mortification of an interview. But it turned out otherwise: the contessina was at home, and De Pretis was expected, as usual, to give the lesson. Slowly he climbed the great staircase, and was admitted.

"Good-day, Sor Maestro," said the liveried footman, who knew him well. "The Signor Conte desires to speak with you to-day, before you go to the signorina."

The maestro's heart sank, and he gripped hard the roll of music in his hand as he followed the servant to the count's cabinet. There was to be a scene of explanation, after all.

The count was seated in his great arm-chair, in a cloud of tobacco smoke, reading a Prussian military journal. His stick leaned against the table by his side, in painful contrast with the glittering cavalry sabres crossed upon the dark red wall opposite. The tall windows looked out on the piazza, and it was raining, or just beginning to rain. The great inkstand on the table was made to represent a howitzer, and the count looked as though he were ready to fire it point-blank at any intruder. There was an air of disciplined luxury in the room, that spoke of a rich old soldier who fed his fancy with titbits from a stirring past. De Pretis felt very uncomfortable, but the nobleman rose to greet him, as he rose to greet everything above the rank of a servant, making himself steady with his stick. When De Pretis was seated, he sat down also. The rain pattered against the window.

" Signor De Pretis," began the count, in tones as hard as chilled steel, " you are an honorable man." There was something interrogative in his voice.

" I hope so," answered the maestro modestly ; " like other Christians, I have a soul " —

" You will your soul take care of in your leisure moments," interrupted the count. " At present you have no leisure."

" As you command, Signor Conte."

" I was yesterday evening at the theatre. The professor you recommended for my daughter is with the new tenor one person." De Pretis spread out his hands and bowed, as if to deprecate any share in the transaction. The count continued,

"You are of the profession, Signor De Pretis. Evidently, you of this were aware."

"It is true," assented Ercole, not knowing what to say.

"Of course it is true. I am therefore to hear your explanation disposed." His gray eyes fastened sternly on the maestro. But the latter was prepared, for he had long foreseen that the count would one day be disposed to hear an explanation, as he expressed it.

"It is quite true," repeated De Pretis. "The young man was very poor, and desired to support himself while he was studying music. He was well fitted to teach our literature, and I recommended him. I hope that, in consideration of his poverty, and because he turned out a very good teacher, you will forgive me, Signor Conte."

"This talented singer I greatly applaud," answered the count stiffly. "As a with-the-capacity-and-learning-requisite-for-teaching-endowed young man deserves he also some commendation. Also will I remember his laudable-and-not-lacking-independence character. Nevertheless, unfitting would it be, should I pay the first tenor of the opera five francs an hour to teach my daughter Italian literature." De Pretis breathed more freely.

"Then you will forgive me, Signor Conte, for endeavoring to promote the efforts of this worthy young man in supporting himself?"

"Signor De Pretis," said the count, with a certain quaint geniality, "I have my precautions observed. I examined Signor Cardegna in Italian literature in my own person, and him proficient found. Had I found him to be ignorant, and had I his talents as an operatic singer later discovered, I would you out of that window have projected." De Pretis was alarmed, for the old count looked as though he would have carried out the threat. "As it is," he concluded, "you are an honorable man, and I wish you good - morning. Lady Hedwig awaits you, as usual." He rose courteously, leaning on his stick, and De Pretis bowed himself out.

He expected that the contessina would immediately begin talking of Nino, but he was mistaken; she never once referred to the opera or the singer, and except that she looked pale and transparent, and sang with a trifle less interest in her music than usual, there was nothing noticeable in her manner. Indeed, she had every reason to be silent.

Early that morning Nino received by a messenger a pretty little note, written in execrable Italian, begging him to come and breakfast with the baroness at twelve, as she much desired to speak with him after his stupendous triumph of the previous night.

Nino is a very good boy, but he is mortal, and after the excitement of the evening he thought nothing could be pleasanter than to spend a few hours in that scented boudoir, among the palms and the beautiful objects and the perfumes, talking with a woman who professed herself ready to help him in his love affair. We have no perfumes, or cushions, or pretty things at number twenty-seven, Santa Catarina dei Funari, though everything is very bright and neat and most proper, and the cat is kept in the kitchen, for the most part. So it is no wonder that he should have preferred to spend the morning with the baroness.

She was half lying, half sitting, in a deep arm-chair, when Nino entered; and she was reading a book. When she saw him she dropped the volume on her knee, and looked up at him from under her lids, without speaking. She must have been a be-witching figure. Nino advanced toward her, bow-ing low, so that his dark curling hair shaded his face.

"Good-day, signora," said he softly, as though fearing to hurt the quiet air. "I trust I do not interrupt you?"

"You never interrupt me, Nino," she said, "ex-cept — except when you go away."

"You are very good, signora."

"For heaven's sake, no pretty speeches," said she, with a little laugh.

"It seems to me," said Nino, seating himself, "that it was you who made the pretty speech, and I who thanked you for it." There was a pause.

"How do you feel?" asked the baroness at last, turning her head to him.

"Grazie — I am well," he answered, smiling.

"Oh, I do not mean that, — you are always well. But how do you enjoy your first triumph?"

"I think," said Nino, "that a real artist ought to have the capacity to enjoy a success at the moment, and the good sense to blame his vanity for enjoying it after it is passed."

"How old are you, Nino?"

"Did I never tell you?" he asked, innocently. "I shall be twenty-one soon."

"You talk as though you were forty, at least."

"Heaven save us!" quoth Nino.

"But really, are you not immensely flattered at the reception you had?"

"Yes."

"You did not look at all interested in the public at the time," said she, "and that Roman nose of yours very nearly turned up in disdain of the applause, I thought. I wonder what you were thinking of all the while."

"Can you wonder, baronessa?" She knew what he meant, and there was a little look of annoyance in her face when she answered.

"Ah, well, of course not, since *she* was there." Her ladyship rose, and taking a stick of Eastern pastil from a majolica dish in a corner made Nino light it from a wax taper.

"I want the smell of the sandal-wood this morning," said she; "I have a headache." She was enchanting to look at, as she bent her softly-shaded face over the flame to watch the burning perfume. She looked like a beautiful lithe sorceress making a love spell, — perhaps for her own use. Nino turned from her. He did not like to allow the one image he loved to be even for a moment disturbed by the one he loved not, however beautiful. She moved away, leaving the pastil on the dish. Suddenly she paused, and turned back to look at him.

"Why did you come to-day?" she asked.

"Because you desired it," answered Nino, in some astonishment.

"You need not have come," she said, bending down to lean on the back of a silken chair. She folded her hands, and looked at him as he stood not three paces away. "Do you not know what has happened?" she asked, with a smile that was a little sad.

"I do not understand," said Nino, simply. He was facing the entrance to the room, and saw the curtains parted by the servant. The baroness had her back to the door, and did not hear.

"Do you not know," she continued, "that you are free now? Your appearance in public has put an end to it all. You are not tied to me any longer, — unless you wish it."

As she spoke these words Nino turned white, for under the heavy curtain, lifted to admit her, stood Hedwig von Lira, like a statue, transfixed and immovable from what she had heard. The baroness noticed Nino's look, and, springing back to her height from the chair on which she had been leaning, faced the door.

"My dearest Hedwig!" she cried, with a magnificent readiness. "I am so very glad you have come. I did not expect you in the least. Do take off your hat, and stay to breakfast. Ah, forgive me: this is Professor Cardegna. But you know him? Yes; now that I think, we all went to the Pantheon together." Nino bowed low, and Hedwig bent her head.

"Yes," said the young girl, coldly. "Professor Cardegna gives me lessons."

"Why, of course; how *bête* I am! I was just telling him that, since he has been successful, and is enrolled among the great artists, it is a pity he is no longer tied to giving Italian lessons, — tied to coming here three times a week, to teach me literature." Hedwig smiled a strange, icy smile, and sat down by the window. Nino was still utterly astonished, but he would not allow the baroness's quibble to go entirely uncontradicted.

"In truth," he said, "the Signora Baronessa's lessons consisted chiefly" —

"In teaching me pronunciation," interrupted the baroness, trying to remove Hedwig's veil and hat, somewhat against the girl's inclination. "Yes, you see how it is. I know a little of singing, but I cannot pronounce, — not in the least. Ah, these Italian vowels will be the death of me! But if there is any one who can teach a poor dilettante to pronounce them," she added, laying the hat away on a chair, and pushing a footstool to Hedwig's feet, "that some one is Signor Cardegna."

By this time Nino had recognized the propriety of temporizing; that is to say, of letting the baroness's fib pass for what it was worth, lest the discussion of the subject should further offend Hedwig, whose eyes wandered irresolutely toward him, as though she would say something if he addressed her.

"I hope, signorina," he said, "that it is not quite as the baroness says. I trust our lessons are not at an end?" He knew very well that they were.

"I think, Signor Cardegna," said Hedwig, with more courage than would have been expected from such a mere child, — she is twenty, but Northern people are not grown up till they are thirty, at least, — "I think it would have been more obliging if, when I asked you so much about your cousin, you had acknowledged that you had no cousin, and that the singer was none other than yourself." She blushed, perhaps, but the curtain of the window hid it.

"Alas, signorina," answered Nino, still standing before her, "such a confession would have deprived me of the pleasure — of the honor of giving you lessons."

"And pray, Signor Cardegna," put in the baroness, "what are a few paltry lessons, compared with the pleasure you ought to have experienced in satisfying the Contessina di Lira's curiosity? Really, you have little courtesy."

Nino shrank into himself, as though he were hurt, and he gave the baroness a look which said worlds. She smiled at him, in joy of her small triumph, for Hedwig was looking at the floor again,

and could not see. But the young girl had strength
in her, for all her cold looks and white cheek. .

"You can atone, Signor Cardegna," she said.
Nino's face brightened.

"How, signorina?" he asked.

"By singing to us now," said Hedwig. The
baroness looked grave, for she well knew what a
power Nino wielded with his music.

"Do not ask him," she protested. "He must be
tired, — tired to death, with all he went through
last night."

"Tired?" ejaculated Nino, with some surprise.
"I tired? I was never tired in my life, of singing.
I will sing as long as you will listen." He went to
the piano. As he turned, the baroness laid her
hand on Hedwig's, affectionately, as though sympa-
thizing with something she supposed to be passing
in the girl's mind. But Hedwig was passive, unless a little shudder at the first touch of the baroness's fingers might pass for a manifestation of feeling. Hedwig had hitherto liked the baroness,
finding in her a woman of a certain artistic sense,
combined with a certain originality. The girl was
an absolute contrast to the woman, and admired in
her the qualities she thought lacking in herself,
though she possessed too much self-respect to attempt
to acquire them by imitation. Hedwig sat like a
Scandinavian fairy princess on the summit of a glass
hill; her friend roamed through life like a beautiful soft-footed wild animal, rejoicing in the sense
of being, and sometimes indulging in a little play-

ful destruction by the way. The girl had heard a
voice in the dark, singing, and ever since then she
had dreamed of the singer; but it never entered
her mind to confide to the baroness her strange
fancies. An undisciplined imagination, securely
shielded from all outward disturbing causes, will
do much with a voice in the dark, — a great deal
more than such a woman as the baroness might imagine.

I do not know enough about these blue-eyed
German girls to say whether or not Hedwig had
ever before thought of her unknown singer as an
unknown lover. But the emotions of the previous
night had shaken her nerves a little, and had she
been older than she was she would have known
that she loved her singer, in a distant and maidenly
fashion, as soon as she heard the baroness speak of
him as having been her property. And now she
was angry with herself, and ashamed of feeling any
interest in a man who was evidently tied to another
woman by some intrigue she could not comprehend.
Her coming to visit the baroness had been as unpre-
meditated as it was unexpected, that morning, and
she bitterly repented it; but being of good blood
and heart, she acted as boldly as she could, and
showed no little tact in making Nino sing, and thus
cutting short a painful conversation. Only when
the baroness tried to caress her and stroke her hand
she shrank away, and the blood mantled up to her
cheeks. Add to all this the womanly indignation
she felt at having been so long deceived by Nino,

and you will see that she was in a very vacillating frame of mind.

The baroness was a subtle woman, reckless and diplomatic by turns, and she was not blind to the sudden repulse she met with from Hedwig, unspoken though it was. But she merely withdrew her hand, and sat thinking over the situation. What she thought, no one knows ; or, at least, we can only guess it from what she did afterwards. As for me, I have never blamed her at all, for she is the kind of woman I should have loved. In the mean time Nino caroled out one love song after another. He saw, however, that the situation was untenable, and after a while he rose to go. Strange to say, although the baroness had asked Nino to breakfast, and the hour was now at hand, she made no effort to retain him. But she gave him her hand, and said many flattering and pleasing things, which, however, neither flattered nor pleased him. As for Hedwig, she bent her head a little, but said nothing, as he bowed before her. Nino therefore went home with a heavy heart, longing to explain to Hedwig why he had been tied to the baroness, — that it was the price of her silence and of the privilege he had enjoyed of giving lessons to the contessina ; but knowing, also, that all explanation was out of the question for the present. When he was gone, Hedwig and the baroness were left together.

" It must have been a great surprise to you, my dear," said the elder lady kindly.

" What ? "

" That your little professor should turn out a great artist in disguise. It was a surprise to me, too, — ah, another illusion destroyed. Dear child! You have still so many illusions, — beautiful, pure illusions. Dieu! how I envy you!" They generally talked French together, though the baroness knows German. Hedwig laughed bravely.

" I was certainly astonished," she said. " Poor man! I suppose he did it to support himself. He never told me he gave you lessons, too." The baroness smiled, but it was from genuine satisfaction this time.

" I wonder at that, since he knew we were intimate, or, at least, that we were acquainted. Of course I would not speak of it last night, because I saw your father was angry."

" Yes, he was angry. I suppose it was natural," said Hedwig.

" Perfectly natural. And you, my dear, were you not angry too, — just a little ? "

" I? No. Why should I be angry? He was a very good teacher, for he knows whole volumes by heart; and he understands them, too."

Soon they talked of other things, and the baroness was very affectionate. But though Hedwig saw that her friend was kind and most friendly, she could not forget the words that were in the air when she chanced to enter, nor could she quite accept the plausible explanation of them which the baroness had so readily invented. For jealousy is the forerunner of love, and sometimes its awakener.

She felt a rival and an enemy, and all the hereditary combativeness of her Northern blood was roused.

Nino, who was in no small perplexity, reflected. He was not old enough or observant enough to have seen the breach that was about to be created between the baroness and Hedwig. His only thought was to clear himself in Hedwig's eyes from the imputation of having been tied to the dark woman in any way save for his love's sake. He at once began to hate the baroness with all the ferocity of which his heart was capable, and with all the calm his bold, square face outwardly expressed. But he was forced to take some action at once, and he could think of nothing better to do than to consult De Pretis.

To the maestro he poured out his woes and his plans. He exhibited to him his position toward the baroness and toward Hedwig in the clearest light. He conjured him to go to Hedwig, and explain that the baroness had threatened to unmask him, and thus deprive him of his means of support, — he dared not put it otherwise, — unless he consented to sing for her and come to her as often as she pleased. To explain, to propitiate, to smooth, — in a word, to reinstate Nino in her good opinion.

"Death of a dog!" exclaimed De Pretis; "you do not ask much! After you have allowed your lady-love, your innamorata, to catch you saying you are bound body and soul to another woman, — and such a woman! ye saints, what a beauty! —

you ask me to go and set matters right! What
the diavolo did you want to go and poke your nose
into such a mousetrap for? Via! I am a fool to
have helped you at all."

"Very likely," said Nino calmly. "But meanwhile there are two of us, and perhaps I am the
greater. You will do what I ask, maestro; is it
not true? And it was not I who said it; it was
the baroness."

"The baroness — yes — and may the maledictions of the inferno overtake her," said De Pretis,
casting up his eyes and feeling in his coat-tail
pockets for his snuff-box. Once, when Nino was
younger, he filled Ercole's snuff-box with soot and
pepper, so that the maestro had a black nose and
sneezed all day.

What could Ercole do? It was true that he had
hitherto helped Nino. Was he not bound to continue that assistance? I suppose so; but if the
whole affair had ended then, and this story with it,
I would not have cared a button. Do you suppose
it amuses me to tell you this tale? Or that if it
were not for Nino's good name I would ever have
turned myself into a common story-teller? Bah!
you do not know me. A page of quaternions gives
me more pleasure than all this rubbish put together, though I am not averse to a little gossip
now and then, of an evening, if people will listen
to my details and fancies. But those are just the
things people will not listen to. Everybody wants
sensation nowadays. What is a sensation compared

with a thought? What is the convulsive gesticulation of a dead frog's leg compared with the intellect of the man who invented the galvanic battery, and thus gave fictitious sensation to all the countless generations of dead frogs' legs that have since been the objects of experiment? Or if you come down to so poor a thing as mere feeling, what are your feelings in reading about Nino's deeds compared with what he felt in doing them? I am not taking all this trouble to please you, but only for Nino's sake, who is my dear boy. You are of no more interest or importance to me than if you were so many dead frogs; and if I galvanize your sensations, as you call them, into an activity sufficient to make you cry or laugh, that is my own affair. You need not say " thank you " to me. I do not want it. Ercole will thank you, and perhaps Nino will thank me, but that is different.

I will not tell you about the interview that Ercole had with Hedwig, nor how skillfully he rolled up his eyes and looked pathetic when he spoke of Nino's poverty, and of the fine part he had played in the whole business. Hedwig is a woman, and the principal satisfaction she gathered from Ercole's explanation was the knowledge that her friend the baroness had lied to her in explaining those strange words she had overheard. She knew it, of course, by instinct; but it was a great relief to be told the fact by some one else, as it always is, even when one is not a woman.

VIII.

SEVERAL days passed after the début without giving Nino an opportunity of speaking to Hedwig. He probably saw her, for he mingled in the crowd of dandies in the Piazza Colonna of an afternoon, hoping she would pass in her carriage and give him a look. Perhaps she did ; he said nothing about it, but looked calm when he was silent and savage when he spoke, after the manner of passionate people. His face aged and grew stern in those few days, so that he seemed to change on a sudden from boy to man. But he went about his business, and sang at the theatre when he was obliged to; gathering courage to do his best and to display his powers from the constant success he had. The papers were full of his praises, saying that he was absolutely without rival from the very first night he sang, matchless and supreme from the moment he first opened his mouth, and all that kind of nonsense. I dare say he is now, but he could not have been really the greatest singer living, so soon. However, he used to bring me the newspapers that had notices of him, though he never appeared to care much for them, nor did he ever keep them himself. He said he hankered for an ideal which he would never attain ; and I told him that if he was never

to attain it he had better abandon the pursuit of it
at once. But he represented to me that the ideal
was confined to his imagination, whereas the reality had a great financial importance, since he daily
received offers from foreign managers to sing for
them, at large advantage to himself, and was hesitating only in order to choose the most convenient.
This seemed sensible, and I was silent. Soon afterwards he presented me with a box of cigars and
a very pretty amber mouthpiece. The cigars were
real Havanas, such as I had not smoked for years,
and must have cost a great deal.

"You may not be aware, Sor Cornelio," he said
one evening, as he mixed the oil and vinegar with
the salad, at supper, "that I am now a rich man,
or soon shall be. An agent from the London opera
has offered me twenty thousand francs for the season in London, this spring."

"Twenty thousand francs!" I cried in amazement. "You must be dreaming, Nino. That is
just about seven times what I earn in a year with
my professorship and my writing."

"No dreams, caro mio. I have the offer in my
pocket." He apparently cared no more about it
than if he had twenty thousand roasted chestnuts
in his pocket.

"When do you leave us?" I asked, when I was
somewhat recovered.

"I am not sure that I will go," he answered,
sprinkling some pepper on his lettuce.

"Not sure! Body of Diana, what a fool you
are!"

"Perhaps," said he, and he passed me the dish.
Just then, Mariuccia came in with a bottle of wine,
and we said no more about it; for Mariuccia is
indiscreet.

Nino thought nothing about his riches, because
he was racking his brains for some good expedient
whereby he might see the contessina and speak with
her. He had ascertained from De Pretis that the
count was not so angry as he had expected, and
that Hedwig was quite satisfied with the explanations of the maestro. The day after the foregoing
conversation he wrote a note to her, wherein he said
that if the Contessina di Lira would deign to be
awake at midnight that evening she would have a
serenade from a voice she was said to admire. He
bid Mariuccia carry the letter to the Palazzo Carmandola.

At half past eleven, at least two hours after supper, Nino wrapped himself in my old cloak, and
took the guitar under his arm. Rome is not a very
safe place for midnight pranks, and so I made him
take a good knife in his waist-belt; for he had con-
fided to me where he was going. I tried to dissuade
him from the plan, saying he might catch cold; but
he laughed at me.

A serenade is an every-day affair, and in the
street one voice sounds about as well as another.
He reached the palace, and his heart sank when he
saw Hedwig's window dark and gloomy. He did
not know that she was seated behind it in a deep
chair, wrapped in white things, and listening for

him against the beatings of her heart. The large moon seemed to be spiked on the sharp spire of the church that is near her house, and the black shadows cut the white light as clean as with a knife. Nino had tuned his guitar in the other street, and stood ready, waiting for the clocks to strike. Presently they clanged out wildly, as though they had been waked from their midnight sleep, and were angry ; one clock answering the other, and one convent bell following another in the call to prayers. For two full minutes the whole air was crazy with ringing, and then it was all still. Nino struck a single chord. Hedwig almost thought he might hear her heart beating all the way down in the street.

"Ah, del mio dolce ardor bramato ogetto," he sang, — an old air in one of Gluck's operas, that our Italian musicians say was composed by Alessandro Stradella, the poor murdered singer. It must be a very good air, for it pleases me ; and I am not easily pleased with music of any kind. As for Hedwig, she pressed her ear to the glass of the window that she might not lose any note. But she would not open nor give any sign. Nino was not so easily discouraged, for he remembered that once before she had opened her window for a few bars he had begun to sing. He played a few chords, and breathed out the "Salve, dimora casta e pura," from Faust, high and soft and clear. There is a point in that song, near to the end, where the words say, "Reveal to me the maiden," and where the music goes away to the highest note that any one can possibly sing. It always appears quite easy for Nino, and he does not squeak like a dying pig, as all the other tenors do on that note. He was looking up as he sang it, wondering whether it would have any effect. Apparently Hedwig lost her head completely, for she gently opened the casement and looked out at the moonlight opposite, over the carved stone mullions of her window. The song ended, he hesitated whether to go or to sing again. She was evidently looking towards him; but he was in the light, for the moon has risen higher, and she, on the other side of the street, was in the dark.

"Signorina!" he called softly. No answer. "Signorina!" he said again, coming across the empty street and standing under the window, which might have been thirty feet from the ground.

"Hush!" came a whisper from above.

"I thank you with all my soul for listening to me," he said in a low voice. "I am innocent of that of which you suspect me. I love you, ah, I love you!" But at this she left the window very quickly. She did not close it, however, and Nino stood long, straining his eyes for a glimpse of the white face that had been there. He sighed, and striking a chord sang out boldly the old air from the Trovatore, "Ah, che la morte ognora è tarda nel venir." Every blind fiddler in the streets plays it, though he would be sufficiently scared if death came any the quicker for his fiddling. But old and

worn as it is, it has a strain of passion in it, and
Nino threw more fire and voice into the ring of it
than ever did famous old Boccardè, when he sang
it at the first performance of the opera, thirty. and
odd years ago. As he played the chords after the
first strophe, the voice from above whispered again :
" Hush, for Heaven's sake ! " Just that, and
something fell at his feet, with a soft little padded
sound on the pavement. He stooped to pick it up,
and found a single rose ; and at that instant the
window closed sharply. Therefore he kissed the
rose and hid it, and presently he strode down the
street, finishing his song as he went, but only humming it, for the joy had taken his voice away. I
heard him let himself in and go to bed, and he
told me about it in the morning. That is how I
know.

Since the day after the début Nino had not seen
the baroness. He did not speak of her, and I am
sure he wished she were at the very bottom of the
Tiber. But on the morning after the serenade he
received a note from her, which was so full of pro-
testations of friendship and so delicately couched
that he looked grave, and reflected that it was his
duty to be courteous, and to answer such a call as
that. She begged him earnestly to come at one
o'clock ; she was suffering from headache, she said,
and was very weak. Had Nino loved Hedwig a
whit the less, he would not have gone. But he felt
himself strong enough to face anything and everything, and therefore he determined to go.

. He found her, indeed, with the manner of a person who is ill, but not with the appearance. She was lying on a huge couch, pushed to the fireside, and there were furs about her. A striped scarf of rich Eastern silk was round her throat, and she held in her hand a new novel, of which she carelessly cut the pages with a broad-hafted Persian knife. But there was color in her dark cheek, and a sort of angry fire in her eyes. Nino thought the clean steel in her hand looked as though it might be used for something besides cutting leaves, if the fancy took her.

"So at last you have honored me with a visit, signore," she said, not desisting from her occupation. Nino came to her, and she put out her hand. He touched it, but could not bear to hold it, for it burned him.

"You used to honor my hand differently from that," she half whispered. Nino sat himself down a little way from her, blushing slightly. It was not at what she had said, but at the thought that he should ever have kissed her fingers.

"Signora," he replied, "there are customs, chivalrous and gentle in themselves, and worthy for all men to practice. But from the moment a custom begins to mean what it should not, it ought to be abandoned. You will forgive me if I no longer kiss your hand."

"How cold you are! — how formal! What should it mean?"

' "It is better to say too little than too much," he answered.

" Bah!" she cried, with a bitter little laugh. " Words are silver, but silence — is very often nothing but silver-plated brass. Put a little more wood on the fire; you make me cold." Nino obeyed.

" How literal you are! " said the baroness petulantly. " There is fire enough, on the hearth."

" Apparently, signora, you are pleased to be enigmatical," said Nino.

" I will be pleased to be anything I please," she answered, and looked at him rather fiercely. " I wanted you to drive away my headache, and you only make it worse."

" I am sorry, signora. I will leave you at once. Permit me to wish you a very good-morning." He took his hat and went towards the door. Before he reached the heavy curtain, she was at his side with a rush like a falcon on the wing, her eyes burning darkly between anger and love.

" Nino! " She laid hold of his arm, and looked into his face.

" Signora," he protested coldly, and drew back.

" You will not leave me so? "

" As you wish, signora. I desire to oblige you."

" Oh, how cold you are! " she cried, leaving his arm, and sinking into a chair by the door, while he stood with his hand on the curtain. She hid her eyes. " Nino, Nino! You will break my heart! " she sobbed; and a tear, perhaps more of anger than of sorrow, burst through her fingers, and coursed down her cheek.

9

Few men can bear to see a woman shed tears. Nino's nature rose up in his throat, and bade him console her. But between him and her was a fair, bright image that forbade him to move hand or foot.

" Signora," he said, with all the calm . he could command, " if I were conscious of having by word or deed of mine given you cause to speak thus, I would humbly implore your forgiveness. But my heart does not accuse me. I beg you to allow me to take leave of you. I will go away, and you shall have no further cause to think of me." He moved again, and lifted the curtain. But she was like a panther, so quick and beautiful. Ah, how I could have loved that woman! She held him, and would not let him go, her smooth fingers fastening round his wrists like springs.

" Please to let me go," he said between his teeth, with rising anger.

" No! I will not let you! " she cried fiercely, tightening her grasp on him. Then the angry fire in her tearful eyes seemed suddenly to melt into a soft flame, and the color came faster to her cheeks. "Ah, how can you let me so disgrace myself! how can you see me fallen so low as to use the strength of my hands, and yet have no pity! Nino, Nino, do not kill me ! "

" Indeed, it would be the better for you if I should," he answered bitterly, but without attempting to free his wrists from her strong, soft grip.

" But you will," she murmured passionately.

"You are killing me by leaving me., Can you not see it?" Her voice melted away in the tearful cadence. But Nino stood gazing at her as stonily as though he were the Sphinx. How could he have the heart? I cannot tell. Long she looked into his eyes, silently; but she might as well have tried to animate a piece of iron, so stern and hard he was. Suddenly, with a strong, convulsive movement, she flung his hands from her.

"Go!" she cried hoarsely. "Go to that wax doll you love, and see whether she will love you, or care whether you leave her or not! Go, go, go! Go to her!" She had sprung far back from him, and now pointed to the door, drawn to her full height and blazing in her wrath.

"I would advise you, madam, to speak with proper respect of any lady with whom you choose to couple my name." His lips opened and shut mechanically, and he trembled from head to foot.

"Respect!" She laughed wildly. "Respect for a mere child whom you happen to fancy! Respect, indeed, for anything you choose to do! I — I — respect Hedwig von Lira? Ha! ha!" and she rested her hand on the table behind her, as she laughed.

"Be silent, madam," said Nino, and he moved a step nearer, and stood with folded arms.

"Ah! You would silence me now, would you? You would rather not hear me speak of your midnight serenades, and your sweet letters dropped from the window of her room, at your feet?" But her rage overturned itself, and with a strange cry she fell into a deep chair, and wept/bitterly, burying her face in her two hands. " Miserable woman that I am!" she sobbed, and her whole lithe body was convulsed.

"You are indeed," said Nino, and he turned once more to go. But as he turned, the servant threw back the curtain.

"The Signor Conte di Lira," he announced in distinct tones. For a moment there was a dead silence, during which, in spite of his astonishment at the sudden appearance of the count, Nino had time to reflect that the baroness had caused him to be watched during the previous night. It might well be, and the mistake she made in supposing the thing Hedwig had dropped to be a letter told him that her spy had not ventured very near.

The tall count came forward under the raised curtains, limping and helping himself with his stick. His face was as gray and wooden as ever, but his mustaches had an irritated, crimped look, that Nino did not like. The count barely nodded to the young man, as he stood aside to let the old gentleman pass; his eyes turned mechanically to where the baroness sat. She was a woman who had no need to simulate passion in any shape, and it must have cost her a terrible effort to control the paroxysm of anger and shame and grief that had overcome her. There was something unnatural and terrifying in her sudden calm, as she forced herself to rise and greet her visitor.

"I fear I come out of season," he said, apologetically, as he bent over her hand.

"On the contrary," she answered; "but forgive me if I speak one word to Professor Cardegna." She went to where Nino was standing.

"Go into that room," she said, in a very low voice, glancing towards a curtained door opposite the windows, "and wait till he goes. You may listen if you choose." She spoke authoritatively.

"I will not," answered Nino, in a determined whisper.

"You will not?" Her eyes flashed again. He shook his head.

"Count von Lira," she said aloud, turning to him, "do you know this young man?" She spoke in Italian, and Von Lira answered in the same language; but as what he said was not exactly humorous, I will spare you the strange construction of his sentences.

"Perfectly," he answered. "It is precisely concerning this young man that I desire to speak with you." The count remained standing because the baroness had not told him to be seated.

"That is fortunate," replied the baroness, "for I wish to inform you that he is a villain, a wretch, a miserable fellow!" Her anger was rising again, but she struggled to control it. When Nino realized what she said, he came forward, and stood near the count, facing the baroness, his arms folded on his breast, as though to challenge accusation. The count raised his eyebrows.

" I am aware that he concealed his real profession so long as he gave my daughter lessons. That, however, has been satisfactorily explained, though I regret it. Pray inform me why you designate him as a villain." Nino felt a thrill of sympathy for this man whom he had so long deceived.

" This man, sir," said she in measured tones, " this low-born singer, who has palmed himself off on us as a respectable instructor in language, has the audacity to love your daughter. For the sake of pressing his odious suit, he has wormed himself into your house, as into mine ; he has sung beneath your daughter's window, and she has dropped letters to him, — love-letters, do you understand ? And now," — her voice rose more shrill and uncontrollable at every word, as she saw Lira's face turn white, and her anger gave desperate utterance to the lie, — "and now he has the effrontery to come to me — to me — to me of all women — and to confess his abominable passion for that pure angel, imploring me to assist him in bringing destruction upon her and you. Oh, it is execrable, it is vile, it is hellish ! " She pressed her hands to her temples as she stood, and glared at the two men. The count was a strong man, easily petulant, but hard to move to real anger. Though his face was white and his right hand clutched his crutch-stick, he still kept the mastery of himself.

" Is what you tell me true, madam ? " he asked in a strange voice.

" Before God, it is true ! " she cried desperately.

The old man looked at her for one moment, and then, as though he had been twenty years younger, he made at Nino, brandishing his stick to strike. But Nino is strong and young, and he is almost a Roman. He foresaw the count's action, and his right hand stole to the table, and grasped the clean, murderous knife; the baroness had used it so innocently to cut the leaves of her book, half an hour before. With one wrench he had disarmed the elder man, forced him back upon a lounge, and set the razor edge of his weapon against the count's throat.

"If you speak one word, or try to strike me, I will cut off your head," he said quietly, bringing his cold, marble face close down to the old man's eyes. There was something so deathly in his voice, in spite of its quiet sound, that the count thought his hour was come, brave man as he was. The baroness tottered back against the opposite wall, and stood staring at the two, disheveled and horrified.

"This woman," said Nino, still holding the cold thing against the flesh, "lies in part, and in part tells the truth. I love your daughter, it is true." The poor old man quivered beneath Nino's weight, and his eyes rolled wildly, searching for some means of escape. But it was of no use. "I love her, and have sung beneath her window; but I never had a written word from her in my life, and I neither told this woman of my love nor asked her assistance. She guessed it at the first; she guessed

the reason of my disguise, and she herself offered
to help me. You may speak now. Ask her."
Nino relaxed his hold, and stood off, still grasping
the knife. The old count breathed, shook himself
and passed his handkerchief over his face before
he spoke. The baroness stood as though she were
petrified.

"Thunder weather, you are a devilish young
man!" said Von Lira, still panting. Then he suddenly recovered his dignity. "You have caused
me to assault this young man, by what you told
me," he said, struggling to his feet. "He defended
himself, and might have killed me, had he chosen.
Be good enough to tell me whether he has spoken
the truth, or you."

"He has spoken — the truth," answered the
baroness, staring vacantly about her. Her fright
had taken from her even the faculty of lying. Her
voice was low, but she articulated the words distinctly. Then, suddenly, she threw up her hands,
with a short, quick scream, and fell forward, senseless, on the floor. Nino looked at the count, and
dropped his knife on a table. The count looked at
Nino.

"Sir," said the old gentleman, "I forgive you
for resisting my assault. I do not forgive you for
presuming to love my daughter, and I will find
means to remind you of the scandal you have
brought on my house." He drew himself up to
his full height. Nino handed him his crutch-stick
civilly.

" Signor Conte," he said, simply, but with all
his natural courtesy, " I am sorry for this affair,
to which you forced me, — or rather the Signora
Baronessa forced us both. I have acted foolishly,
perhaps, but I am in love. And permit me to
assure you, sir, that I will yet marry the Signorina
di Lira, if she consents to marry me."

" By the name of Heaven," swore the old count,
"if she wants to marry a singer, she shall." He
limped to the door in sullen anger, and went out.
Nino turned to the prostrate figure of the poor
baroness. The continued strain on her nerves had
broken her down, and she lay on the floor in a dead
faint. Nino put a cushion from the lounge under
her head, and rang the bell. The servant appeared
instantly.

" Bring water quickly!" he cried. " The signora
has fainted." He stood looking at the senseless
figure of the woman, as she lay across the rich
Persian rugs that covered the floor.

" Why did you not bring salts, cologne, her
maid — run, I tell you!" he said to the man, who
brought the glass of water on a gilded tray. He
had forgotten that the fellow could not be expected
to have any sense. When her people came at
last, he had sprinkled her face, and she had unconsciously swallowed enough of the water to have
some effect in reviving her. She began to open
her eyes, and her fingers moved nervously. Nino
found his hat, and, casting one glance around the
room that had just witnessed such strange doings,

passed through the door and went out. The baroness was left with her servants. Poor woman! She did very wrong, perhaps, but anybody would have loved her — except Nino. She must have been terribly shaken, one would have thought, and she ought to have gone to lie down, and should have sent for the doctor to bleed her. But she did nothing of the kind.

She came to see me. I was alone in the house, late in the afternoon, when the sun was just gilding the tops of the houses. I heard the doorbell ring, and I went to answer it myself. There stood the beautiful baroness, alone, with all her dark soft things around her, as pale as death, and her eyes swollen sadly with weeping. Nino had come home and told me something about the scene in the morning, and I can tell you I gave him a piece of my mind about his follies.

"Does Professor Cornelio Grandi live here?" she asked, in a low voice.

"I am he, signora," I answered. "Will you please to come in?" And so she came into our little sitting-room, and sat over there in the old green arm-chair. I shall never forget it as long as I live.

I cannot tell you all she said in that brief half hour, for it pains me to think of it. She spoke as though I were her confessor, so humbly and quietly, — as though it had all happened ten years ago. There is no stubbornness in those tiger women when once they break down.

She said she was going away; that she had done my boy a great wrong, and wished to make such reparation as she could by telling me, at least, the truth. She did not scruple to say that she had loved him, nor that she had done everything in her power to keep him; though he had never so much as looked at her, she added pathetically. She wished to have me know exactly how it happened, no matter what I might think of her.

" You are a nobleman, count," she said to me at last, " and I can trust you as one of my own people, I am sure. Yes, I know: you have been unfortunate, and are now a professor. But that does not change the blood. I can trust you. You need not tell him I came, unless you wish it. I shall never see him again. I am glad to have been here, to see where he lives." She rose, and moved to go. I confess that the tears were in my eyes. There was a pile of music on the old piano. There was a loose leaf on the top, with his name written on it. She took it in her hand, and looked inquiringly at me out of her sad'eyes. I knew she wanted to take it, and I nodded.

" I shall never see him again, you know." Her voice was gentle and weak, and she hastened to the door; so that almost before I knew it she was gone. The sun had left the red-tiled roofs opposite, and the goldfinch was silent in his cage. So I sat down in the chair where she had rested, and folded my hands, and thought, as I am always thinking ever since, how I could have loved such a woman as that; so passionate, so beautiful, so piteously sorry for what she had done that was wrong. Ah me! for the years that are gone away so cruelly, for the days so desperately dead! Give me but one of those golden days, and I would make the pomp of emperors ridiculous. A greater man than I said that, — a man over the seas, with a great soul, who wrote in a foreign tongue, but spoke a language germane to all human speech. But even he cannot bring back one of those dear days. I would give much to have that one day back, when she came and told me all her woes. But that is impossible.

When they came to wake her in the morning — the very morning after that — she was dead in her bed; the color gone forever from those velvet cheeks, the fire quenched out of those passionate eyes, past power of love or hate to rekindle. Requiescat in pace, and may God give her eternal rest and forgiveness for all her sins. Poor, beautiful, erring woman!

IX.

At nine o'clock on the morning of the baroness's death, as Nino was busy singing scales, there was a ring at the door, and presently Mariuccia came running in as fast as her poor old legs could carry her, and whiter than a pillow-case, to say that there was a man at the door with two gendarmes, asking for Nino; and before I could question her, the three men walked unbidden into the room, demanding which was Giovanni Cardegna, the singer. Nino started, and then said quietly that he was the man. I have had dealings with these people, and I know what is best to be done. They were inclined to be rough and very peremptory. I confess I was frightened; but I think I am more cunning when I am a little afraid.

"Mariuccia," I said, as she stood trembling in the doorway, waiting to see what would happen, "fetch a flask of that old wine, and serve these gentlemen, — and a few chestnuts, if you have some. Be seated, signori," I said to them, "and take one of these cigars. My boy is a singer, and you would not hurt his voice by taking him out so early on this raw morning. Sit down, Nino, and ask these gentlemen what they desire." They all sat down, somewhat sullenly, and the gendarmes' sabres clanked on the brick floor.

"What do you wish from me?" asked Nino, who was not much moved after the first surprise.

"We regret to say," answered the man in plain clothes, "that we are here to arrest you."

"May I inquire on what charge?" I asked. "But first let me fill your glasses. Dry throats make surly answers, as the proverb says." They drank. It chanced that the wine was good, being from my own vineyard, — my little vineyard that I bought outside of Porta Salara, — and the men were cold and wet, for it was raining.

"Well," said the man who had spoken before, — he was clean-shaved and fat, and he smacked his lips over the wine, — "it is not our way to answer questions. But since you are so civil, I will tell you that you are arrested on suspicion of having poisoned that Russian baroness, with the long name, at whose house you have been so intimate."

"Poisoned? The baroness poisoned? Is she very ill, then?" asked Nino, in great alarm.

"She is dead," said the fat man, wiping his mouth, and twisting the empty glass in his hand.

"Dead!" cried Nino and I together.

"Dead — yes; as dead as St. Peter," he answered irreverently. "Your wine is good, Signor Professore. Yes, I will take another glass — and my men, too. Yes, she was found dead this morning, lying in her bed. You were there yesterday, Signor Cardegna, and her servant says he saw you giving her something in a glass of water." He drank a long draught from his glass. "You would have done better to give her some of this wine, my friend. She would certainly be alive to-day." But Nino was dark and thoughtful. He must have been pained and terribly shocked at the sudden news, of course, but he did not admire her as I did.

"Of course this thing will soon be over," he said at last. "I am very much grieved to hear of the lady's death, but it is absurd to suppose that I was concerned in it, however it happened. She fainted suddenly in the morning when I was there, and I gave her some water to drink, but there was nothing in it." He clasped his hands on his knee, and looked much distressed.

"It is quite possible that you poisoned her," remarked the fat man, with annoying indifference. "The servant says he overheard high words between you" —

"He overheard?" cried Nino, springing to his feet. "Cursed beast, to listen at the door!" . He began to walk about excitedly. "How long is this affair to keep me?" he asked suddenly. "I have to sing to-night — and that poor lady lying there dead — oh, I cannot!"

"Perhaps you will not be detained more than a couple of hours," said the fat man. "And perhaps you will be detained until the Day of Judgment," he added, with a sly wink at the gendarmes, who laughed obsequiously. "By this afternoon, the doctors will know of what she died; and if there was no poison, and she died a natural death, you can go to the theatre and sing, if you have the stomach. I would, I am sure. You see, she is a great lady, and the people of her embassy are causing everything to be done very quickly. If you had poisoned that old lady who brought us this famous wine a minute ago, you might have had to wait till next year, innocent or guilty." It struck me that the wine was producing its effect.

"Very well," said Nino, resolutely; "let us go. You will see that I am perfectly ready, although the news has shaken me much; and so you will permit me to walk quietly with you, without attracting any attention?"

"Oh, we would not think of incommoding you," said the fat man. "The orders were expressly to give you every convenience, and we have a private carriage below. Signor Grandi, we thank you for your civility. Good-morning — a thousand excuses." He bowed, and the gendarmes rose to their feet, refreshed and ruddy with the good wine. Of course I knew I could not accompany them, and I was too much frightened to have been of any use. Poor Mariuccia was crying in the kitchen.

"Send word to Jacovacci, the manager, if you do not hear by twelve o'clock," Nino called back from the landing, and the door closed behind them all. I was left alone, sad and frightened, and I felt very old, — much older than I am.

It was tragic. Mechanically I sank into the old green arm-chair, where she had sat but yesterday evening, — she whom I had seen but twice, once in the theatre and once here, but of whom I had heard so much. And she was dead, so soon. If Nino could only have heard her last words and seen her last look, he would have been more hurt when he heard of her sudden death. But he is of stone, that man, save for his love and his art. He seems to have no room left for sympathy with human ills, nor even for fear on his own account. Fear! — how I hate the word! Nino did not seem frightened at all, when they took him away. But as for me — well, it was not for myself this time, at least. That is some comfort. I think one may be afraid for other people.

Mariuccia was so much disturbed that I was obliged to go myself to get De Pretis, who gave up all his lessons that day and came to give me his advice. He looked grave and spoke very little, but he is a broad-shouldered, genial man, and very comforting. He insisted on going himself at once to see Nino, to give him all the help he could. He would not hear of my going, for. he said I ought to be bled and have some tea of mallows to calm me. And when I offered him a cigar from the box of good ones Nino had given me, he took six or seven, and put them in his pocket without saying a word. But I did not grudge them to him; for though he is very ridiculous, with his skull-cap and his snuff-box, he is a leal man, as we say, who stands by his friends and snaps his fingers at the devil.

I cannot describe to you the anxiety I felt through all that day. I could not eat, nor drink, nor write. I could not smoke, and when I tried to

10

go to sleep that cat — an apoplexy on her! — climbed up on my shoulder and clawed my hair. Mariuccia sat moaning in the kitchen, and could not cook at all, so that I was half starved.

At three o'clock De Pretis came back.

" Courage, conte mio! " he cried; and I knew it was all right. " Courage! Nino is at liberty again, and says he will sing to-night to show them he is not a clay doll, to be broken by a little knocking about. Ah, what a glorious boy Nino is ! "

" But where is he ? " I asked, when I could find voice to speak, for I was all trembling.

" He is gone for a good walk, to freshen his nerves, poverino. I wonder he has any strength left. For Heaven's sake, give me a match that I may light my cigar, and then I will tell you all about it. Thank you. And I will sit down, comfortably — so. Now you must know that the baroness — *requiescat!* — was not poisoned by Nino, or by any-one else."

" Of course not ! Go on."

" Piano, — slow and sure. They had a terrific scene, yesterday. You know? Yes. Then she went out and tired herself, poor soul, so that when she got home she had an attack of the nerves. Now these foreigners, who are a pack of silly people, do not have themselves bled and drink malva water as we do when we get a fit of anger. But they take opium; that is, a thing they call chloral. God knows what it is made of, but it puts them to sleep, like opium. When the doctors came to look at the poor lady, they saw at once what was the matter, and called the maid. The maid said her mistress certainly had some queer stuff in a little bottle, which she often used to take; and when they inquired further they heard that the baroness had poured out much more than usual the night before, while the maid was combing her hair, for she seemed terribly excited and restless. So they got the bottle and found it nearly empty. Then the doctors said, 'At what time was this young man who is now arrested seen to give her the glass of water?' The man-servant said it was about two in the afternoon. So the doctors knew that if Nino had given her the chloral she could not have gone out afterwards, and have been awake at eleven in the evening when her maid was with her, and yet have been hurt by what he gave her. And so, as Jacovacci was raising a thousand devils in every corner of Rome because they had arrested his principal singer on false pretenses, and was threatening to bring suits against everybody, including the Russian embassy, the doctors, and the government, if Nino did not appear in Faust to-night, according to his agreement, the result was that, half an hour ago, Nino was conducted out of the police precincts with ten thousand apologies, and put into the arms of Jacovacci, who wept for joy, and carried him off to a late breakfast at Morteo's. And then I came here. But I made Nino promise to take a good walk for his digestion, since the weather has changed.

For a breakfast at three in the afternoon may be called late, even in Rome. And that reminds me to ask you for a drop of wine; for I am still fasting, and this talking is worse for the throat than a dozen high masses."

Mariuccia had been listening at the door, as usual, and she immediately began crying for joy; for she is a weak-minded old thing, and dotes on Nino. I was very glad myself, I can tell you; but I could not understand how Nino could have the heart to sing, or should lack heart so much as to be fit for it. Before the evening he came home, `silent and thoughtful. I asked him whether he were not glad to be free so easily.

"That is not a very intelligent question for a philosopher like you to ask," he answered. "Of course I am glad of my liberty; any man would be. But I feel that I am as much the cause of that poor lady's death as though I had killed her with my own hands. I shall never forgive myself."

"Diana!" I cried, "it is a horrible tragedy; but it seems to me that you could not help it if she chose to love you."

"Hush!" said he, so sternly that he frightened me. "She is dead. God give her soul rest. Let us not talk of what she did."

"But," I objected, "if you feel so strongly about it, how can you sing at the opera to-night?"

"There are plenty of reasons why I should sing. In the first place, I owe it to my engagement with Jacovacci. He has taken endless trouble to have me cleared at once, and I will not disappoint him. Besides, I have not lost my voice, and might be half ruined by breaking contract so early. Then, the afternoon papers are full of the whole affair, some right and some wrong, and I am bound to show the Contessina di Lira that this unfortunate accident does not touch my heart, however sorry I may be. If I did not appear, all Rome would say it was because I was heart-broken. If she does not go to the theatre, she will at least hear of it. Therefore I will sing." It was very reasonable of him to think so.

" Have any of the papers got hold of the story of your giving lessons ? "

" No, I think not ; and there is no mention of the Lira family."

" So much the better."

Hedwig did not go to the opera. Of course she was quite right. However she might feel about the baroness, it would have been in the worst possible taste to go to the opera the very day after her death. That is the way society puts it. It is bad taste ; they never say it is heartless, or unkind, or brutal. It is simply bad taste. Nino sang, on the whole, better than if she had been there, for he put his whole soul in his art, and won fresh laurels. When it was over he was besieged by the agent of the London manager to come to some agreement.

." I cannot tell yet," he said. " I will tell you soon." He was not willing to leave Rome, — that was the truth of the matter. He thought of nothing, day or night, but of how he might see Hedwig; and his heart writhed in his breast when it seemed more and more impossible. He dared not risk compromising her by another serenade, as he felt sure that it had been some servant of the count who had betrayed him to the baroness. At last he hit upon a plan. The funeral of the baroness was to take place on the afternoon of the next day. He felt sure that the Graf von Lira would go to it, and he was equally certain that Hedwig would not. It chanced to be the hour at which De Pretis went to the Palazzo to give her the singing lesson.

"I suppose it is a barbarous thing for me to do," he said to himself, "but I cannot help it. Love first, and tragedy afterwards."

In the afternoon, therefore, he sallied out, and went boldly to the Palazzo Carmandola. He inquired of the porter whether the Signor Conte had gone out, and just as he had expected, so he found it. Old Lira had left the house ten minutes earlier, to go to the funeral. Nino ran up the stairs and rang the bell. The footman opened the door, and Nino quickly slipped a five-franc note into his hand, which he had no difficulty in finding. On asking if the signorina were at home, the footman nodded, and added that Professor De Pretis was with her, but she would doubtless see Professor Cardegna as well. And so it turned out. He was ushered into the great drawing-room, where the piano was. Hedwig came forward a few steps from

where she had been standing beside De Pretis, and
Nino bowed low before her. She had on a long
dark dress, and no ornament whatever, save her
beautiful bright hair, so that her face was like a
jewel set in gold and velvet. But, when I think
of it, such a combination would seem absurdly vulgar by the side of Hedwig von Lira. She was so
pale and exquisite and sad that Nino could hardly
look at her. He remembered that there were violets, rarest of flowers in Rome in January, in her
belt.

To tell the truth, Nino had expected to find her
stern and cold, whereas she was only very quiet
and sorrowful.

" Will you forgive me, signorina, for this rashness? " he asked in a low voice.

" In that I receive you I forgive you, sir," she
said. He glanced toward De Pretis, who seemed
absorbed in some music at the piano and was playing over bits of an accompaniment. She understood, and moved slowly to a window at the other
end of the great room, standing among the curtains.
He placed himself in the embrasure. She looked
at him long and earnestly, as if finally reconciling
the singer with the man she had known so long.
She found him changed, as I had, in a short time.
His face was sterner and thinner and whiter than
before, and there were traces of thought in the deep
shadows beneath his eyes. Quietly observing him,
she saw how perfectly simple and exquisitely careful was his dress, and how his hands bespoke that

attention which only a gentleman gives to the details of his person. She saw that, if he were not handsome, he was in the last degree striking to the eye, in spite of all his simplicity, and that he would not lose by being contrasted with all the dandies and courtiers in Rome. As she looked, she saw his lip quiver slightly, the only sign of emotion he ever gives, unless he loses his head altogether, and storms, as he sometimes does.

"Signorina," he began, "I have come to tell you a story; will you listen to it?"

"Tell it me," said she, still looking in his face.

"There was once a solitary castle in the mountains, with battlement and moat both high and broad. Far up in a lonely turret dwelt a rare maiden, of such surpassing beauty and fairness that the peasants thought she was not mortal, but an angel from heaven, resting in that tower from the doing of good deeds. She had flowers up there in her chamber, and the seeds of flowers; and as the seasons passed by, she took from her store the dry germs, and planted them one after another in a little earth on the window-sill. And the sun shone on them and they grew, and she breathed upon them and they were sweet. But they withered and bore no offspring, and fell away, so that year by year her store became diminished. At last there was but one little paper bag of seed left, and upon the cover was written in a strange character, 'This is the Seed of the Thorn of the World.' But the beautiful maiden was sad when she saw this, for

she said, 'All my flowers have been sweet, and
now I have but this thing left, which is a thorn!'
And she opened the paper and looked inside, and
saw one poor little seed, all black and shriveled.
Through that day she pondered what to do with it,
and was very unhappy. At night she said to herself, 'I will not plant this one; I will throw it
away, rather than plant it.' And she went to the
window, and tore the paper, and threw out the little
seed into the darkness."

" Poor little thing!" said Hedwig. She was listening intently.

" She threw it out, and, as it fell, all the air was
full of music, sad and sweet, so that she wondered
greatly. The next day she looked out of the window, and saw, between the moat and the castle wall,
a new plant growing. It looked black and uninvit-
ing, but it had come up so fast that it had already
laid hold on the rough gray stones. At the falling
of the night it reached far up towards the turret, a
great sharp-pointed vine, with only here and there a
miserable leaf on it. 'I am sorry I threw it out,'
said the maiden. 'It is the Thorn of the World,
and the people who pass will think it defaces my
castle.' But when it was dark again the air was
full of music. The maiden went to the window,
for she could not sleep, and she called out, asking
who it was that sang. Then a sweet, low voice
came up to her from the moat. 'I am the Thorn,'
it said, 'I sing in the dark, for I am growing.'
'Sing on, Thorn,' said she, 'and grow if you will.'

But in the morning, when she awoke, her window was darkened, for the Thorn had grown to be a mighty tree, and its topmost shoots were black against the sky. She wondered whether this uncouth plant would bear anything but music. So she spoke to it.

"'Thorn,' she said, 'why have you no flowers?'

"'I am the Thorn of the World,' it answered, 'and I can bear no flowers until the hand that planted me has tended me, and pruned me, and shaped me to be its own. If you had planted me like the rest, it would have been easy for you. But you planted me unwillingly, down below you by the moat, and I have had far to climb.'

"'But my hands are so delicate,' said the maiden. 'You will hurt me, I am sure.'

"'Yours is the only hand in the world that I will not hurt,' said the voice, so tenderly and softly and sadly that the gentle fingers went out to touch the plant and see if it were real. And touching it they clung there, for they had no harm of it. Would you know, my lady, what happened then?"

"Yes, yes — tell me!" cried Hedwig, whose imagination was fascinated by the tale.

"As her hands rested on the spiked branches, a gentle trembling went through the Thorn, and in a moment there burst out such a blooming and blossoming as the maiden had never seen. Every prick became a rose, and they were so many that the light of the day was tinged with them, and their sweetness was like the breath of paradise. But below

her window the Thorn was as black and forbidding
as ever, for only the maiden's presence could make
its flowers bloom. But she smelled the flowers,
and pressed many of them to her cheek.

"'I thought you were only a Thorn,' she said
softly.

"'Nay, fairest maiden,' answered the glorious
voice of the bursting blossom, 'I am the Rose of
the World forever, since you have touched me.'

"That is my story, signorina. Have I wearied
you?"

Hedwig had unconsciously moved nearer to him
as he was speaking, for he never raised his voice,
and she hung on his words. There was color in
her face, and her breath came quickly through her
parted lips. She had never looked so beautiful.

"Wearied me, signore? Ah no; it is a gentle
tale of yours."

"It is a true tale — in part," said he.

"In part? I do not understand" — But the
color was warmer in her cheek, and she turned her
face half away, as though looking out.

"I will tell you," he replied, coming closer, on
the side from which she turned. "Here is the
window. You are the maiden. The thorn — it is
my love for you;" he dropped his voice to a whisper. "You planted it carelessly, far below you in
the dark. In the dark it has grown and sung to
you, and grown again, until now it stands in your
own castle window. Will you not touch it and
make its flowers bloom for you?" He spoke fer-

vently. She had turned her face quite from him now, and was resting her forehead against one hand that leaned upon the heavy frame of the casement. The other hand hung down by her side toward him, fair as a lily against her dark gown. Nino touched it, then took it. He could see the blush spread to her white throat, and fade again. Between the half-falling curtain and the great window he bent his knee and pressed her fingers to his lips. She made as though she would withdraw her hand, and then left it in his. Her glance stole to him as he kneeled there, and he felt it on him, so that he looked up. She seemed to raise him with her fingers, and her eyes held his and drew them; he stood up, and, still holding her hand, his face was near to hers. Closer and closer yet, as by a spell, each gazing searchingly into the other's glance, till their eyes could see no more for closeness, and their lips met in life's first virgin kiss, — in the glory and strength of a twofold purity, each to each.

Far off at the other end of the room De Pretis struck a chord on the piano. They started at the sound.

" When ? " whispered Nino, hurriedly.

" At midnight, under my window," she answered quickly, not thinking of anything better in her haste. " I will tell you then. You must go ; my father will soon be here. No, not again," she protested. But he drew her to him, and said good-by in his own manner. She lingered an instant, and tore herself away. De Pretis was playing loudly. Nino had to pass near him to go out, and the maestro nodded carelessly as he went by.

"Excuse me, maestro," said Hedwig, as Nino bowed himself out; "it was a question of arranging certain lessons."

"Do not mention it," said he indifferently; "my time is yours, signorina. Shall we go through with this solfeggio once more?"

The good maestro did not seem greatly disturbed by the interruption. Hedwig wondered, dreamily, whether he had understood. It all seemed like a dream. The notes were upside down in her sight, and her voice sought strange minor keys unconsciously, as she vainly tried to concentrate her attention upon what she was doing.

"Signorina," said Ercole at last, "what you sing is very pretty, but it is not exactly what is written here. I fear you are tired."

"Perhaps so," said she. "Let us not sing any more to-day." Ercole shut up the music and rose. She gave him her hand, a thing she had never done before; and it was unconscious now, as everything she did seemed to be. There is a point when dreaming gets the mastery, and appears infinitely more real than the things we touch.

Nino, meanwhile, had descended the steps, expecting every moment to meet the count. As he went down the street, a closed carriage drove by with the Lira liveries. The old count was in it, but Nino stepped into the shadow of a doorway to let the equipage pass, and was not seen. The wooden face of the old nobleman almost betrayed something akin to emotion. He was returning from the funeral, and it had pained him; for he had liked the wild baroness, in a fatherly, reproving way. But the sight of him sent a home thrust to Nino's heart.

"Her death is on my soul forever," he muttered between his set teeth. Poor innocent boy, it was not his fault if she had loved him so much. Women have done things for great singers that they have not done for martyrs or heroes. It seems so certain that the voice that sings so tenderly is speaking to them individually. Music is such a fleeting, passionate thing that a woman takes it all to herself; how could he sing like that for any one else? And yet there is always some one for whom he does really pour out his heart, and all the rest are the dolls of life, to be looked at, and admired for their dress and complexion, and to laugh at when the fancy takes him to laugh; but not to love.

At midnight Nino was at his post, but he waited long and patiently for a sign. It was past two, and he was thinking it hopeless to wait longer, when his quick ear caught the sound of a window moving on its hinges, and a moment later something fell at his feet with a sharp, metallic click. The night was dark and cloudy, so that the waning moon gave little light. He picked up the thing, and found a small pocket handkerchief wrapped about a minute pair of scissors, apparently to give it weight. He expected a letter, and groped on the damp pavement with his hands. Then he struck a match, shaded it from the breeze with his hand, and saw that the handkerchief was stained with ink and that the stains were letters, roughly printed to make them distinct. He hurried away to the light of a street lamp to read the strange missive.

X.

He went to the light and spread out the handkerchief. It was a small thing, of almost transparent stuff, with a plain " H. L." and a crown in the corner. The steel pen had torn the delicate fibres here and there.

"They know you have been here. I am watched. Keep away from the house till you hear."

That was all the message, but it told worlds. He knew from it that the count was informed of his visit, and he tortured himself by trying to imagine what the angry old man would do. His heart sank like a stone in his breast when he thought of Hedwig so imprisoned, guarded, made a martyr of, for his folly. He groaned aloud when he understood that it was in the power of her father to take her away suddenly and leave no trace of their destination, and he cursed his haste and impetuosity in having shown himself inside the house. But with all this weight of trouble upon him, he felt the strength and indomitable determination within him which come only to a man who loves, when he knows he is loved again. He kissed the little handkerchief, and even the scissors she had used to weight it with, and he put them in his breast. But he stood irresolute, leaning against the lamp-post, as a man will who is trying to force his thoughts to overtake events, trying to shape the future out of the present. Suddenly, he was aware of a tall figure in a fur coat standing near him on the sidewalk. He would have turned to go, but something about the stranger's appearance struck him so oddly that he stayed where he was and watched him.

The tall man searched for something in his pockets, and finally produced a cigarette, which he leisurely lighted with a wax match. As he did so his eyes fell upon Nino. The stranger was tall and very thin. He wore a pointed beard and a heavy mustache, which seemed almost dazzlingly white, as were the few locks that appeared, neatly brushed over his temples, beneath his opera hat. His sanguine complexion, however, had all the freshness of youth, and his eyes sparkled merrily, as though amused at the spectacle of his nose, which was immense, curved, and polished, like an eagle's beak. He wore perfectly fitting kid gloves and the collar of his fur wrapper, falling a little open, showed that he was in evening dress.

It was so late — past two o'clock — that Nino had not expected anything more than a policeman or some homeless wanderer, when he raised his eyes to look on the stranger. He was fascinated by the strange presence of the aged dandy, for such he seemed to be, and returned his gaze boldly. He was still more astonished, however, when the old gentleman came close to him, and raised his hat, displaying, as he did so, a very high and narrow forehead, crowned with a mass of smooth white hair. There was both grace and authority in the courteous gesture, and Nino thought the old gentleman moved with an ease that matched his youthful complexion rather than his hoary locks.

" Signor Cardegna, the distinguished artist, if I mistake not?" said the stranger, with a peculiar foreign accent, the like of which Nino had never heard. He, also, raised his hat, extremely surprised that a chance passer-by should know him. He had not yet learned what it is to be famous. But he was far from pleased at being addressed in his present mood.

"The same, signore," he replied coldly. " How can I serve you?"

" You can serve the world you so well adorn better than by exposing your noble voice to the midnight damps and chills of this infernal — I would say, eternal — city," answered the other. " Forgive me. I am, not unnaturally, concerned at the prospect of losing even a small portion of the pleasure you know how to give to me and to many others."

" I thank you for your flattery," said Nino, drawing his cloak about him, " but it appears to me that my throat is my own, and whatever voice there may be in it. Are you a physician, signore? And pray why do you tell me that Rome is an infernal city?"

" I have had some experience of Rome, Signor Cardegna," returned the foreigner, with a peculiar smile, "and I hate no place so bitterly in all this world — save one. And as for my being a physician, I am an old man, a very singularly old man in fact, and I know something of the art of healing."

"When I need healing, as you call it," said Nino rather scornfully, "I will inquire for you. Do you desire to continue this interview amid the 'damps and chills' of our 'infernal city'? If not, I will wish you good-evening."

"By no means," said the other, not in the least repulsed by Nino's coldness. "I will accompany you a little way, if you will allow me." Nino stared hard at the stranger, wondering what could induce him to take so much interest in a singer. Then he nodded gravely, and turned toward his home, inwardly hoping that his aggressive acquaintance lived in the opposite direction. But he was mistaken. The tall man blew a quantity of smoke through his nose and walked by his side. He strode over the pavement with a long, elastic step.

"I live not far from here," he said, when they had gone a few steps, "and if the Signor Cardegna will accept of a glass of old wine and a good cigar I shall feel highly honored." Somehow an invitation of this kind was the last thing Nino had expected or desired, least of all from a talkative stranger who seemed determined to make his acquaintance.

"I thank you, signore," he answered, "but I have supped, and I do not smoke."

"Ah — I forgot. You are a singer, and must of

course be careful. That is perhaps the reason why
you wander about the streets when the nights are
dark and damp. But I can offer you something
more attractive than liquor and tobacco. A great
violinist lives with me, a queer, nocturnal bird, —
and if you will come he will be enchanted to play
for you. I assure you he is a very good musician,
the like of whom you will hardly hear nowadays.
He does not play in public any longer, from some
odd fancy of his."

Nino hesitated. Of all instruments he loved the
violin best, and in Rome he had had but little opportunity of hearing it well played. Concerts were
the rarest of luxuries to him, and violinists in Rome
are rarer still.

" What is his name, signore?" he asked, unbending a little.

" You must guess that when you hear him," said
the old gentleman, with a short laugh. " But I give
you my word of honor he is a great musician. Will
you come, or must I offer you further attractions?"

" What might they be?" asked Nino.

" Nay; will you come for what I offer you? If
the music is not good, you may go away again."
Still Nino hesitated. Sorrowful and fearful of the
future as he was, his love gnawing cruelly at his
heart, he would have given the whole world for a
strain of rare music if only he were not forced to
make it himself. Then it struck him that this might
be some pitfall. I would not have gone.

" Sir," he said at last, " if you meditate any foul

play, I would advise you to retract your invitation.
I will come, and I am well armed." He had my
long knife about him somewhere. It is one of my
precautions. But the stranger laughed long and
loud at the suggestion, so that his voice woke queer
echoes in the silent street. Nino did not understand why he should laugh so much, but he found
his knife under his cloak, and made sure it was
loose in its leathern sheath. Presently the stranger
stopped before the large door of an old palazzo, —
every house is a palazzo that has an entrance for
carriages, — and let himself in with a key. There
was a lantern on the stone pavement inside, and
seeing a light, Nino followed him boldly. The old
gentleman took the lantern and led the way up the
stairs, apologizing for the distance and the darkness. At last they stopped, and, entering another
door, found themselves in the stranger's apartment.

"A cardinal lives down-stairs," said he, as he
turned up the light of a couple of large lamps that
burned dimly in the room they had reached. "The
secretary of a very holy order has his office on the
other side of my landing, and altogether this is a
very religious atmosphere. Pray take off your
cloak; the room is warm."

Nino looked about him. He had expected to be
ushered into some princely dwelling, for he had
judged his interlocutor to be some rich and eccen-
tric noble, unless he were an erratic scamp. He
was somewhat taken aback by the spectacle that
met his eyes. The furniture was scant, and all in

the style of the last century. The dust lay half an
inch thick on the old gilded ornaments and chande-
liers.   A great pier-glass was cracked from corner
to corner, and the metallic backing seemed to be
scaling off behind.   There were two or three open
valises on the marble floor, which latter, however,
seemed to have been lately swept.   A square table
was in the centre, also free from dust, and a few
high-backed leathern chairs, studded with brass
nails, were ranged about it.   On the table stood
one of the lamps, and the other was placed on a
marble column in a corner, that once must have supported a bust, or something of the kind.   Old curtains, moth-eaten and ragged with age, but of a rich
material, covered the windows.   Nino glanced at the
open trunks on the floor, and saw that they contained a quantity of wearing apparel and the like.
He guessed that his acquaintance had lately arrived.

" I do not often inhabit this den," said the old
gentleman, who had divested himself of his furs,
and now showed his thin figure arrayed in the extreme of full dress.   A couple of decorations hung
at his button-hole.   " I seldom come here, and on
my return, the other day, I found that the man I
had left in charge was dead, with all his family,
and the place has gone to ruin.   That is always my
luck," he added, with a little laugh.

" I should think he must have been dead some
time," said Nino, looking about him.   " There is a
great deal of dust here."

" Yes, as you say, it is some years," returned his acquaintance, still laughing. He seemed a merry old soul, fifty years younger than his looks. He produced from a case a bottle of wine and two silver cups, and placed them on the table.

" But where is your friend, the violinist? " inquired Nino, who was beginning to be impatient; for except that the place was dusty and old, there was nothing about it sufficiently interesting to take his thoughts from the subject nearest his heart.

" I will introduce him to you," said the other, going to one of the valises and taking out a violin case, which he laid on the table and proceeded to open. The instrument was apparently of great age, small and well shaped. The stranger took it· up and began to tune it.

" Do you mean to say that you are yourself the violinist? " he asked, in astonishment. But the stranger vouchsafed no answer, as he steadied the fiddle with his bearded chin and turned the pegs with his left hand, adjusting the strings.

Then, suddenly and without any preluding, he began to make music, and from the first note Nino sat enthralled and fascinated, losing himself in the wild sport of the tones. The old man's face became ashy white as he played, and his white hair appeared to stand away from his head. The long, thin fingers of his left hand chased each other in pairs and singly along the delicate strings, while the bow glanced in the lamplight as it dashed like lightning across the instrument, or remained almost stationary, quivering in his magic hold as quickly as the wings of the humming-bird strike the summer air. Sometimes he seemed to be tearing the heart from the old violin; sometimes it seemed to murmur soft things in his old ear, as though the imprisoned spirit of the music were pleading to be free on the wings of sound: sweet as love that is strong as death; feverish and murderous as jealousy that is as cruel as the grave; sobbing great sobs of a terrible death-song, and screaming in the outrageous frenzy of a furious foe; wailing thin cries of misery, too exhausted for strong grief; dancing again in horrid madness, as the devils dance over some fresh sinner they have gotten themselves for torture; and then at last, as the strings bent to the commanding bow, finding the triumph of a glorious rest in great, broad chords, splendid in depth and royal harmony, grand, enormous, and massive as the united choirs of heaven.

Nino was beside himself, leaning far over the table, straining eyes and ears to understand the wonderful music that made him drunk with its strength. As the tones ceased he sank back in his chair, exhausted by the tremendous effort of his senses. Instantly the old man recovered his former appearance. With his hand he smoothed the thick white hair; the fresh color came back to his cheeks; and as he tenderly laid his violin on the table, he was again the exquisitely dressed and courtly gentleman who had spoken to Nino in the street. The musician disappeared, and the man of the world returned. He poured wine into the plain silver cups, and invited Nino to drink; but the boy pushed the goblet away, and his strange host drank alone.

"You asked me for the musician's name," he said, with a merry twinkle in his eye, from which every trace of artistic inspiration had faded; "can you guess it now?" Nino seemed tongue-tied still, but he made an effort.

"I have heard of Paganini," he said, "but he died years ago."

"Yes, he is dead, poor fellow! I am not. Paganini."

"I am at a loss, then," said Nino dreamily. "I do not know the names of many violinists, but you must be so famous that I ought to know yours."

"No; how should you? I will tell you. I am Benoni, the Jew." The tall man's eyes twinkled more brightly than ever. Nino stared at him, and saw that he was certainly of a pronounced Jewish type. His brown eyes were long and oriental in shape, and his nose was unmistakably Semitic.

"I am sorry to seem so ignorant," said Nino, blushing, "but I do not know the name. I perceive, however, that you are indeed a very great musician, — the greatest I ever heard." The compliment was perfectly sincere, and Benoni's face beamed with pleasure. He evidently liked praise.

"It is not extraordinary," he said, smiling. "In the course of a very long life it has been my only solace, and if I have some skill it is the result of constant study. I began life very humbly."

" So did I," said Nino thoughtfully, " and I am
not far from the humbleness yet."

" Tell me," said Benoni, with a show of interest,
" where you come from, and why you are a singer."

" I was a peasant's child, an orphan, and the
good God gave me a voice. That is all I know
about it. A kind-hearted gentleman, who once
owned the estate where I was born, brought me up,
and wanted to make a philosopher of me. But I
wanted to sing, and so I did."

" Do you always do the things you want to do ? "
asked the other. " You look as though you might.
You look like Napoleon, — that man always interested me. That is why I asked you to come and
see me. I have heard you sing, and you are a great
artist, — an additional reason. All artists should
be brothers. Do you not think so ? "

" Indeed, I know very few good ones," said Nino
simply; " and even among them I would like to
choose before claiming relationship — personally.
But Art is a great mother, and we are all her
children."

" More especially we who began life so poorly,
and love Art because she loves us." Benoni seated
himself on the arm of one of the old chairs, and
looked down across the worm-eaten table at the
young singer. " We," he continued, " who have
been wretchedly poor know better than others that
art is real, true, and enduring; medicine in sick-
ness and food in famine ; wings to the feet of youth
and a staff for the steps of old age. Do you think

I exaggerate, or do you feel as I do?" He paused for a reply, and poured more wine into his goblet.

"Oh, you know I feel as you do!" cried Nino, with rising enthusiasm.

"Very good; you are a genuine artist. What you have not felt yet, you will feel hereafter. You have not suffered yet."

"You do not know about me," said Nino in a low voice. "I am suffering now."

Benoni smiled. "Do you call that suffering? Well, it is perhaps very real to you, though I do not know what it is. But art will help you through it all, as it has helped me."

"What were you?" asked Nino. "You say you were poor."

"Yes. I was a shoemaker, and a poor one at that. I have worn out more shoes than I ever made. But I was brought up to it for many years."

"You did not study music from a child, then?"

"No. But I always loved it; and I used to play in the evenings, when I had been cobbling all day long."

"And one day you found out you were a great artist and became famous. I see! What a strange beginning!" cried Nino.

"Not exactly that. It took a long time. I was obliged to leave my home, for other reasons, and then I played from door to door, and from town to town, for whatever coppers were thrown to me. I had never heard any good music, and so I played the things that came into my head. By and by

people would make me stay with them awhile, for
my music's sake.   But I never stayed long."

"Why not?"

"I cannot tell you now," said Benoni, looking
grave and almost sad : "it is a very long story.   I
have traveled a great deal, preferring a life of adventure.   But of late money has grown to be so
important a thing that I have given a series of
great concerts, and have become rich enough to
play for my own pleasure.   Besides, though I travel
so much, I like society, and I know many people
everywhere.   To-night, for instance, though I have
been in Rome only a week, I have been to a dinner
party, to the theatre, to a reception, and to a ball.
Everybody invites me as soon as I arrive.   I am
very popular, — and yet I am a Jew," he added,
laughing in an odd way.

"But you are a merry Jew," said Nino, laughing too, "besides being a great genius.   I do not
wonder people invite you."

"It is better to be merry than sad," replied Benoni.   "In the course of a long life I have found
out that."

"You do not look so very old," said Nino.
"How old are you?"

"That is a rude question," said his host, laughing.   "But I will improvise a piece of music for
you."   He took his violin, and stood up before the
broken pier-glass.   Then he laid the bow over the
strings and struck a chord.   "What is that?" he
asked, sustaining the sound.

" The common chord of A minor," answered
Nino immediately.

" You have a good ear," said Benoni, still playing the same notes, so that the constant monotony
of them buzzed like a vexatious insect in Nino's
hearing. Still the old man sawed the bow over the
same strings without change. On and on, the
same everlasting chord, till Nino thought he must
go mad.

" It is intolerable; for the love of Heaven stop ! "
he cried, pushing back his chair and beginning to
pace the room. Benoni only smiled, and went on
as unchangingly as ever. Nino could bear it no
longer, being very sensitive about sounds, and he
made for the door.

" You cannot get out, — I have the key in my
pocket," said Benoni, without stopping.

Then Nino became nearly frantic, and made at
the Jew to wrest the instrument from his hands.
But Benoni was agile, and eluded him, still playing
the one chord, till Nino cried aloud, and sank in a
chair, entirely overcome by the torture, that seemed
boring its way into his brain like a corkscrew.

" This," said Benoni, the bow still sawing the
strings, " is life without laughter. Now let us laugh
a little, and see the effect."

It was indeed wonderful. With his instrument
he imitated the sound of a laughing voice, high
up above the monotonous chord : softly at first, as
though far in the distance ; then louder and nearer,
the sustaining notes of the minor falling away one

after the other and losing themselves, as the merriment gained ground on the sadness; till finally, with a burst of life and vitality of which it would be impossible to convey any idea, the whole body of mirth broke into a wild tarantella movement, so vivid and elastic and noisy that it seemed to Nino that he saw the very feet of the dancers, and heard the jolly din of the tambourine and the clattering, clappering click of the castanets.

" That," said Benoni, suddenly stopping, " is life with laughter, be it ever so sad and monotonous before. Which do you prefer ? "

" You are the greatest artist in the world ! " cried Nina enthusiastically ; " but I should have been a raving madman if you had played that chord any longer."

" Of course," said Benoni, " and I should have gone mad if I had not laughed. Poor Schumann, you know, died insane because he fancied he always heard one note droning in his ears."

" I can understand that," said Nino. " But it is late, and I must be going home. Forgive my rudeness and reluctance to come with you. I was moody and unhappy. You have given me more pleasure than I can tell you."

" It will seem little enough to-morrow, I dare say," replied Benoni. " That is the way with pleasures. But you should get them all the same, when you can, and grasp them as tightly as a drowning man grasps a straw. Pleasures and money, money and pleasures."

Nino did not understand the tone in which his host made this last remark. He had learned dif-' ferent doctrines from me.

" Why do you speak so selfishly, after showing that you can give pleasure so freely, and telling me that we are all brothers ? " he asked.

" If you are not in a hurry, I will explain to you that money is the only thing in this world worth having," said Benoni, drinking another cup of the wine, which appeared to have no effect whatever on his brain.

" Well ? " said Nino, curious to hear what he had to say.

" In the first place you will allow that from the noblest moral standpoint a man's highest aim should be to do good to his fellow creatures ? Yes, you allow that. And to do the greatest possible good to the greatest possible number ? Yes, you allow that, also. Then, I say, other things being alike, a good man will do the greatest possible amount of good in the world when he has the greatest possible amount of money. The more money, the more good ; the less money, the less good. Of course money is only the means to the end, but nothing tangible in the world can ever be anything else. All art is only a means to the exciting of still more perfect images in the brain ; all crime is a means to the satisfaction of passion, or avarice which is itself a king-passion ; all good itself is a means to the attainment of heaven. Everything is bad or good in the world, except art, which is a thing sep-

arate, though having good and bad results. But
the attainment of heaven is the best object to keep
in view. To that end, do the most good ; and to
do it, get the most money. Therefore, as a means,
money is the only thing in the world worth having,
since you can most benefit humanity by it, and consequently be the most sure of going to heaven when
you die. Is that clear ? "

" Perfectly," said Nino, " provided a man is himself good."

" It is very reprehensible to be bad," said Benoni, with a smile.

" What a ridiculous truism! " said Nino, laughing outright.

" Very likely," said the other. " But I never
heard any preacher, in any country, tell his con-
gregation anything else. And people always listen
with attention. In countries where rain is entirely
unknown, it is not a truism to say that ' when it
rains it is damp.' On the contrary, in such countries that statement would be regarded as requiring
demonstration, and, once demonstrated, it would be
treasured and taught as an interesting scientific
fact. Now it is precisely the same with congrega-
tions of men. They were never bad, and never
can be ; in fact, they doubt, in their dear innocent
hearts, whether they know what a real sin is. Consequently they listen with interest to the statement
that sin is bad, and promise themselves that if ever
that piece of information should be unexpectedly
needed by any of their friends, they will remember it."

"You are a satirist, Signor Benoni," said Nino. "Anything you like," returned the other. "I have been called worse names than that, in my time. So much for heaven, and the prospect of it. But a gentleman has arisen in a foreign country who says that there is no heaven anywhere, and that no one does good except in the pursuit of pleasure here or hereafter. But as his hereafter is nowhere, disregard it in the argument, and say that man should only do, or actually does, everything solely for the sake of pleasure here; say that pleasure is good, so long as it does not interfere with the pleasures of others, and good is pleasure. Money may help a man to more of it, but pleasure is the thing. Well, then, my young brother artist, what did I say?—'money and pleasure, pleasure and money.' The means are there; and as, of course, you are good, like everybody else, and desire pleasure, you will get to heaven hereafter, if there is such a place; and if not, you will get the next thing to it, which is a paradise on earth." Having reached the climax, Signor Benoni lit a cigarette, and laughed his own peculiar laugh.

Nino shuddered involuntarily at the hideous sophistry. For Nino is a good boy, and believes very much in heaven, as well as in a couple of other places. Benoni's quick brown eyes saw the movement, and understood it, for he laughed longer yet, and louder.

"Why do you laugh like that? I see nothing to laugh at. It is very bitter and bad to hear, all

12

this that you say. I would rather hear your music.
You are badly off, whether you believe in heaven
or not. For if you do, you are not likely to get
there; and if you do not believe in it, you are a heretic, and will be burned forever and ever."

"Not so badly answered, for an artist; and in a
few words, too," said Benoni approvingly. "But,
my dear boy, the trouble is that I shall not get to
heaven either way, for it is my great misfortune to
be already condemned to everlasting flames."

"No one is that," said Nino gravely.

"There are some exceptions, you know," said
Benoni.

"Well," answered the young man thoughtfully,
"of course there is the Wandering Jew, and such
tales, but nobody believes in him."

"Good-night," said Benoni. "I am tired, and
must go to bed."

Nino found his way out alone, but carefully
noted the position of the palazzo before he went
home through the deserted streets. It was four in
the morning.

EARLY in the morning after Nino's visit to Signor Benoni, De Pretis came to my house, wringing his hands and making a great trouble and noise. I had not yet seen Nino, who was sound asleep, though I could not imagine why he did not wake. But De Pretis was in such a temper that he shook the room and everything in it, as he stamped about the brick floor. It was not long before he had told me the cause of his trouble. He had just received a formal note from the Graf von Lira, inclosing the amount due to him for lessons, and dispensing with his services for the future.

Of course this was the result of the visit Nino had so rashly made; it all came out afterwards, and I will not now go through the details that De Pretis poured out, when we only half knew the truth. The count's servant who admitted Nino had pocketed the five francs as quietly as you please, and the moment the count returned he told him how Nino had come and had stayed three quarters of an hour, just as if it were an every-day affair. The count, being a proud old man, did not encourage him to make further confidences, but sent him about his business. He determined to make a prisoner of his daughter until he could remove her from Rome. He accordingly confined her in the little suite of ·apartments that were her own, and set an old soldier, whom he had brought from Germany as a body-servant, to keep watch at the outer door. He did not condescend to explain even to Hedwig the cause of his conduct, and she, poor girl, was as proud as he, and would not ask why she was shut up, lest the answer should be a storm of abuse against Nino. She cared not at all how her father had found out her secret, so long as he knew it, and she guessed that submission would be the best policy.

Meanwhile, active preparations were made for an immediate departure. The count informed his friends that he was going to pass Lent in Paris, on account of his daughter's health, which was very poor, and in two days everything was ready. They would leave on the following morning. In the evening the count entered his daughter's apartments, after causing himself to be formally announced by a servant, and briefly informed her that they would start for Paris on the following morning. Her maid had been engaged in the mean time in packing her effects, not knowing whither her mistress was going. Hedwig received the announcement in silence, but her father saw that she was deadly white and her eyes heavy from weeping. I have anticipated this much to make things clearer. It was on the first morning of Hedwig's confinement that De Pretis came to our house.

Nino was soon waked by the maestro's noise, and

came to the door of his chamber, which opens into
the little sitting-room, to inquire what the matter
might be. Nino asked if the maestro were ped-
dling cabbages, that he should scream so loudly.

"Cabbages, indeed! cabbage yourself, silly boy!"
cried Ercole, shaking his fist at Nino's head, just
visible through the crack of the door. "A pretty
mess you have made, with your ridiculous love affair! Here am I"—

"I see you are," retorted Nino; "and do not
call any affair of mine ridiculous, or I will throw
you out of the window. Wait a moment!" With
that he slammed his door in the maestro's face, and
went on with his dressing. For a few minutes De
Pretis raved at his ease, venting his wrath on me.
Then Nino came out.

"Now, then," said he, preparing for a tussle,
"what is the matter, my dear maestro?" But Ercole had expended most of his fury already.

"The matter!" he grumbled. "The matter is
that I have lost an excellent pupil through you.
Count Lira says he does not require my services
any longer, and the man who brought the note says
they are going away."

"Diavolo!" said Nino, running his fingers
through his curly black hair, "it is indeed serious.
Where are they going?"

"How should I know?" asked De Pretis angrily. "I care much more about losing the lesson
than about where they are going. I shall not follow them, I promise you. I cannot take the basil-

ica of St. Peter about with me in my pocket, can I ? "

And so he was angry at first, and at length he was pacified, and finally he advised Nino to discover immediately where the count and his daughter were going ; and, if it were to any great capital, to endeavor to make a contract to sing there. Lent came early that year, and Nino was free at the end of Carnival, — not many days longer to wait. This was the plan that had instantly formed itself in Nino's brain. De Pretis is really a most obliging man, but one cannot wonder that he should be annoyed at the result of Nino's four months' courtship under such great difficulties, when it seemed that all their efforts had led only to the sudden departure of his lady-love. As for me, I advised Nino to let the whole matter drop then and there. I told him he would soon get over his foolish passion, and that a statue like Hedwig could never suffer anything, since she could never feel. But he glared at me, and did as he liked, just as he always has done.

The message on the handkerchief that Nino had received the night before warned him to keep away from the Palazzo Carmandola. Nino reflected that this warning was probably due to Hedwig's anxiety for his personal safety, and he resolved to risk anything rather than remain in ignorance of her destination. It must be a case of giving some signal. But this evening he had to sing at the theatre, and therefore, without more ado, he left us and went to bed again, where he stayed until twelve o'clock. Then he went to rehearsal, arriving an hour behind time, at least, a matter which he treated with the coolest indifference. After that he got a pound of small shot, and amused himself with throwing a few at a time at the kitchen window from the little court at the back of our house, where the well is. It seemed a strangely childish amusement for a great singer.

Having sung successfully through his opera that night, he had supper with us, as usual, and then went out. Of course he told me afterwards what he did. He went to his old post under the windows of the Palazzo Carmandola, and as soon as all was dark he began to throw small shot up at Hedwig's window. He now profited by his practice in the afternoon, for he made the panes rattle with the little bits of lead, several times. At last he was rewarded. Very slowly the window opened, and Hedwig's voice spoke in a low tone : —

"Is it you?"

"Ah, dear one! Can you ask?" began Nino.

"Hush! I am still locked up. We are going away, — I cannot tell where."

"When, dearest love?"

"I cannot tell. What *shall* we do?" very tearfully.

"I will follow you immediately; only let me know when and where."

"If you do not hear by some other means, come here to-morrow night. I hear steps. Go at once."

" Good-night, dearest," he murmured ; but the window was already closed, and the fresh breeze that springs up after one o'clock blew from the air the remembrance of the loving speech that had passed upon it.

On the following night he was at his post, and again threw the shot against the pane for a signal. After a long time Hedwig opened the window very cautiously.

"Quick !" she whispered down to him, " go ! they are all awake," and she dropped something heavy and white. Perhaps she added some word, but Nino would not tell me, and never would read me the letter. But it contained the news that Hedwig and her father were to leave Rome for Paris on the following morning ; and ever since that night Nino has worn upon his little finger a plain gold ring, — I cannot tell why, and he says he found it.

The next day he ascertained from the porter of the Palazzo Carmandola that the count and contessina, with their servants, had actually left Rome that morning for Paris. From that moment he was sad as death, and went about his business heavily, being possessed of but one idea, namely, to sign an engagement to sing in Paris as soon as possible. In that wicked city the opera continues through Lent, and after some haggling, in which De Pretis insisted on obtaining for Nino the most advantageous terms, the contract was made out and signed.

I see very well that unless I hurry myself I shall never reach the most important part of this story, which is, after all, the only part worth telling. I am sure I do not know how I can ever tell it so quickly, but I will do my best, and you must have a little patience; for though I am not old, I am not young, and Nino's departure for Paris was a great shock to me, so that I do not like to remember it, and the very thought of it sickens me. If you have ever had any education, you must have seen an experiment in which a mouse is put in a glass jar, and all the air is drawn away with a pump, so that the poor little beast languishes and rolls pitifully on its side, gasping and wheezing with its tiny lungs for the least whiff of air. That is just how I felt when Nino went away. It seemed as though I could not breathe in the house or in the streets, and the little rooms at home were so quiet that one might hear a pin fall, and the cat purring through the closed doors. Nino left at the beginning of the last ten days of Carnival, when the opera closed, so that it was soon Lent; and everything is quieter then.

But before he left us there was noise enough and bustle of preparation, and I did not think I should miss him; for he always was making music, or walking about, or doing something to disturb me, just at the very moment when I was most busy with my books. Mariuccia, indeed, would ask me from time to time what I should do when Nino was gone, as if she could foretell what I was to feel. I suppose she knew I was used to him, after fourteen

years of it, and would be inclined to black humors
for want of his voice. But she could not know just
what Nino is to me, nor how I look on him as my
own boy. These peasants are quick-witted and
foolish; they guess a great many things better
than I could, and then reason on them like idiots.

Nino himself was glad to go. I could see his face
grow brighter as the time approached; and though
he appeared to be more successful than ever in his
singing, I am sure that he cared nothing for the applause he got, and thought only of singing as well
as he could for the love of it. But when it came
to the parting we were left alone.

"Messer Cornelio," he said, looking at me affectionately, "I have something to say to you to-night,
before I go away."

"Speak, then, my dear boy," I answered, "for
no one hears us."

"You have been very good to me. A father
could not have loved me better, and such a father as
I had could not have done a thousandth part what
you have done for me. I am going out into the
world for a time, but my home is here, — or, rather,
where my home is will always be yours. You
have been my father, and I will be your son; and
it is time you should give up your professorship.
No, not that you are at all old; I do not mean
that."

"No, indeed," said I, "I should think not."

"It would be much more proper if you retired
into an elegant leisure, so that you might write as

many books as you desire, without wearing yourself
out in teaching those students every day. Would
you not like to go back to Serveti ? "

" Serveti ! — ah, beautiful, lost Serveti, with its
castle and good vinelands ! "

" You shall have it again before long, my father," he said. He had never called me father before, the dear boy ! I suppose it was because he
was going away. But Serveti again ! The thing
was impossible, and I said so.

" It is not impossible," he answered placidly.
" Successful singers make enough money in a year
to buy Serveti. A year is soon passed. But now
let us go to the station, or I shall not be in time for
the train."

" God bless you, Nino mio," I said, as I saw him
off. It seemed to me that I saw two or three Ni-
nos. But the train rolled away and took them all
from me, — the ragged little child who first came
to me, the strong-limbed, dark-eyed boy with his
scales and trills and enthusiasm, and the full-
grown man with the face like the great emperor,
mightily triumphing in his art and daring in his
love. They were all gone in a moment, and I was
left alone on the platform of the station, a very sorrowful and weak old man. Well, I will not think
about that day.

The first I heard of Nino was by a letter he
wrote from Paris, a fortnight after he had left me.
It was characteristic of him, being full of eager
questions about home and De Pretis and Mariuccia

and Rome. Two things struck me in his writing. In the first place, he made no mention of the count or Hedwig, which led me to suppose that he was recovering from his passion, as boys do when they travel. And secondly, he had so much to say about me that he forgot all about his engagement, and never even mentioned the theatre. On looking carefully through the letter again, I found he had written across the top the words " Rehearsals satisfactory." That was all.

It was not long after the letter came, however, that I was very much frightened by receiving a telegram, which must have cost several francs to send all that distance. By this he told me that he had no clue to the whereabouts of the Liras, and he implored me to make inquiries and discover where they had gone. He added that he had appeared in Faust successfully. Of course he would succeed. If a singer can please the Romans, he can please anybody. But it seemed to me that if he had received a very especially flattering reception he would have said so. I went to see De Pretis, whom I found at home over his dinner. We put our heads together and debated how we might discover the Paris address of the Graf von Lira. In a great city like that it was no wonder Nino could not find them ; but De Pretis hoped that some of his pupils might be in correspondence with the contessina, and would be willing to give the requisite directions for reaching her. But days passed, and a letter came from Nino written immediately after sending the telegram, and still we had accomplished nothing. The letter merely amplified the telegraphic message.

"It is no use," I said to De Pretis. "And besides, it is much better that he should forget all about it."

"You do not know that boy," said the maestro, taking snuff. He was quite right, as it turned out.

Suddenly Nino wrote from London. He had made an arrangement, he said, by which he was allowed to sing there for three nights only. The two managers had settled it between them, being friends. He wrote very despondently, saying that although he had been far more fortunate in his appearances than he had expected, he was in despair at not having found the contessina, and had accepted the arrangement which took him to London because he had hopes of finding her there. On the day which brought me this letter I had a visitor. Nino had been gone nearly a month. It was in the afternoon, towards sunset, and I was sitting in the old green armchair watching the goldfinch in his cage, and thinking sadly of the poor dear baroness, and of my boy, and of many things. The bell rang, and Mariuccia brought me a card in her thick fingers which were black from peeling potatoes, so that the mark of her thumb came off on the white pasteboard. The name on the card was "Baron Ahasuerus Benoni," and there was no address. I told her to show the signore into the sitting-room, and he was not long in coming. I immediately recognized the man Nino had described, with his unearthly freshness of complexion, his eagle nose, and his snow-white hair. I rose to greet him.

"Signor Grandi," he said, "I trust you will pardon my intrusion. I am much interested in your boy, the great tenor."

"Sir," I replied, "the visit of a gentleman is never an intrusion. Permit me to offer you a chair." He sat down, and crossed one thin leg over the other. He was dressed in the height of the fashion ; he wore patent-leather shoes, and carried a light ebony cane with a silver head. His hat was perfectly new, and so smoothly brushed that it reflected a circular image of the objects in the room. But he had a certain dignity that saved his foppery from seeming ridiculous.

"You are very kind," he answered. "Perhaps you would like to hear some news of Signor Cardegna,— your boy, for he is nothing else."

"Indeed," I said, "I should be very glad. Has he written to you, baron ? "

"Oh, no ! We are not intimate enough for that. But I ran on to Paris the other day, and heard him three or four times, and had him to supper at Bignon's. He is a great genius, your boy, and has won all hearts."

"That is a compliment of weight from so distinguished a musician as yourself," I answered ; for, as you know, Nino had told me all about his playing. Indeed, the description was his, which is the reason why it is so enthusiastic.

" Yes," said Benoni, " I am a great traveler, and often go to Paris for a day or two. I know every one there. Cardegna had a perfect ovation. All the women sent him flowers, and all the men asked him to dinner."

" Pardon my curiosity," I interrupted, " but as you know every one in Paris, could you inform me whether Count von Lira and his daughter are there at present? He is a retired Prussian officer." Benoni stretched out one of his long arms and ran his fingers along the keys of the piano without striking them. He could just reach so far from where he sat. He gave no sign of intelligence, and I felt sure that Nino had not questioned him.

" I know them very well," he said presently, " but I thought they were here."

" No, they left suddenly for Paris, a month ago."

"-I can very easily find out for you," said Benoni, his bright eyes turning on me with a searching look. " I can find out from Lira's banker, who is probably also mine. What is the matter with that young man? He is as sad as Don Quixote."

" Nino? He is probably in love," I said, rather indiscreetly.

" In love? Then of course he is in love with Mademoiselle de Lira, and has gone to Paris to find her, and cannot. That is why you ask me." I was so much astonished at the quickness of his guess-work that I stared, open-mouthed.

" He must have told you ! " I exclaimed at last.

"Nothing of the kind. In the course of a long life I have learned to put two and two together, that is all. He is in love, he is your boy, and you are looking for a certain young lady. It is as clear as day." But in reality he had guessed the secret long before.

"Very well," said I humbly, but doubting him, all the same, " I can only admire your perspicacity. But I would be greatly obliged if you would find out where they are, those good people. You seem to be a friend of my boy's, baron. Help him, and he will be grateful to you. It is not such a very terrible thing that a great artist should love a noble's daughter, after all, though I used to think so." Benoni laughed, that strange laugh which Nino had described, — a laugh that seemed to belong to another age.

" You amuse me with your prejudices about nobility," he said, and his brown eyes flashed and twinkled again. " The idea of talking about nobility in this age ! You might as well talk of the domestic economy of the Garden of Eden."

" But you are yourself a noble — a baron," I objected.

" Oh, I am anything you please," said Benoni. " Some idiot made a baron of me, the other day, because I lent him money and he could not pay it. But I have some right to it, after all, for I am a Jew. The only real nobles are Welshmen and Jews. You cannot call anything so ridiculously recent as the European upper classes a nobility.

Now I go straight back to the creation of the world, like all my countrymen. The Hibernians get a factitious reputation for antiquity by saying that Eve married an Irishman after Adam died, and that is about as much claim as your European nobles have to respectability. Bah! I know their beginnings, — very small indeed."

"You, also, seem to have strong prejudices on the subject," said I, not wishing to contradict a guest in my house.

"So strong that it amounts to having no prejudices at all. Your boy wants to marry a noble damosel. In Heaven's name, let him do it. Let us manage it amongst us. Love is a grand thing. I have loved several women all their lives. Do not look surprised. I am a very old man; they have all died, and at present I am not in love with anybody. I suppose it cannot last long, however. I loved a woman once on a time" — Benoni paused. He seemed to be on the verge of a soliloquy, and his strange, bright face, which seemed illuminated always with a deathless vitality, became dreamy and looked older. But he recollected himself, and rose to go. His eye caught sight of the guitar that hung on the wall.

"Ah," he cried suddenly, "music is better than love, for it lasts; let us make music." He dropped his hat and stick and seized the instrument. In an instant it was tuned, and he began to perform the most extraordinary feats of agility with his fingers that I ever beheld. Some of it was very beautiful,

13

and some of it very sad and wild, but I understood
Nino's enthusiasm. I could have listened to the
old guitar in his hands for hours together, — I,
who care little for music; and I watched his face.
He stalked about the room with the thing in his
hands, in a sort of wild frenzy of execution. His
features grew ashy pale, and his smooth white hair
stood out wildly from his head. He looked, then,
more than a hundred years old, and there was a
sadness and a horror about him that would have
made the stones cry aloud for pity. I could not
believe he was the same man. At last he was tired,
and stopped.

"You are a great artist, baron," I said. "Your
music seems to affect you much."

"Ah, yes, it makes me feel like other men, for
the time," said he, in a low voice. "Did you know
that Paganini always practiced on the guitar? It
is true. Well, I will find out about the Liras for
you in a day or two, before I leave Rome again."

I thanked him, and he took his leave.

XII.

BENONI had made an impression on me that nothing could efface. His tall, thin figure and bright eyes got into my dreams and haunted me, so that I thought my nerves were affected. For several days I could think of nothing else, and at last had myself bled, and took some cooling barley water, and gave up eating salad at night, but without any perceptible effect.

Nino wrote often, and seemed very much excited about the disappearance of the contessina, but what could I do? I asked every one I knew, and nobody had heard of them, so that at last I quite gave it over, and wrote to tell him so. A week passed, then a fortnight, and I had heard nothing from Benoni. Nino wrote again, inclosing a letter addressed to the Contessina di Lira, which he implored me to convey to her, if I loved him. He said he was certain that she had never left Italy. Some instinct seemed to tell him so, and she was evidently in neither London nor Paris, for he had made every inquiry, and had even been to the police about it. Two days after this, Benoni came. He looked exactly as he did the first time I saw him.

"I have news," he said briefly, and sat down in the armchair, striking the dust from his boot with his little cane.

"News of the Graf?" I inquired.

"Yes. I have found out something. They never left Italy at all, it seems. I am rather mystified, and I hate mystification. The old man is a fool; all old men are fools, excepting myself. Will you smoke? No? Allow me, then. It is a modern invention, but a very good one." He lit a cigarette. "I wish your Liras were in Tophet," he continued, presently. "How can people have the bad taste to hide? It only makes ingenious persons the more determined to find them." He seemed talkative, and as I was so sad and lonely I encouraged him by a little stimulus of doubt. I wish I had doubted him sooner, and differently.

"What is the use?" I asked. "We shall never find them."

"'Never' is a great word," said Benoni. "You do not know what it means. I do. But as for finding them, you shall see. In the first place, I have talked with their banker. He says the count gave the strictest orders to have his address kept a secret. But, being one of my people, he allowed himself to make an accidental allusion which gave me a clue to what I wanted. They are hidden somewhere in the mountains."

"Diavolo! among the brigands, they will not be very well treated," said I.

"The old man will be careful. He will keep clear of danger. The only thing is to find them."

"And what then?" I asked.

"That depends on the most illustrious Signor

Cardegna," said Benoni, smiling. "He only asked you to find them. He probably did not anticipate that I would help you."

It did not appear to me that Benoni had helped me much, after all. You might as well look for a needle in a haystack as try to find any one who goes to the Italian mountains. The baron offered no further advice, and sat calmly smoking and looking at me. I felt uneasy, opposite him. He was a mysterious person, and I thought him disguised. It was really not possible that with his youthful manner his hair should be naturally so white, or that he should be so old as he seemed. I asked him the question we always find it interesting to ask foreigners, hoping to lead him into conversation.

"How do you like our Rome, Baron Benoni?"

"Rome? I loathe and detest it," he said, with a smile. "There is only one place in the whole world that I hate more."

"What place is that?" I asked, remembering that he had made the same remark to Nino before.

"Jerusalem," he answered, and the smile faded on his face. I thought I guessed the reason of his dislike in his religious views. But I am very liberal about those things.

"I think I understand you," I said; "you are a Hebrew, and the prevailing form of religion is disagreeable to you."

"No, it is not exactly that, — and yet, perhaps it is." He seemed to be pondering on the reason of his dislike. .

"But why do you visit these places, if they do not please you?"

"I come here because I have so many agreeable acquaintances. I never go to Jerusalem. I also come here from time to time to take a bath. The water of the Trevi has a peculiarly rejuvenating effect upon me, and something impels me to bathe in it."

"Do you mean in the fountain? Ah, foreigners say that if you drink the water by moonlight you will return to Rome."

"Foreigners are all weak-minded fools. I like that word. The human race ought to be called fools generically, as distinguished from the more intelligent animals. If you went to England, you would be as great a fool as any Englishman that comes here and drinks Trevi water by moonlight. But I assure you I do nothing so vulgar as to patronize the fountain, any more than I would patronize Mazzarino's church, hard by. I go to the source, the spring, the well where it rises."

"Ah, I know the place well," I said. "It is near to Serveti."

"Serveti? Is not that in the vicinity of Horace's villa?"

"You know the country well, I see," said I, sadly.

"I know most things," answered the Jew, with complacency. "You would find it hard to hit upon anything I do not know. Yes, I am a vain man, it is true, but I am very frank and open about it. Look at my complexion. Did you ever see anything like it? It is Trevi water that does it." I thought such excessive vanity very unbecoming in a man of his years, but I could not help looking amused. It was so odd to hear the old fellow descanting on his attractions. He actually took a small mirror from his pocket, and looked at himself in most evident admiration.

"I really believe," he said at length, pocketing the little looking-glass, "that a woman might love me still. What do you say?"

"Doubtless," I answered politely, although I was beginning to be annoyed, "a woman might love you at first sight. But it would be more dignified for you not to love her."

"Dignity!" He laughed long and loud, a cutting laugh, like the breaking of glass. "There is another of your phrases. Excuse my amusement, Signor Grandi, but the idea of dignity always makes me smile." He called that thing a smile! "It is in everybody's mouth, — the dignity of the state, the dignity of the king, the dignity of woman, the dignity of father, mother, schoolmaster, soldier. Psh! an apoplexy, as you say, on all the dignities you can enumerate. There is more dignity in a poor, patient ass toiling along a rough road under a brutal burden than in the entire human race put together, from Adam to myself. The conception of dignity is notional, most· entirely. I never see a poor wretch of a general, or king, or any such animal, adorned in his toggery of dignity, without laughing at him, and his dignity again leads him to

suppose that my smile is the result of the pleasur-
able sensations his appearance excites in me. Nature has dignity at times; some animals have it;
but man, never. What man mistakes for it in himself is his vanity, — a vanity much more pernicious
than mine, because it deceives its possessor, who is
also wholly possessed by it, and is its slave. I have
had many illusions in my life, Signor Grandi."

"One would say, baron, that you had parted
with them."

"Yes, and that is my chief vanity, — the vanity
of vanities which I prefer to all the others. It is
only a man of no imagination who has no vanity.
He cannot imagine himself any better than he is.
A creative genius makes for his own person a ' self '
which he thinks he is, or desires other people to believe him to be. It makes little difference whether
he succeeds or not, so long as he flatters himself he
does. He complacently takes all his images from
the other animals, or from natural objects and phe-
nomena, depicting himself bold as an eagle, brave
as a lion, strong as an ox, patient as an ass, vain as
a popinjay, talkative as a parrot, wily as a serpent,
gentle as a dove, cunning as a fox, surly as a bear;
his glance is lightning, his voice thunder, his heart
stone, his hands are iron, his conscience a hell,
his sinews of steel, and his love like fire. In short,
he is like anything alive or dead, except a man,
saving when he is mad. Then he is a fool. Only
man can be a fool. It distinguishes him from the
higher animals."

I cannot describe the unutterable scorn that
blazed in his eyes as Benoni poured out the vials
of his wrath on the unlucky human race. With
my views, we were not likely to agree in this matter.
"Who are you?" I asked. "What right can
you possibly have to abuse us all in such particularly strong terms? Do you ever make proselytes to
your philosophy?"

"No," said he, answering my last question, and
recovering his serenity with that strange quickness
of transition I had remarked when he had made
music during his previous visit. "No, they all die
before I have taught them anything."

"That does not surprise me, baron," said I. He
laughed a little.

"Well, perhaps it would surprise you even less
if you knew me better," he replied. "But really, I
came here to talk about Cardegna, and not to chatter about that contemptible creature, man, who is
not worth a moment's notice, I assure you. I believe I can find these people, and I confess it would
amuse me to see the old man's face when we walk
in upon him. I must be absent for a few days on
business in Austria, and shall return immediately,
for I have not taken my bath yet, that I spoke of.
Now, if it is agreeable to you, I would propose that
we go to the hills, on my return, and prosecute our
search together; writing to Nino in the mean time
to come here as soon as he has finished his engagement in Paris. If he comes quickly, he may go
with us; if not, he can join us. At all events, we

can have a very enjoyable tour among the natives, who are charming people, quite like animals, as you ought to know."

I think I must be a very suspicious person. Circumstances have made me so, and perhaps my suspicions are very generally wrong. It may be. At all events, I did suspect the rich and dandified old baron of desiring to have a laugh by putting Nino into some absurd situation. He had such strange views, or, at least, he talked so oddly, that I did not believe half he said. It is not possible that anybody should seriously hold the opinions he professed.

When he was gone I sat alone, pondering on the situation, which was like a very difficult problem in a nightmare, that could not or would not look sensible, do what I would. It chanced that I got a letter from Nino that evening, and I confess I was reluctant to open it, fearing that he would reproach me with not having taken more pains to help him. I felt as though, before opening the envelope, I should like to go back a fortnight and put forth all my strength to find the contessina, and gain a comforting sense of duty performed. If I had only done my best, how easy it would have been to face a whole sheet of complaints! Meanwhile the letter was come, and I had done nothing worth mentioning. I looked at the back of it, and my conscience smote me ; but it had to be accomplished, and at last I tore the cover off and read.

Poor Nino ! He said he was ill with anxiety, and

feared it would injure his voice. He said that to break his engagement and come back to Rome would be ruin to him. He must face it out, or take the legal consequences of a breach of contract, which are overwhelming* to a young artist. He detailed all the efforts he had made to find Hedwig, pursuing every little sign and clue that seemed to present itself; all to no purpose. The longer he thought of it, the more certain he was that Hedwig was not in Paris or London. She might be anywhere else in the whole world, but she was certainly not in either of those cities. Of that he was convinced. He felt like a man who had pursued a beautiful image to the foot of a precipitous cliff; the rock had opened and swallowed up his dream, leaving him standing alone in hopeless despair; and a great deal more poetic nonsense of that kind.

I do not believe I had ever realized what he so truly felt for Hedwig, until I sat at my table with his letter before me, overcome with the sense of my own weakness in not having effectually checked this mad passion at its rise; or, since it had grown so masterfully, of my wretched procrastination in not having taken my staff in my hand and gone out into the world to find the woman my boy loved and bring her to him. By this time, I thought, I should have found her. I could not bear to think of his being ill, suffering, heart-broken, — ruined, if he lost his voice by an illness, — merely because I had not had the strength to do the best thing for him. Poor Nino, I thought, you shall never say

again that Cornelio Grandi has not done what was
in his power to make you happy.

"That baron! an apoplexy on him! has illuded
me with his promises of help," I said to myself.
"He has no more intention of helping me or Nino
than he has of carrying off the basilica of St. Peter.
Courage, Cornelio! thou must gird up thy loins,
and take a little money in thy scrip, and find Hedwig von Lira."

All that night I lay awake, trying to think how
I might accomplish this end ; wondering to which
point of the compass I should turn, and above all
reflecting that I must make great sacrifices. But
my boy must have what he wanted, since he was
consuming himself, as we say, in longing for it. It
seemed to me no time for counting the cost, when
every day might bring upon him a serious illness.
If he could only know that I was acting, he would
allow his spirits to revive and take courage.

In the watches of the night I thought over my
resources, which, indeed, were meagre enough ; for
I am a very poor man. It was necessary to take
a great deal of money, for once away from Rome
no one could tell when I might return. My salary
as professor is paid to me quarterly, and it was yet
some weeks to the time when it was due. I had
only a few francs remaining, — not more than
enough to pay my rent and to feed Mariuccia and
me. I had paid at Christmas the last installment
due on my vineyard out of Porta Salara, and
though I owed no man anything I had no money,

and no prospect of any for some time. And yet I could not leave home on a long journey without at least two hundred scudi in my pocket. A scudo is a dollar, and a dollar has five francs, so that I wanted a thousand francs. You see, in spite of the baron's hint about the mountains, I thought I might have to travel all over Italy before I satisfied Nino.

A thousand francs is a great deal of money, — it is a Peru, as we say. I had not the first sou toward it. I thought a long time. I wondered if the old piano were worth anything; whether anybody would give me money for my manuscripts, the results of patient years of labor and study; my old gold scarf-pin, my seal ring, and even my silver watch, which keeps really very good time, — what were they worth? But it would not be much, not the tenth part of what I wanted. I was in despair, and I tried to sleep. Then a thought came to me.

"I am a donkey," I said. "There is the vineyard itself, — my little vineyard beyond Porta Salara. It is mine, and is worth half as much again as I need." And I slept quietly till morning.

It is true, and I am sure it is natural, that in the daylight my resolution looked a little differently to me than it did in the quiet night. I had toiled and scraped a great deal more than you know to buy that small piece of land, and it seemed much more my own than all Serveti had ever been in my better days. Then I shut myself up in my room and read

Nino's letter over again, though it pained me very much ; for I needed courage. And when I had read it, I took some papers in my pocket, and put on my hat and my old cloak, which Nino will never want any more now for his midnight serenades, and I went out to sell my little vineyard.

"It is for my boy," I said, to give myself some comfort.

But it is one thing to want to buy, and it is quite another thing to want to sell. All day I went from one man to another with my papers, — all the agents who deal in those things; but they only said they thought it might be sold in time; it would take many days, and perhaps weeks.

"But I want to sell it to-day," I explained.

"We are very sorry," said they, with a shrug of the shoulders; and they showed me the door.

I was extremely down-hearted, and though I could not sell my piece of land I spent three sous in buying two cigars to smoke, and I walked about the Piazza Colonna in the sun; I would not go home to dinner until I had decided what to do. There was only one man I had not tried, and he was the man who had sold it to me. Of course I knew people who do this business, for I had had enough trouble to learn their ways when I had to sell Serveti, years ago. But this one man I had not tried yet, because I knew that he would drive a cruel bargain with me when he saw I wanted the money. But at last I went to him, and told him just what my wishes were.

" Well," he said, " it is a very bad time for selling land. But to oblige you, because you are a
customer, I will give you eight hundred francs for
your little place. That is really much more than I
can afford."

" Eight hundred francs!" I exclaimed in despair. " But I have paid you nearly twice as much
for it in the last three years! What do you take
me for? To sell such a gem of a vineyard for
eight hundred francs! If you offer me thirteen
hundred I will discuss the matter with you."

" I have known you a long time, Signor Grandi,
and you are an honest man. I am sure you do not
wish to deceive me. I will give you eight hundred
and fifty."

Deceive him, indeed! The very man who had
received fifteen hundred from me said I deceived
him when I asked thirteen hundred for the same
piece of land! But I needed it very much, and so,
bargaining and wrangling, I got one thousand and
seventy-five francs in bank-notes ; and I took care
they should all be good ones, too. It was a poor
price, I know, but I could do no better, and I went
home happy. But I dared not tell Mariuccia. She
is only my servant, to be sure, but she would have
torn me in pieces.

Then I wrote to the authorities at the university
to say that I was obliged to leave Rome suddenly,
and would of course not claim my salary during
my absence. But I added that I hoped they would
not permanently supplant me. If they did, I knew

I should be ruined. Then I told Mariuccia that I was going away for some days to the country, and I left her the money to pay the rent, and her wages, and a little more, so that she might be provided for if I were detained very long. I went out again and telegraphed to Nino, to say I was going at once in search of the Liras, and begging him to come home as soon as he should have finished his engagement.

- To tell the truth, Mariuccia was very curious to know where I was going, and asked me many questions, which I had some trouble in answering. But at last it was night again, and the old woman went to bed and left me. Then I went on tiptoe to the kitchen, and found a skein of thread and two needles, and set to work.

I knew the country whither I was going very well, and it was necessary to hide the money I had in some ingenious way. So I took two waistcoats, — one of them was quite good still, — and I sewed them together, and basted the bank-notes between them. It was a clumsy piece of tailoring, though it took me so many hours to do it. But I had put the larger waistcoat outside very cunningly, so that when I had put on the two, you could not see that there was anything beneath the outer one. I think I was very clever to do this without a woman to help me. Then I looked to my boots, and chose my oldest clothes, — and you may guess, from what you know of me, how old they were, — and I made a little bundle that I could carry in my hand, with

a change of linen, and the like. These things I
made ready before I went to bed, and I slept with
the two waistcoats and the thousand francs under
my pillow, though I suppose nobody would have
chosen that particular night for robbing me.

. All these preparations had occupied me so much
that I had not found any time to grieve over my
poor little vineyard that I had sold ; and besides, I
was thinking all the while of Nino, and how glad
he would be to know that I was really searching for
Hedwig.   But when I thought of the vines, it hurt   ,
me ; and I think it is only long after the deed that
it seems more blessed to give than to receive.

But at last I slept, as tired folk will, leaving care
to the morrow ; and when I awoke it was daybreak,
and Mariuccia was clattering angrily with the tin
coffee-pot outside.   It was a bright morning, and
the goldfinch sang, and I could hear him scattering
the millet · seed about his cage while I dressed.
And then the parting grew very near, and I drank
my coffee silently, wondering how soon it would be
over, and wishing that the old woman would go
out and let me have my house alone.   But she
would not, and to my surprise she made very little
worry or trouble, making a great show of being
busy.   When I was quite ready, she insisted on
putting a handful of roasted chestnuts into my
pocket, and she said she would pray for me.   The
fact is, she thought, foolish old creature as she is,
that I was old and in poor health, and she had·
often teased me to go into the country for a few

14

days, so that she was not ill pleased that I should seem to take her advice. She stood looking after me as I trudged along the street, with my bundle and my good stick in my right hand, and a lighted cigar in my left.

I had made up my mind that I ought first to try the direction hinted at by the baron, since I had absolutely no other clue to the whereabouts of the Count von Lira and his daughter. I therefore got into the old stage that still runs to Palestrina and the neighboring towns, for it is almost as quick as going by rail, and much cheaper ; and half an hour later we rumbled out of the Porta San Lorenzo, and I had entered upon the strange journey to find Hedwig von Lira, concerning which frivolous people have laughed so unkindly. And you may call me a foolish old man if you like. I did it for my boy.

XIII.

I WENT to Palestrina because all foreigners go there, and are to be heard of from other parts of the mountains in that place. It was a long and tiresome journey; the jolting stage-coach shook me very much. There was a stout woman inside, with a baby that squealed; there was a very dirty old country curate, who looked as though he had not shaved for a week, or changed his collar for a month. But he talked intelligently, though he talked too much, and he helped to pass the time until I was weary of him. We jolted along over the dusty roads, and were at least thankful that it was not yet hot.

In the evening we arrived at Palestrina, and stopped before the inn in the market-place, as tired and dusty as might be. The woman went one way, and the priest the other, and I was left alone. I soon found the fat old host, and engaged a room for the night. He was talkative and curious, and sat by my side when he had prepared my supper in the dingy dining-room down-stairs. I felt quite sure that he would be able to tell me what I wanted, or at least to give me a hint from hearsay. But he at once began to talk of last year, and how much better his business had been then than it was now, as country landlords invariably do.

It was to no purpose that I questioned him about the people that had passed during the fortnight, the month, the two months, back; it was clear that no one of the importance of my friends had been heard of. At last I was tired, and he lit a wax candle, which he would carefully charge in the bill afterwards, at double its natural price, and he showed me the way to my room. It was a very decent little room, with white curtains and a good bed and a table, — everything I could desire. A storm had come up since I had been at my supper, and it seemed a comfortable thing to go to bed, although I was disappointed at having got no news.

But when I had blown out my candle, determining to expostulate with the host in the morning, if he attempted to make me pay for a whole one, I lay thinking of what I should do ; and turning on my side, I observed that a narrow crack of the door admitted rays of light into the darkness of my chamber. Now I am very sensitive to draughts and inclined to take cold, and the idea that there was a door open troubled me, so that at last I made up my mind to get up and close it. As I rose to my feet, I perceived that it was not the door by which I had entered ; and so, before shutting it, I called out, supposing there might be some one in the next room.

" Excuse me," I said loudly, " I will shut this door." But there was no reply.

Curiosity is perhaps a vice, but it is a natural one. Instead of pulling the door to its place, I pushed it a little, knocking with my knuckles at the same time. But as no one answered, I pushed it further, and put in my head. It was a disagreeable thing I saw.

The room was like mine in every way, save that the bed was moved to the middle of the open space, and there were two candles on two tables. On the bed lay a dead man. I felt what we call a brivido, — a shiver like an ague.

It was the body of an old man, with a face like yellow wax, and a singularly unpleasant expression even in death. His emaciated hands were crossed on his breast, and held a small black crucifix. The candles stood, one at the head and one at the foot, on little tables. I entered the room and looked long at the dead old man. I thought it strange that there should be no one to watch him, but I am not afraid of dead men, after the first shudder is past. It was a ghastly sight enough, however, and the candles shed a glaring, yellowish light over it all.

"Poor wretch," I said to myself, and went back to my room, closing the door carefully behind me.

At first I thought of rousing the host, and explaining to him my objections to being left almost in the same room with a corpse. But I reflected that it would be foolish to seem afraid of it, when I was really not at all timid, and so I went to bed, and slept until dawn. But when I went down-stairs I found the innkeeper, and gave him a piece of my mind.

"What sort of an inn do you keep? What manners are these?" I cried angrily. "What diavolo put into your pumpkin head to give me a sepulchre for a room?"

He seemed much disturbed at what I said, and broke out into a thousand apologies. But I was not to be so easily pacified.

"Do you think," I demanded, "that I will ever come here again, or advise any of my friends to come here? It is insufferable. I will write to the police" — But at this he began to shed tears and to wring his hands, saying it was not his fault.

"You see, signore, it was my wife who made me arrange it so. Oh! these women — the devil has made them all! It was her father — the old dead man you saw. He died yesterday morning, — may he rest! — and we will bury him to-day. You see every one knows that unless a dead man is watched by some one from another town his soul will not rest in peace. My wife's father was a jettatore; he had the evil eye, and people knew it for miles around, so I could not persuade any one from the other villages to sit by him and watch his body, though I sent everywhere all day yesterday. At last that wife of mine — maledictions on her folly! — said, 'It is my father, after all, and his soul must rest, at any price. If you put a traveler in the next room, and leave the door open, it will be the same thing; and so he will be in peace.' That

is the way it happened, signore," he continued,
after wiping away his tears; " you see I could not
help it at all. But if you will overlook it, I will
not make any charges for your stay. My wife shall
pay me. She has poultry by the hundred. I will
pay myself with her chickens."

 " Very good," said I, well pleased at having
got so cheap a lodging. "But I am a just man,
and I will pay for what I have eaten and drunk,
and you can take the night's lodging out of your
wife's chickens, as you say." So we were both satisfied.[1]

The storm of the night had passed away, leaving everything wet and the air cool and fresh. I
wrapped my cloak about me, and went into the
market-place, to see if I could pick up any news.
It was already late, for the country, and there were
few people about. Here and there, in the streets,
a wine-cart was halting on its way to Rome, while
the rough carter went through the usual arrangement of exchanging some of his employer's wine
for food for himself, filling up the barrel with good
pure water, that never hurt any one. I wandered
about, though I could not expect to see any face
that I knew; it is so many years since I lived at
Serveti, that even were the carters from my old
place, I should have forgotten how they looked.
Suddenly, at the corner of a dirty street, where
there was a little blue and white shrine to the Ma-

[1] This incident actually occurred, precisely as related.—
F. M. C.

donna, I stumbled against a burly fellow with a gray beard, carrying a bit of salt codfish in one hand and a cake of corn bread in the other, eating as he went.

"Gigi!" I cried in delight, when I recognized the old carrettiere who used to bring me grapes and wine, and still does when the fancy takes him.

"Dio mio! Signor Conte!" he cried with his mouth full, and holding up the bread and fish with his two hands, in astonishment. When he recovered himself, he instantly offered to share his meal with me, as the poorest wretch in Italy will offer his crust to the greatest prince, out of politeness. "Vuol favorire?" he said, smiling.

I thanked him and declined, as you may imagine. Then I asked him how he came to be in Palestrina; and he told me that he was often there in the winter, as his sister had married a vine-dresser of the place, of whom he bought wine occasionally. Very well-to-do people, he explained eagerly, proud of his prosperous relations.

We clambered along through the rough street together, and I asked him what was the news from Serveti and from that part of the country, well knowing that if he had heard of any rich foreigners in that neighborhood he would at once tell me of it. But I had not much hope. He talked about the prospects of the vines, and such things, for some time, and I listened patiently.

"By the bye," he said at last, "there is a gran signore who is gone to live in Fillettino, — a crazy man, they say, with a beautiful daughter, but really beautiful, as an angel."

I was so much surprised that I made a loud exclamation.

" What is the matter?" asked Gigi.

" It is nothing, Gigi," I answered, for I was afraid lest he should betray my secret, if I let him guess it. " It is nothing. I struck my foot against a stone. But you were telling about a foreigner who is gone to live somewhere. Fillettino? Where is that?"

' " Oh, the place of the diavolo! I do not wonder you do not know, conte, for gentlemen never go there. It is in the Abruzzi, beyond Trevi. Did you ever hear of the Serra di Sant' Antonio, where so many people have been killed?"

" Diana! I should think so! In the old days " —

" Bene," said Gigi, " Fillettino is there, at the beginning of the pass."

" Tell me, Gigi mio," I said, " are you not very thirsty?" The way to the heart of the wine carter lies through a pint measure. Gigi was thirsty, as I supposed, and we sat down in the porch of my inn, and the host brought a stoup of his best wine and set it before us.

" I would like to hear about the crazy foreigner who is gone to live in the hills among the briganti," I said, when he had wet his throat.

" What I know I will tell you, Signor Conte," he answered, filling his pipe with bits that he broke off a cigar. " But I know very little. He must

be a foreigner, because he goes to such a place;
and he is certainly crazy, for he shuts his daughter
in the old castle, and watches her as though she
was made of wax, like the flowers you have in
Rome under glass."

"How long have they been there, these queer
folks?" I asked.

"What do I know? It may be a month or two.
A man told me, who had come that way from
Fucino, and that is all I know."

"Do people often travel that way, Gigi?"

"Not often, indeed," he answered, with a grin.
"They are not very civil, the people of those
parts." Gigi made a gesture, or a series of gestures. He put up his hands as though firing a gun.
Then he opened his right hand and closed it, with
a kind of insinuating twirl of the fingers, which
means "to steal." Lastly he put his hand over
his eyes, and looked through his fingers as though
they were bars, which means "prison." From this
I inferred that the inhabitants of Fillettino were
addicted to murder, robbery, and other pastimes,
for which they sometimes got into trouble. The
place he spoke of is about thirty miles, or something more, from Palestrina, and I began planning
how I should get there as cheaply as possible. I
had never been there, and wondered what kind of a
habitation the count had found; for I knew it must
be the roughest sort of mountain town, with some
dilapidated castle, or other, overhanging it. But the
count was rich, and he had doubtless made himself

very comfortable. I sat in silence, while Gigi
finished his wine, and chatted about his affairs between the whiffs of his pipe.

"Gigi," I said at last, "I want to buy a donkey."

"Eh, your excellency can be accommodated;
and a saddle, too, if you wish."

"I think I could ride without a saddle," I said,
for I thought it a needless piece of extravagance.

"Madonna mia!" he cried. "The Signor Conte
ride bareback on a donkey! They would laugh at
you. But my brother-in-law can sell you a beast
this very day, and for a mere song."

"Let us go and see the beast," I said. I felt a
little ashamed of having wished to ride without a
saddle. But as I had sold all I had, I wanted to
make the money last as long as possible; or at least
I would spend as little as I could, and take something back, if I ever went home at all. We had
not far to go, and Gigi opened a door in the street
and showed me a stable, in which something moved
in the darkness. Presently he led out an animal
and began to descant upon its merits.

"Did you ever see a more beautiful donkey?"
asked Gigi admiringly. "It looks like a horse!"
It was a little ass, with sad eyes, and ears as long
as its tail. It was also very thin, and had the hair
rubbed off its back from carrying burdens. But it
had no sore places, and did not seem lame.

"He is full of fire," said Gigi, poking the donkey
in the ribs to excite a show of animation. "You
should see him gallop up hill with my brother on

his back, and a good load into the bargain. Brrrr! Stand still, will you!" he cried, holding tight by the halter, though the animal did not seem anxious to run away.

"And then," said Gigi, "he eats nothing,—positively nothing."

"He does not look as though he had eaten much of late," I said.

"Oh, my brother-in-law is as good to him as though he were a Christian. He gives him corn bread and fish, just like his own children. But this ass prefers straw."

"A frugal ass," I said, and we began to bargain. I will not tell you what I gave Gigi's brother-in-law for the beast, because you would laugh. And I bought an old saddle, too. It was really necessary, but it was a dear bargain, though it was cheaper than hiring; for I sold the donkey and the saddle again, and got back something.

It is a wild country enough that lies behind the mountains towards the sources of the Aniene,— the river that makes the falls at Tivoli. You could not half understand how in these times, under the new government, and almost within a long day's ride from Rome, such things could take place as I am about to tell you of, unless I explained to you how very primitive that country is which lies to the southeast of the capital, and which we generally call the Abruzzi. The district is wholly mountainous, and though there are no very great elevations there are very ragged gorges and steep precipices, and now and then an -inaccessible bit of forest far up among the rocks, which no man has ever thought of cutting down. It would be quite impossible to remove the timber. The people are mostly shepherds in the higher regions, where there are no vines, and when opportunity offers they will waylay the unwary traveler and rob him, and even murder him, without thinking very much about it. In the old days, the boundary between the Papal States and the kingdom of Naples ran through these mountains, and the contrabbandieri — the smugglers of all sorts of wares — used to cross from one dominion to the other by circuitous paths and steep ways of which only a few had knowledge. The better known of these passes were defended by soldiers and police, but there have been bloody fights fought, within a few years, between the law and its breakers. Foreigners never penetrate into the recesses of these hills, and even the English guidebooks, which are said to contain an account of everything that the Buon Dio ever made, compiled from notes taken at the time of the creation, make no mention of places which surpass in beauty all the rest of Italy put together.

No railroad or other modern innovation penetrates into those Arcadian regions, where the goatherd plays upon his pipe all the day long, the picture of peace and innocence, or prowls in the passes with a murderous long gun, if there are foreigners in the air. The women toil at carrying their scant supply of drinking-water from great distances dur-

ing a part of the day, and in the evening they spin
industriously by their firesides or upon their door-
steps, as the season will have it. It is an old life,
the same to-day as a thousand years ago, and perhaps as it will be a thousand years hence. The
men are great travelers, and go to Rome in the
winter to sell their cheese, or to milk a flock of
goats in the street at daybreak, selling the foaming
canful for a sou. But their visits to the city do
not civilize them; the outing only broadens the ho-
rizon of their views in regard to foreigners, and
makes them more ambitious to secure one, and see
what he is like, and cut off his ears, and get his
money. Do not suppose that the shepherd of the
Abruzzi lies all day on the rocks in the sun, waiting for the foreign gentleman to come within reach.
He might wait a long time. Climbing has strength-
ened the muscles of his legs into so much steel,
and a party of herdsmen have been known to come
down from the Serra to the plains around Velletri,
and to return to their inaccessible mountains, after
doing daring deeds of violence, in twenty-four hours
from the time of starting; covering at least from
eighty to ninety miles by the way. They are extraordinary fellows, as active as tigers, and fabu-
lously strong, though they are never very big.

This country begins behind the range of Sabine
mountains seen from Rome across the Campagna,
and the wild character of it increases as you go towards the southeast.

Since I have told you this much, I need not

weary you with further descriptions. I do not like descriptions, and it is only when Nino gives me his impressions that I write them, in order that you may know how beautiful things impress him, and the better judge of his character.

I do not think that Gigi really cheated me so very badly about the donkey. Of course I do not believe the story of his carrying the brother-in-law and the heavy load uphill at a gallop; but I am thin and not very heavy, and the little ass carried me well enough through the valleys, and when we came to a steep place I would get off and walk, so as not to tire him too much. If he liked to crop a thistle or a blade of grass, I would stop a moment, for I thought he would grow fatter in that way, and I should not lose so much when I sold him again. But he never grew very fat.

Twice I slept by the way, before I reached the end of my journey, — once at Olevano, and once at Trevi; for the road from Olevano to Trevi is long, and some parts are very rough, especially at first. I could tell you just how every stone on the road looks — Rojate, the narrow pass beyond, and then the long valley with the vines; then the road turns away and rises as you go. along the plateau of Arcinazzo, which is hollow beneath, and you can hear the echoes as you tread; then at the end of that the desperate old inn, called by the shepherds the Madre dei Briganti, — the mother of brigands, — smoke-blackened within and without, standing alone on the desolate heath; further on, a broad bend of the valley to the left, and you see Trevi rising before you, crowned with an ancient castle, and overlooking the stream that becomes the Aniene afterwards; from Trevi through a rising valley that grows narrower at every step, and finally seems to end abruptly, as indeed it does, in a dense forest far up the pass. And just below the woods lies the town of Fillettino, where the roads ends; for there is a road which leads to Tivoli, but does not communicate with Olevano, whence I had come.

Of course I had made an occasional inquiry by the way, when I could do so without making people too curious. When any one asked me where I was going, I would say I was bound for Fucino, to buy beans for seed at the wonderful model farm that Torlonia has made by draining the old lake. And then I would ask about the road; and sometimes I was told there was a strange foreigner at Fillettino, who made everybody wonder about him by his peculiar mode of life. Therefore, when I at last saw the town, I was quite sure that the count was there, and I got off my little donkey, and let him drink in the stream, while I myself drank a little higher up. The road was dusty, and my donkey and I were thirsty.

I thought of all I would do, as I sat on the stone by the water, and the beast cropped the wretched grass; and soon I came to the conclusion that I did not know in the least what I should do. I had unexpectedly found what I wanted, very soon, and I was thankful enough to have been so lucky. But

I had not the first conception of what course I was to pursue when once I had made sure of the count. Besides, it was barely possible that it was not he, after all, but another foreigner, with another daughter. The thought frightened me, but I drove it away. If it were really old Lira who had chosen this retreat in which to imprison his daughter and himself, I asked myself whether I could do anything, save send word to Nino as soon as possible.

I felt like a sort of Don Quixote, suddenly chilled into the prosaic requirements of common sense. Perhaps if Hedwig had been my Dulcinea, instead of Nino's, the crazy fit would have lasted, and I would have attempted to scale the castle wall and carry off the prize by force. There is no telling what a sober old professor of philosophy may not do, when he is crazy. But meanwhile I was sane. Graf von Lira had a right to live anywhere he pleased with his daughter, and the fact that I had discovered the spot where he pleased to live did not constitute an introduction. Or finally, if I got access to the old count, what had I to say to him? Ought I to make a formal request for Nino? I looked at my old clothes, and almost smiled.

But the weather was cold, though the roads were dusty; so I mounted my ass and jogged along, meditating deeply.

15

XIV.

FILLETTINO is a trifle cleaner than most towns of the same kind. Perhaps it rains more often, and there are fewer people. Considering that its vicinity has been the scene of robbery, murder, and all manner of adventurous crime from time immemorial, I had expected to find it a villainous place. It is nothing of the kind. There is a decent appearance about it that is surprising; and though the houses are old and brown and poor, I did not see pigs in many rooms, nor did the little children beg of me, as they beg of every one elsewhere. The absence of the pigs struck me particularly, for in the Sabine towns they live in common with the family, and go out only in the daytime to pick up what they can get.

I went to the apothecary — there is always an apothecary in these places — and inquired for a lodging. Before very long I had secured a room, and it seemed that the people were accustomed to travelers, for it was surprisingly clean. The bed was so high that I could touch the ceiling when I sat on it, and the walls were covered with ornaments, such as glazed earthenware saints, each with a little basin for holy water, some old engravings of other saints, a few paper roses from the last fair, and a weather-beaten game-pouch of leather. The window looked out over a kind of square, where a great quantity of water ran into a row of masonry tanks out of a number of iron pipes projecting from an overhanging rock. Above the rock was the castle, the place I had come to see, towering up against the darkening sky.

It is such a strange place that I ought to describe it to you, or you will not understand the things that happened there. There is a great rock, as I said, rising above the town, and upon this is built the feudal stronghold, so that the walls of the building do not begin less than forty feet from the street level. The height of the whole castle consequently seems enormous. The walls, for the most part, follow the lines of the gray rock, irregularly, as chance would have it, and the result is a three-cornered pile, having a high square tower at one angle, where also the building recedes some yards from the edge of the cliff, leaving on that side a broad terrace guarded by a stone parapet. On another side of the great isolated bowlder a narrow roadway heads up a steep incline, impracticable for carriages, but passable for four-footed beasts; and this path gives access to the castle through a heavy gate opening upon a small court within. But the rock itself has been turned to account, and there are chambers within it, which formerly served as prisons, opening to the right and left of a narrow staircase, hewn out of the stone, and leading from the foot of the tower to the street below; upon which it opens through a low square door, set in the rock and studded with heavy iron nails.

Below the castle hangs the town, and behind it rises the valley, thickly wooded with giant beech-trees. Of course I learned the details of the interior little by little, and I gathered also some interesting facts regarding the history of Fillettino, which are not in any way necessary to my story. The first thing I did was to find out what means of communication there were with Rome. There was a postal service twice a week, and I was told that Count von Lira, whose name was no secret in the village, sent messengers very often to Subiaco. The post left that very day, and I wrote to Nino to tell him that I had found his friends in villeggiatura at Fillettino, advising him to come as soon as he could, and recruit his health and his spirits.

I learned, further, from the woman who rented me my lodging, that there were other people in the castle besides the count and his daughter. At least, she had seen a tall gentleman on the terrace with them during the last two days; and it was not true that the count kept Hedwig a prisoner. On the contrary, they rode out together almost every day, and yesterday the tall gentleman had gone with them. The woman also went into many details; telling me how much money the count had spent in a fortnight, bringing furniture and a real piano and immense loads of baskets, which the porters were told contained glass and crockery, and must be carefully handled. It was clear that the count was settled for some time. He had probably taken the old place for a year, by a lease from the Roman family to whom Fillettino and the neighboring estates belong. He would spend the spring and the summer there, at least.

Being anxious to see who the tall gentleman might be, of whom my landlady had spoken, I posted myself in the street, at the foot of the inclined bridle-path leading to the castle gate. I walked up and down for two hours, about the time I supposed they would all ride, hoping to catch a glimpse of the party. Neither the count nor his daughter knew me by sight, I was sure, and I felt quite safe. It was a long time to wait, but at last they appeared, and I confess that I nearly fell down against the wall when I saw them.

There they were on their horses, moving cautiously down the narrow way above me. First came the count, sitting in his saddle as though he were at the head of his old regiment, his great gray mustaches standing out fiercely from his severe, wooden face. Then came Hedwig, whom I had not seen for a long time, looking as white and sorrowful as the angel of death, in a close black dress, or habit, so that her golden hair was all the color there was to be seen about her.

But the third rider, — there was no mistaking that thin, erect figure, dressed in the affectation of youth; those fresh pink cheeks, with the snowy mustache, and the thick white hair showing beneath the jaunty hat; the eagle nose and the bright eyes. Baron Benoni, and no other.

My first instinct was to hide myself; but before I could retreat, Benoni recognized me, even with my old clothes. Perhaps they are not so much older than the others, compared with his fashionable garments. He made no sign as the three rode by; only I could see by his eyes, that were fixed angrily upon me, that he knew me, and did not wish to show it. As for myself, I stood stock still in amazement.

I had supposed that Benoni had really gone to Austria, as he had told me he was about to do. I had thought him ignorant of the count's retreat, save for the hint which had so luckily led me straight to the mark. I had imagined him to be but a chance acquaintance of the Lira family, having little or no personal interest in their doings. Nevertheless, I had suspected him, as I have told you. Everything pointed to a deception on his part. He had evidently gone immediately from Rome to Fillettino. He must be intimate with the count, or the latter would not have invited him to share a retreat seemingly intended to be kept a secret. He also, I thought, must have some very strong reason for consenting to bury himself in the mountains in company with a father and daughter who could hardly be supposed to be on good terms with each other.

But again, why had he seemed so ready to help me and to forward Nino's suit? Why had he given me the smallest clue to the count's whereabouts? Now I am not a strong man in action, perhaps, but I am a very cunning reasoner. I remembered the man, and the outrageous opinions he had expressed, both to Nino and to me. Then I understood my suspicions. It would be folly to expect such a man to have any real sympathy or sense of friendship for any one. He had amused himself by promising to come back and go with me on my search, perhaps to make a laughing-stock of me, or even of my boy, by telling the story to the Liras afterwards. He had entertained no idea that I would go alone, or that, if I went, I could be successful. He had made a mistake, and was very angry; his eyes told me that. Then I made a bold resolution. I would see him and ask him what he intended to do; in short, why he had deceived me.

There would probably be no difficulty in the way of obtaining an interview. I was not known to the others of the party, and Benoni would scarcely refuse to receive me. I thought he would excuse himself, with ready cynicism, and pretend to continue his offers of friendship and assistance. I confess, I regretted that I was so humbly clad, in all my old clothes; but, after all, I was traveling, you know.

It was a bold resolution, I think, and I revolved the situation in my mind during two days, thinking over what I should say. But with all my thought I only found that everything must depend on Benoni's answer to my own question — " Why? "

On the third day, I made myself look as fine as

I could, and though my heart beat loudly as I mounted the bridle-path, I put on a bold look and rang the bell.   It was a clanging thing, that seemed to creak on a hinge, as I pulled the stout string from outside.   A man appeared, and on my inquiry said I might wait in the porch behind the great wooden gate, while he delivered my message to his excellency the baron.   It seemed to take a long time, and I sat on a stone bench, eyeing the court-yard curiously from beneath the archway.   It was sunny and clean, with an old well in the middle, but I could see nothing save a few windows open-ing upon it.   At last the man returned and said that I might come with him.

I found Benoni, clad in a gorgeous dressing-gown, stalking up and down a large vaulted apart-ment, in which there were a few new armchairs, a table covered with books, and a quantity of ancient furniture, that looked unsteady and fragile, although it had been carefully dusted. · A plain green baize carpet covered about half the floor, and the re-mainder was of red brick.   The morning sun streamed in through tall windows, and played in a rainbow-like effulgence on the baron's many colored dressing-gown, as he paused in his walk to greet me.

"Well, my friend," said Benoni gayly, "how in the name of the devil did you get here?"   I thought I had been right; he was going to play at being my friend again.

"Very easily, by the help of your little hint," I

replied; and I seated myself, for I felt that I was master of the situation.

"Ah, if I had suspected you of being so intelligent, I would not have given you any hint at all. You see I have not been to Austria on business, but am here in this good old flesh of mine, such as it is."

"Consequently" — I began, and then stopped. I suddenly felt that Benoni had turned the tables upon me, I could not tell how.

"Consequently," said he, continuing my sentence, "when I told you that I was going to Austria I was lying."

"The frankness of the statement obliges me to believe that you are now telling the truth," I answered angrily. I felt uneasy. Benoni laughed in his peculiar way.

"Precisely," he continued again, "I was lying. I generally do, for so long as I am believed I deceive people; and when they find me out, they are confused between truth and lying, so that they do not know what to believe at all. By the bye, I am wandering. I am sorry to see you here. I hope you understand that." He looked at me with the most cheerful expression. I believe I was beginning to be angry at his insulting calmness. I did not answer him.

"Signor Grandi," he said in a moment, seeing I was silent, "I am enchanted to see you, if you prefer that I should be. But may I imagine if I can do anything more for you, now that you have heard from my own lips that I am a liar? I say it again, — I like the word, — I am a liar, and I wish I were a better one. What can I do for you?"

"Tell me why you have acted this comedy," said I, recollecting at the right moment the gist of my reflections during the past two days.

"Why? To please myself, good sir; for the sovereign pleasure of myself."

"I would surmise," I retorted, "that it could not have been for the pleasure of any one else."

"Perhaps you mean, because no one else could be base enough to take pleasure in what amuses me?" I nodded savagely at his question. "Very good. Knowing this of me, do you further surmise that I should be so simple as to tell you how I propose to amuse myself in the future?" I recognized the truth of this, and I saw myself checkmated at the outset. I therefore smiled and endeavored to seem completely satisfied, hoping that his vanity would betray him into some hint of the future. He seemed to have before taken pleasure in misleading me with a fragment of truth, supposing that I could not make use of it. I would endeavor to lead him into such a trap again.

"It is a beautiful country, is it not?" I remarked, going to the window before which he stood, and looking out. "You must enjoy it greatly, after the turmoil of society." You see, I was once as gay as any of them, in the old days; and so I made the reflection that seemed natural to his case, wondering how he would answer.

" It is indeed a very passable landscape," he said
indifferently. " With horses and a charming companion one may kill a little time here, and find a
satisfaction in killing it." I noticed the slip, by
which he spoke of a single companion instead of
two.

" Yes," I replied, " the count is said to be a most
agreeable man."

He paused a moment, and the hesitation seemed
to show that the count was not the companion he
had in his mind.

" Oh, certainly," he said, at length, " the count is
very agreeable, and his daughter is the paragon of
all the virtues and accomplishments." There was
something a little disparaging in his tone as he
made the last remark, which seemed to me a clumsy
device to throw me off the scent, if scent there
were. Considering his surpassing personal vanity, of which I had received an ocular demonstration when he visited me in Rome, I fancied that if
there were nothing more serious in his thoughts he
would have given me to understand that Hedwig
found him entirely irresistible. Since he was able
to control his vanity, there must be a reason for it.

" I should think that the contessina must be
charmed at having so brilliant a companion as
yourself in her solitude," I said, feeling my way
to the point.

" With me? I am an old man. Children of
that age detest old men." I thought his manner
constrained, and it was unlike him not to laugh as

he made the speech. The conviction grew upon
me that Hedwig was the object of his visit. Moreover, I became persuaded that he was but a poor
sort of villain, for he was impulsive, as villains
should never be. We leaned over the stone sill of
the window, which he had opened during the conversation. There was a little trail of ants climbing
up and down the wall at the side, and he watched
them. One of the small creatures, heavily laden
with a seed of some sort, and toiling painfully
under the burden, had been separated from the
rest, and clambered over the edge of the window-
sill. On reaching the level surface it paused, as
though very weary, and looked about, moving its
tiny horns. Benoni looked at it a moment, and
then with one finger he suddenly whisked the poor
little thing into space. It hurt me to see it, and
I knew he must be cruel, for he laughed aloud.
Somehow, it would have seemed less cruel to have
brushed away the whole trail of insects, rather
than to pitch upon this one small, tired workman,
overladen and forgotten by the rest.

"Why did you do that?" I asked involuntarily.

"Why? Why do I do anything? Because I
please, the best of all reasons."

"Of course, it was foolish of me to ask you.
That is probably the cause of your presence here.
You would like to hurl my boy Nino from the
height he has reached in his love, and to satisfy
your cruel instincts you have come here to attack
the heart of an innocent girl." I watched him nar-

rowly, and I have often wondered how I had the courage to insult him. It was a bold shot at the truth, and his look satisfied me that I was not very wide of the mark. To accuse a gray-haired old man of attempting to win the affections of a young girl would seem absurd enough. But if you had ever seen Benoni, you would understand that he was anything but old, save for his snowy locks. Many a boy might envy the strange activity of his thin limbs, the bloom and freshness of his eager face, and the fire of his eyes. He was impulsive, too ; for instead of laughing at the absurdity of the thing, or at what should have been its absurdity, as a more accomplished villain would have done, he was palpably angry. He looked quickly at me and moved savagely, so that I drew back, and it was not till some moments later that it occurred to him that he ought to seem amused.

"How ridiculous!" he cried at last, mastering his anger. "You are joking."

"Oh, of course I am joking," I answered, leaving the window. "And now I must wish you good-morning, with many apologies for my intrusion." He must have been glad to be rid of me, but he politely insisted on showing me to the gate. Perhaps he wanted to be sure that I should not ask questions of the servants.

As we passed through an outer hall, we came suddenly upon Hedwig, entering from the opposite direction, dressed in black, and looking like a beautiful shadow of pain. As I have told you, she did

not know me.   Benoni bowed to the ground, as she
went by, making some flattering speech about her
appearance.   She had started slightly on first seeing us, and then she went on without speaking;
but there was on her face a look of such sovereign
scorn and loathing as I never saw on the features
of any living being.   And more than scorn, for
there was fear and hatred with it; so that if a
glance could tell a whole history, there would have
been no detail of her feeling for Benoni left to
guess.

This meeting produced a profound impression on
me, and I saw her face in my dreams that night.
Had anything been wanting to complete, in my
judgment, the plan of the situation in the castle,
that something was now supplied.   The Jew had
come there to get her for himself.   She hated him
for his own sake; she hated him because she was
faithful to Nino; she hated him because he perhaps knew of her secret love for my boy.   Poor
maiden, shut up for days and weeks to come with
a man she dreaded and scorned at once!   The
sight of her recalled to me that I had in my pocket
the letter Nino had sent me for her, weeks before,
and which I had found no means of delivering since
I had been in Fillettino.   Suddenly I was seized
with a mad determination to deliver it at any cost.
The baron bowed me out of the gate, and I paused
outside when the ponderous door had swung on its
hinges and his footsteps were echoing back through
the court.

I sat down on the parapet of the bridle-path, and with my knife cut some of the stitches that sewed my money between my two waistcoats. I took out one of the bills of a hundred francs that were concealed within, I found the letter Nino had sent me for Hedwig, and I once more rang the bell. The man who had admitted me came again, and looked at me in some astonishment. But I gave him no time to question me.

" Here is a note for a hundred francs," I said. " Take it, and give this letter to the Signora Contessina. If you bring me a written answer here to-morrow at this hour, I will give you as much more." The man was dumfounded for a moment, after which he clutched the money and the letter greedily, and hid them in his coat.

" Your excellency shall be punctually obeyed," he said, with a deep bow, and I went away.

It was recklessly extravagant of me to do this, but there was no other course. A small bribe would have been worse than none at all. If you can afford to pay largely, it is better to bribe a servant than to trust a friend. Your friend has nothing to gain by keeping your secret, whereas the servant hopes for more money in the future, and the prospect of profit makes him as silent as the grave.

I would certainly not have acted as I did, had I not met Hedwig in the hall. But the sight of her pale face and heavy eyes went to my heart, and I would have given the whole of my little fortune to bring some gladness to her, even though I might not see it. The situation, too, was so novel and alarming that I felt obliged to act quickly, not knowing what evils delay might produce.

On the following morning I went up to the gateway again and rang the bell. The same man appeared. He slipped a note into my hand, and I slipped a bill into his. But, to my surprise, he did not shut the door and retire.

" The signorina said your excellency should read the note, and I should accompany you," he said ; and I saw he had his hat in his hand, as if ready to go. I tore open the note. It merely said that the servant was trustworthy, and would " instruct the Signor Grandi " how to act.

"You told the contessina my name, then ? " I said to the man. He had announced me to the baron, and consequently knew who I was. He nodded, closed the door behind him, and came with me. When we were in the street, he explained that Hedwig desired to speak with me. He expounded the fact that there was a staircase in the rock, leading to the level of the town. Furthermore, he said that the old count and the baron occasionally drank deeply, as soldiers and adventurers will do, to pass the evening. The next time it occurred, he, the faithful servant, would come to my lodging and conduct me into the castle by the aforesaid passage, of which he had the key.

I confess I was unpleasantly alarmed at the prospect of making a burglarious entrance in such romantic fashion. It savored more of the last century than of the quiet and eminently respectable age in which we live. But then, the castle of Fillettino was built hundreds of years ago, and it is not my fault if it has not gone to ruin, like so many others of its kind. The man recommended me to be always at home after eight o'clock in the evening, in case I were wanted, and to avoid seeing the baron when he was abroad. He came and saw where I lived, and with many bows he left me.

You may imagine in what anxiety I passed my time. A whole week elapsed, and yet I was never summoned. Every evening at seven, an hour before the time named, I was in my room, waiting for some one who never came. I was so much disturbed in mind that I lost my appetite and thought of being bled again. But I thought it too soon, and contented myself with getting a little tamarind from the apothecary.

One morning the apothecary, who is also the postmaster, gave me a letter from Nino, dated in Rome. His engagement was over, he had reached Rome, and he would join me immediately.

16

XV.

As it often happens that, in affairs of importance, the minor events which lead to the ultimate result seem to occur rapidly, and almost to stumble over each other in their haste, it came to pass that on the very evening after I had got Nino's letter I was sent for by the contessina.

When the man came to call me, I was sitting in my room, from force of habit, though the long delay had made the possibility of the meeting seem shadowy. I was hoping that Nino might arrive in time to go in my place, for I knew that he would not be many hours behind his letter. He would assuredly travel as fast as he could, and if he had understood my directions he was not likely to go astray. But in spite of my hopes the summons came too soon, and I was obliged to go myself.

Picture to yourselves how I looked and how I felt: a sober old professor, as I am, stealing out in the night, all wrapped in a cloak as dark and shabby as any conspirator's; armed with a good knife in case of accidents; with beating heart, and doubting whether I could use my weapon if needful; and guided to the place of tryst by the confidential servant of a beautiful and unhappy maiden. I have often laughed since then at the figure I must have cut, but I did not laugh at the time. It was a very serious affair.

We skirted the base of the huge rock on which the castle is built, and reached the small, low door without meeting any one. It was a moonlit night, — the Paschal moon was nearly at the full, — and the whiteness made each separate iron rivet in the door stand out distinct, thrown into relief by its own small shadow on the seamed oak. My guide produced a ponderous key, which screamed hoarsely in the lock under the pressure of his two hands, as he made it turn in the rusty wards. The noise frightened me, but the man laughed, and said they could not hear where they sat, far up in the vaulted chamber, telling long stories over their wine. We entered, and I had to mount a little way up the dark steps to give him room to close the door behind us, by which we were left in total darkness. I confess I was very nervous and frightened until he lighted a taper which he had brought and made enough light to show the way. The stairs were winding and steep, but perfectly dry, and when he had passed me I followed him, feeling that at all events the door behind was closed, and there was some one between me and any danger ahead.

The man paused in front of me, and when I had rounded the corner of the winding steps I saw that a brighter light than ours shone from a small doorway opening directly upon the stair. In another moment I was in the presence of Hedwig von Lira. The man retired, and left us.

She stood, dressed in black, against the rough stone; the strong light of a gorgeous gilt lamp that was placed on the floor streamed upward on her white face. Her eyes caught the brightness, and seemed to burn like deep, dark gems, though they appeared so blue in the day. She looked like a person tortured past endurance, so that the pain of the soul has taken shape, and the agony of the heart has assumed substance. Tears shed had hollowed the marble cheeks, and the stronger suffering that cannot weep had chiseled out great shadows beneath her brows. Her thin clasped hands seemed wringing each other into strange shapes of woe; and though she stood erect as a slender pillar against the black rock, it was rather from the courage of despair than because she was straight and tall by her own nature.

I bent low before her, awed by the extremity of suffering I saw.

"Are you Signor Grandi?" she asked, in a low and trembling voice.

"Most humbly at your service, Signora Contessina," I answered. She put out out her hand to me, and then drew it back quickly, with a timid, nervous look as I moved to take it.

"I never saw you," she said, "but I feel as though you *must* be a friend " — She paused.

"Indeed, signorina, I am here for that reason," said I, trying to speak stoutly, and so to inspire her with some courage. "Tell me how I can best serve you; and though I am not young and strong like

Nino Cardegna, my boy, I am not so old but that I can do whatsoever you command."

" Then, in God's name, save me from this " — But again the sentence died upon her lips, and she glanced anxiously at the door. I reflected that if any one came we should be caught like mice in a trap, and I made as though I would look out upon the stairs. But she stopped me.

" I am foolishly frightened," she said. " That man is faithful, and will keep watch." I thought it time to discover her wishes.

" Signorina," said I, " you ask me to save you. You do not say from what. I can at least tell you that Nino Cardegna will be here in a day or two " — At this sudden news she gave a little cry, and the blood rushed to her cheeks, in strange contrast with their deathly whiteness. She seemed on the point of speaking, but checked herself, and her eyes, that had looked me through and through a moment before, drooped modestly under my glance.

" Is it possible ? " she said at last, in a changed voice. " Yes, if he comes, I think the Signor Cardegna will help me."

" Madam," I said, very courteously, for I guessed her embarrassment, " I can assure you that my boy is ready to give you his life in return for the kindness he received at your hands in Rome." She looked up, smiling through her tears, for the sudden happiness had moistened the drooping lids.

" You are very kind, Signor Grandi. Signor Cardegna is, I believe, a good friend of mine. You say he will be here ? "

"I received a letter from him to-day, dated in Rome, in which he tells me that he will start immediately. He may be here to-morrow morning," I answered. Hedwig had regained her composure, perhaps because she was reassured by my manner of speaking about Nino. I, however, was anxious to hear from her own lips some confirmation of my suspicions concerning the baron. "I have no doubt," I continued, presently, "that, with your consent, my boy will be able to deliver you from this prison"— I used the word at a venture. Had Hedwig suffered less, and been less cruelly tormented, she would have rebuked me for the expression. But I recalled her to her position, and her self-control gave way at once.

"Oh, you are right to call it a prison!" she cried. "It is as much a prison as this chamber hewed out of the rock, where so many a wretch has languished hopelessly; a prison from which I am daily taken out into the sweet sun, to breathe and be kept alive, and to taste how joyful a thing liberty must be! And every day I am brought back, and told that I may be free if I will consent. Consent! God of mercy!" she moaned, in a sudden tempest of passionate despair. "Consent ever to belong, body — and soul — to be touched, polluted, desecrated, by that inhuman monster; sold to him, to a creature without pity, whose heart is a toad, a venomous creeping thing, — sold to him for this life, and to the vengeance of God hereafter; bartered, traded, and told that I am so vile and lost that the very price I am offered is an honor to me, being so much more than my value." She came toward me as she spoke, and the passionate, un- shed tears that were in her seemed to choke her, so that her voice was hoarse.

"And for what — for what?" she cried wildly, seizing my arm and looking fiercely into my eyes. "For what, I say? Because I gave him a poor rose; because I let him see me once; because I loved his sweet voice; because — because — I love him, and will love him, and do love him, though I die!"

The girl was in a frenzy of passion and love and hate all together, and did not count her words. The white heat of her tormented soul blazed from her pale face and illuminated every feature, though she was turned from the light, and she shook my arm in her grasp so that it pained me. The marble was burned in the fire, and must consume itself to ashes. The white and calm statue was become a pillar of flame in the life-and-death struggle for love. I strove to speak, but could not, for fear and wonder tied my tongue. And indeed she gave me short time to think.

"I tell you I love him, as he loves me," she con- tinued, her voice trembling upon the rising cadence, "with all my whole being. Tell him so. Tell him he must save me, and that only he can: that for his sake I am tortured, and scorned, and disgraced, and sold; my body thrown to dogs, and worse than dogs; my soul given over to devils that tempt me to kill and be free, — by my own father, for his

sake. Tell him that these hands he kissed are
wasted with wringing small pains from each other,
but the greater pain drives them to do worse. Tell
him, good sir, — you are kind and love him, but
not as I do, — tell him that this golden hair of
mine has streaks of white in these terrible two
months; that these eyes he loved are worn with
weeping. Tell him " —

But her voice failed her, and she staggered
against the wall, hiding her face in her hands. A
trembling breath, a struggle, a great wild sob: the
long-sealed tears were free, and flowed fast over her
hands.

" Oh, no, no," she moaned, "you must not tell
him that." Then choking down her agony she
turned to me: " You will not — you cannot tell
him of this? I am weak, ill, but I will bear everything for — for him." The great effort exhausted
her, and I think that if I had not caught her she
would have fallen, and she would have hurt herself
very much on the stone floor. But she is young,
and I am not very strong, and could not have held
her up. So I knelt, letting her weight come on my
shoulder.

The fair head rested pathetically against my old
coat, and I tried to wipe away her tears with her
long, golden hair ; for I had not any handkerchief.
But very soon I could not see to do it. I was
crying myself, for the pity of it all, and my tears
trickled down and fell on her thin hands. And
so I kneeled, and she half lay and half sat upon

the floor, with her head resting on my shoulder. I
was glad then to be old, for I felt that I had a right
to comfort her.

Presently she looked up into my face, and saw
that I was weeping. She did not speak, but found
her little lace handkerchief, and pressed it to my
eyes, — first to one, and then to the other; and the
action brought a faint maidenly flush to her cheeks
through all her own sorrow. A daughter could not
have done it more kindly.

"My child," I said at last, "be sure that your
secret is safe with me. But there is one coming
with whom it will be safer."

"You are so good," she said, and her head sank
once more, and nestled against my breast, so that
I could just see the bright tresses through my gray
beard. But in a moment she looked up again, and
made as though she would rise; and then I helped
her, and we both stood on our feet.

Poor, beautiful, tormented Hedwig! I can remember it, and call up the whole picture to my
mind. She still leaned on my arm, and looked up
to me, her loosened hair all falling back upon her
shoulders; and the wonderful lines of her delicate
face made ethereal and angelic by her sufferings.

"My dear," I said at last, smoothing her golden
hair with my hand, as I thought her mother would
do, if she had a mother, — "my dear, your interview with my boy may be a short one, and you may
not have an opportunity to meet at all for days. If
it does not pain you too much, will you tell me just

what your troubles are, here? I can then tell him, so that you can save the time when you are together." She gazed into my eyes for some seconds, as though to prove me, whether I were a true man.

" I think you are right," she answered, taking courage. " I will tell you in two words. My father treats me as though I had committed some unpardonable crime, which I do not at all understand. He says my reputation is ruined. Surely, that is not true?" She asked the question so innocently and simply that I smiled.

" No, my dear, it is not true," I replied.

" I am sure I cannot understand it," she continued; " but he says so, and, insists that my only course is to accept what he calls the advantageous offer which has suddenly presented itself. He insists very roughly." She shuddered slightly. " He gives me no peace. It appears that this creature wrote to ask my father for my hand, when we left Rome, two months ago. The letter was forwarded, and my father began at once to tell me that I must make up my mind to the marriage. At first I used to be very angry; but seeing we were alone, I finally determined to seem indifferent, and not to answer him when he talked about it. Then he thought my spirit was broken, and he sent for Baron Benoni, who arrived a fortnight ago. Do you know him, Signor Grandi? You came to see him, so I suppose you do." The same look of hatred and loathing came to her face that I had noticed when Benoni and I met her in the hall.

" Yes, I know him. He is a traitor, a villain," I said earnestly.

" Yes, and more than that. But he is a great banker in Russia " —

" A banker ? " I asked, in some astonishment.

" Did you not know it? Yes ; he is very rich, and has a great firm, if that is the name for it. But he wanders incessantly, and his partners take care of his affairs. My father says that I shall marry him, or end my days here."

" Unless you end his for him ! " I cried indignantly.

" Hush ! " said she, and trembled violently. " He is my father, you know," she added earnestly.

" But you cannot consent " — I began.

" Consent ! " she interrupted, with a bitter laugh. " I will die rather than consent."

" I mean, you cannot consent to be shut up in this valley forever."

" If need be, I will," she said, in a low voice.

" There is no need," I whispered.

" You do not know my father. He is a man of iron," she answered sorrowfully.

" You do not know my boy. He is a man of his word," I replied.

We were both silent, for we both knew very well what our words meant. From such a situation there could be but one escape.

" I think you ought to go now," she said at last. " If I were missed it would all be over. But I am sorry to let you go, you are so kind. How can you let me know"— She stopped, with a blush, and stooped to raise the lamp from the floor.

"Can you not meet here to-morrow night, when they are asleep?" I suggested, knowing what her question would have been.

"I will send the same man to you to-morrow evening, and let you know what is possible," she said. "And now I will show you the way out of my house," she added, with the first faint shadow of a smile. With the slight gilt lamp in her hand, she went out of the little rock chamber, listened a moment, and began to descend the steps.

"But the key?" I asked, following her light footsteps with my heavier tread.

"It is in the door," she answered, and went on.

When we reached the bottom, we found it as she had said. The servant had left the key on the inside, and with some difficulty I turned the bolts. We stood for one moment in the narrow space, where the lowest step was set close against the door. Her eyes flashed strangely in the lamplight.

"How easy it would be!" I said, understanding her glance. She nodded, and pushed me gently out into the street; and I closed the door, and leaned against it as she locked it.

"Good-night," she said from the other side, and I put my mouth to the keyhole. "Good-night. Courage!" I answered. I could hear her lightly mounting the stone steps. It seemed wonderful to me that she should not be afraid to go back alone. But love makes people brave.

The moon had risen higher during the time I had been within, and I strolled round the base of the rock, lighting a cigar as I went. The terrible adventure I had dreaded was now over, and I felt myself again. In truth, it was a curious thing to happen to a man of my years and my habits; but the things I had heard had so much absorbed my attention that, while the interview lasted, I had forgotten the strange manner of the meeting. I was horrified at the extent of the girl's misery, more felt than understood from her brief description and passionate outbreaks. There is no mistaking the strength of a suffering that wastes and consumes the mortal part of us as wax melts at the fire.

And Benoni — the villain! He had written to ask Hedwig in marriage before he came to see me in Rome. There was something fiendish in his almost inviting me to see his triumph, and I cursed him as I kicked the loose stones in the road with my heavy shoes. So he was a banker, as well as a musician and a wanderer. Who would have thought it?

"One thing is clear," I said to myself, as I went to bed: "unless something is done immediately, that poor girl will consume herself and die." And all that night her poor thin face and staring eyes were in my dreams; so that I woke up several times, thinking I was trying to comfort her and could not. But toward dawn I felt sure that Nino was coming, and that all would be well.

I was chatting with my old landlady the next morning, and smoking to pass the time, when there was suddenly a commotion in the street. That is to say, some one was arriving, and all the little children turned out in a body to run after the stranger, while the old women came to their doors with their knitting, and squinted under the bright sunlight to see what was the matter.

It was Nino, of course — my own boy, riding on a stout mule, with a countryman by his side upon another. He was dressed in plain gray clothes, and wore high boots. His great felt hat drooped half across his face, and hid his eyes from me; but there was no mistaking the stern, square jaw and the close, even lips. I ran toward him, and called him by name. In a moment he was off his beast, and we embraced tenderly.

"Have you seen her?" were the first words he spoke. I nodded, and hurried him into the house where I lived, fearful lest some mischance should bring the party from the castle riding by. He sent his man with the mules to the inn, and when we were at last alone together he threw himself into a chair, and took off his hat.

Nino too was changed in the two months that had passed. He had traveled far, had sung lustily, and had been applauded to the skies; and he had seen the great world. But there was more than all that in his face. There were lines of care and of thought that well became his masculine features. There was a something in his look that told of a set purpose, and there was a light in his dark eyes that spoke a world of warning to any one who might dare to thwart him. But he seemed thinner, and his cheeks were as white as the paper I write on.

Some men are born masters, and never once relax the authority they exercise on those around them. Nino has always commanded me, as he seems to command everybody else, in the fewest words possible. But he is so true and honest and brave that all who know him love him; and that is more than can be said for most artists. As he sat in his chair, hesitating what question to ask first, or waiting for me to speak, I thought that if Hedwig von Lira had searched the whole world for a man able to deliver her from her cruel father and from her hated lover she could have chosen no . better champion than Nino Cardegna, the singer. Of course you all say that I am infatuated with the boy, and that I helped him to do a reckless thing, simply because I was blinded by my fondness. But I maintain, and shall ever hold, that Nino did right in this matter, and I am telling my story merely in order that honest men may judge.

He sat by the window, and the sun poured through the panes upon his curling hair, his traveling dress, and his dusty boots. The woman of the house brought in some wine and water; but he only sipped the water, and would not touch the wine.

"You are a dear, kind father to me," he said, putting out his hand from where he sat, "and before we talk I must tell you how much I thank you." Simple words, as they look on paper; but another man could not have, said so much in an hour, as his voice and look told me.

XVI.

"NINO mio," I began, "I saw the contessina last night. She is in a very dramatic and desperate situation. But she greets you, and looks to you to save her from her troubles." Nino's face was calm, but his voice trembled a little as he answered : —

"Tell me quickly, please, what the troubles are."

"Softly — I will tell you all about it. You must know that your friend Benoni is a traitor to you, and is here. Do not look astonished. He has made up his mind to marry the contessina, and she says she will die rather than take him, which is quite right of her." At the latter piece of news, Nino sprang from his chair.

"You do not seriously mean that her father is trying to make her marry Benoni?" he cried.

"It is infamous, my dear boy; but it is true."

"Infamous! I should think you could find a stronger word. How did you learn this?" I detailed the circumstances of our meeting on the previous night. While I talked, Nino listened with intense interest, and his face changed its look from anger to pity, and from pity to horror. When I had finished, he was silent.

"You can see for yourself," I said, "that the case is urgent."

" I will take her away," said Nino, at last. " It will be very unpleasant for the count. He would have been wiser to allow her to have her own way."

" Do nothing rash, Nino mio. Consider a little what the consequences would be if you were caught in the act of violently carrying off the daughter of a man as powerful as Von Lira."

" Bah! You talk of his power as though we lived under the Colonnesi and the Orsini, instead of under a free monarchy. If I am once married to her, what have I to fear? Do you think the count would go to law about his daughter's reputation? Or do you suppose he would try to murder me? "

" I would do both, in his place," I answered. "But perhaps you are right, and he will yield when he sees that he is outwitted. Think again, and suppose that the contessina herself objects to such a step."

"That is a different matter. She shall do nothing save by her own free will. You do not imagine I would try to take her away unless she were willing? " He sat down again beside me, and affectionately laid one hand on my shoulder.

" Women, Nino, are women," I remarked.

" Unless they are angels," he assented.

" Keep the angels for Paradise, and beware of taking them into consideration in this working-day world. I have often told you, my boy, that I am older than you."

" As if I doubted that! " he laughed.

" Very well. I know something about women. A

17

hundred women will tell you that they are ready to
flee with you; but not more than one in the hundred will really leave everything and follow you to
the end of the world, when the moment comes for
running away. They always make a fuss at the
last, and say it is too dangerous, and you may be
caught. That is the way of them. You will be
quite ready with a ladder of ropes, like one of Boc-
caccio's men, and a roll of bank-notes for the journey, and smelling-salts, and a cushion for the puppy
dog, and a separate conveyance for the maid, just
according to the directions she has given you;
then, at the very last, she will perhaps say that she
is afraid of hurting her father's feelings by leaving
him without any warning. Be careful, Nino ! "

" As for that," he answered sullenly enough, " if
she will not, she will not ; and I would not attempt
to persuade her against her inclination. But unless you have very much exaggerated what you saw
in her face, she will be ready at five minutes' notice. It must be very like hell, up there in that
castle, I should think."

" Messer Diavolo, who rules over the house, will
not let his prey escape him so easily as you think."

" Her father ? " he asked.

" No ; Benoni. There is no creature so relent-
less as an old man in pursuit of a young woman."

" I am not afraid of Benoni."

" You need not be afraid of her father," said I,
laughing. " He is lame, and cannot run after you."
I do not know why it is that we Romans laugh at

lame people; we are sorry for them, of course, as we are for other cripples.

"There is something more than fear in the matter," said·Nino seriously. "It is a great thing to have upon one's soul."

"What?" I asked.

"To take a daughter away from her father without his consent, — or at least without consulting him. I would not like to do it."

"Do you mean to ask the old gentleman's consent before eloping with his daughter? You are a little donkey, Nino, upon my word."

"Donkey, or anything else you like, but I will act like a galantuomo. I will see the count, and ask him once more whether he is willing to let his daughter marry me. If not, so much the worse; he will be warned."

"Look here, Nino," I said, astonished at the idea. "I have taught you a little logic. Suppose you meant to steal a horse, instead of a woman. Would you go to the owner of the horse, with your hat in your hand, and say, 'I trust your worship will not be offended if I steal this horse, which seems to be a good animal and pleases me;' and then would you expect him to allow you to steal his horse?"

"Sor Cornelio, the case is not the same. Women have a right to be free, and to marry whom they please; but horses are slaves. However, as I am not a thief, I would certainly ask the man for the horse; and if he refused it, and I conceived that I had a right to have it, I would take it by force, and not by stealth."

" It appears to me that if you meant to get possession of what was not yours you might as well get it in the easiest possible way," I objected. " But we need not argue the case. There is a much better reason why you should not consult the count."

" I do not believe it," said Nino stubbornly.

" Nevertheless, it is so. The Contessina di Lira is desperately unhappy, and if nothing is done she may die. Young women have died of broken hearts before now. You have no right to endanger her life by risking failure. Answer me that, if you can, and I will grant you are a cunning sophist, but not a good lover."

" There is reason in what you say now," he answered. " I had not thought of that desperateness of the case which you speak of. You have seen her." He buried his face in his hand, and seemed to be thinking.

" Yes, I have seen her, and I wish you had been in my place. You would think differently about asking her father's leave to rescue her." From having been anxious to prevent anything rash, it seemed that I was now urging him into the very jaws of danger. I think that Hedwig's face was before me, as it had been in reality on the previous evening. " As Curione said to Cæsar, delay is injurious to any one who is fully prepared for action. I remember also to have read somewhere that such waste of time in diplomacy and palavering is the favorite resource of feeble and timid minds, who regard the use of dilatory and ambiguous measures as an evidence of the most admirable and consummate prudence."

"Oh, you need not use so much learning with me," said Nino. "I assure you that I will be neither dilatory nor ambiguous. In fact, I will go at once, without even dusting my boots, and I will say, Give me your daughter, if you can ; and if you cannot, I will still hope to marry her. He will probably say 'No,' and then I will carry her off. It appears to me that is simple enough."

"Take my advice, Nino. Carry her off first, and ask permission afterwards. It is much better. The real master up there is Benoni, I fancy, and not the count. Benoni is a gentleman who will give you much trouble. If you go now to see Hedwig's father, Benoni will be present at the interview." Nino was silent, and sat stretching his legs before him, his head on his breast. "Benoni," I continued, "has made up his mind to succeed. He has probably taken this fancy into his head out of pure wickedness. Perhaps he is bored, and really wants a wife. But I believe he is a man who delights in cruelty and would as lief break the contessina's heart by getting rid of you as by marrying her." I saw that he was not listening.

"I have an idea," he said at last. "You are not very wise, Messer Cornelio, and you counsel me to be prudent and to be rash in the same breath."

"You make very pretty compliments, Sor Nino,"

I answered tartly. He put out his hand deprecatingly.

"You are as wise as any man can be who is not in love," he said, looking at me with his great eyes. But love is the best counselor."

"What is your idea?" I asked, somewhat pacified.

"You say they ride together every day. Yes — very good. The contessina will not ride to-day; partly because she will be worn out with fatigue from last night's interview, and partly because she will make an effort to discover whether I have arrived to-day or not. You can count on that."

"I imagine so."

"Very well," he continued; "in that case one of two things will happen: either the count will go out alone, or they will all stay at home."

"Why will Benoni not go out with the count?"

"Because Benoni will hope to see Hedwig alone, if he stays at home, and the count will be very glad to give him the opportunity."

"I think you are right, Nino. You are not so stupid as I thought."

"In war," continued the boy, "a general gains a great advantage by separating his adversary's forces. If the count goes out alone, I will present myself to him in the road, and tell him what I want."

"Now you are foolish again. You should, on the contrary, enter the house when the count is away, and take the signorina with you then and there.

Before he could return you would be miles on the road to Rome."

"In the first place, I tell you once and for all, Sor Cornelio," he said slowly, "that such an action would be dishonorable, and I will not do anything of the kind. Moreover, you forget that, if I followed your advice, I should find Benoni at home, — the very man from whom you think I have everything to fear. No ; I must give the count one fair chance." I was silent, for I saw he was determined, and yet I would not let him think that I was satisfied.

,The idea of losing an advantage by giving an enemy any sort of warning before the attack seemed to me novel in the extreme ; but I comprehended that Nino saw in his scheme a satisfaction to his conscience, and smelled in it a musty odor of forgotten knight-errantry that he had probably learned to love in his theatrical experiences. I had certainly not expected that Nino Cardegna, the peasant child, would turn out to be the pink of chivalry and the mirror of honor. But I could not help admiring his courage, and wondering if it would not play him false at the perilous moment. I did not half know him then, though he had been with me for so many years. But I was very anxious to ascertain from him what he meant to do, for I feared that his bold action would make trouble, and I had visions of the count and Benoni together taking sudden and summary vengeance on myself.

"Nino," I said, " I have made great sacrifices to

help you in finding these people," — I would not tell him I had sold my vineyard to make preparation for a longer journey, though he has since found it out, — " but if you are going to do anything rash I will get on my little ass, and ride a few miles from the village until it is over." Nino laughed aloud.

" My dear professor," he said, " do not be afraid. I will give you plenty of time to get out of the way. Meanwhile, the contessina is certain to send the confidential servant of whom you speak, to give me instructions. If I am not here, you ought to be, in order to receive the message. Now listen to me."

I prepared to be attentive and to listen to his scheme. I was by no means expecting the plan he proposed.

" The count may take it into his head to ride at a different hour, if he rides alone," he began. " I will therefore have my mule saddled now, and will station my man — a countryman from Subiaco and good for any devilry — in some place where he can watch the entrance to the house, or the castle, or whatever you call this place. So soon as he sees the count come out he will call me. As a man can ride in only one of two directions in this valley, I shall have no trouble whatever in meeting the old gentleman, even if I cannot overtake him with my mule."

" Have you any arms, Nino ? "

" No. I do not want weapons to face an old man in broad daylight ; and he is too much of a soldier to attack me if I am defenceless. If the servant comes after I am gone, you must remember every detail of what he says, and you must also arrange a little matter with him. Here is money, as much as will keep any Roman servant quiet. The man will be rich before we have done with him. I will write a letter, which he must deliver; but he must also know what he has to do."

"At twelve o'clock to-night the contessina must positively be at the door of the staircase by which you entered yesterday. *Positively* — do you understand? She will then choose for herself between what she is suffering now and flight with me." If she chooses to fly, my mules and my countryman will be ready. The servant who admits me had better make the best of his way to Rome, with the money he has got There will be difficulties in the way of getting the contessina to the staircase, especially as the count will be in a towering passion with me, and will not sleep much. But he will not have the smallest idea that I shall act so suddenly, and he will fancy that when once his daughter is safe within the walls for the night she will not think of escaping. I do not believe he even knows of the existence of this staircase. At all events, it appears, from your success in bribing the first man you met, that the servants are devoted to her interests and their own, and not at all to those of her father."

"I cannot conceive, Nino," said I, "why you do not put this bold plan into execution without seeing the count first, and making the whole thing so dan-

gerous. If he takes alarm in the night, he will
catch you fast enough on his good horses, before
you are at Trevi."

"I am determined to act as I proposed," said
Nine, "because it is a thousand times more honorable, and because I am certain that the contessina
would not have me act otherwise. She will also
see for herself that flight is best; for I am sure
the count will make a scene of some kind when he
comes home from meeting me. If she knows she
can escape to-night she will not suffer from what
he has to say; but without the prospect of freedom
she would suffer very much."

"Where did you learn to understand women, my
boy?" I asked.

"I do not understand women in general," he answered, "but I understand very well the only woman who exists for me personally. I know that she
is the soul of honor, and that at the same time she
has enough common sense to perceive the circumstances of her situation."

"But how will you make sure of not being overtaken?" I objected, making a last feeble stand
against his plan.

"That is simple enough. My countryman from
Subiaco knows every inch of these hills. He says
that the pass above Fillettino is impracticable for
any animals save men, mules, and donkeys. A
horse would roll down at every turn. My mules
are the best of their kind, and there are none like

them here. By sunrise I shall be over the Serra and well on the way to Ceprano, or whatever place I may choose for joining the railroad."

"And I? Will you leave me here to be murdered by that Prussian devil?" I asked, in some alarm.

"Why, no, padre mio. If you like, you can start for Rome at sunset, or as soon as I return from meeting the count; or you can get on your donkey and go up the pass, where we shall overtake you. Nobody will harm you, in your disguise, and your donkey is even more sure-footed than my mules. It will be a bright night, too, for the moon is full."

"Well, well, Nino," said I at last, "I suppose you will have your own way, as you always do in the world. And if it must be so, I will go up the pass alone, for I am not afraid at all. It would be against all the proprieties that you should be riding through a wild country alone at night with the young lady you intend to marry; and if I go with you there will be nothing to be said, for I am a very proper person, and hold a responsible position in Rome. But for charity's sake, do not undertake anything of this kind again "—

"Again?" exclaimed Nino, in surprise. "Do you expect me to spend my life in getting married, — not to say in eloping?"

"Well, I trust that you will have enough of it this time."

"I cannot conceive that when a man has once

married the woman he loves he should ever look at another," said Nino gravely.

"You are a most blessed fellow," I exclaimed.

Nino found my writing materials, which consisted of a bad steel pen, some coarse ruled paper, and a wretched little saucer of ink, and began writing an epistle to the contessina. I watched him as he wrote, and I smoked a little to pass the time. As I looked at him, I came to the conclusion that to-day, at least, he was handsome. His thick hair curled about his head, and his white skin was as pale and clear as milk. I thought that his complexion had grown less dark than it used to be, perhaps from being so much in the theatre at night. That takes the dark blood out of the cheeks. But any woman would have looked twice at him. Besides, there was, as there is now, a certain marvelous neatness and spotlessness about his dress; but for his dusty boots, you would not have guessed he had been traveling. Poor Nino! When he had not a penny in the world but what he earned by copying music, he used to spend it all with the washerwoman, so that Mariuccia was often horrified, and I reproved him for the extravagance.

At last he finished writing, and put his letter into the only envelope there was left. He gave it to me, and said he would go out and order his mules to be ready.

"I may be gone all day," he said, "and I may return in a few hours. I cannot tell. In any case, wait for me, and give the letter and all the instructions to the man, if he comes." Then he thanked me once more very affectionately, and having embraced me he went out.

I watched from the window, and he looked up and waved his hand. I remember it very distinctly — just how he looked. His face was paler than ever, his lips were close set, though they smiled, and his eyes were sad. He is an incomprehensible boy — he always was.

I was left alone, with plenty of time for meditation, and I assure you my reflections were not pleasant. O love, love, what madness you drive us into, by day and night! Surely it is better to be a sober professor of philosophy than to be in love, ever so wildly, or sorrowfully, or happily. I do not wonder that a parcel of idiots have tried to prove that Dante loved philosophy and called it Beatrice. He would have been a sober professor, if that were true, and a happier man. But I am sure it is not true, for I was once in love myself.

XVII

It fell out as Nino had anticipated, and when he told me all the details, some time afterwards, it struck me that he had shown an uncommon degree of intelligence in predicting that the old count would ride alone that day. He had, indeed, so made his arrangements that even if the whole party had come out together nothing worse would have occurred than a postponement of the interview he sought. But he was destined to get what he wanted that very day, namely, an opportunity of speaking with Von Lira alone.

It was twelve o'clock when he left me, and the midday bell was ringing from the church, while the people bustled about, getting their food. Every old woman had a piece of corn cake, and the ragged children got what they could, gathering the crumbs in their mothers' aprons. A few rough fellows who were not away at work in the valley munched the maize bread with a leek and a bit of salt fish, and some of them had oil on it. Our mountain people eat scarcely anything else, unless it be a little meat on holidays, or an egg when the hens are laying. But they laugh and chatter over the coarse fare, and drink a little wine when they can get it. Just now, however, was the season for fasting, being the end of Holy Week, and the people made a virtue of necessity and kept their eggs and their wine for Easter.

When Nino went out he found his countryman and explained to him what he was to do. The man saddled one of the mules and put himself on the watch, while Nino sat by the fire in the quaint old inn and ate some bread. It was the end of March when these things happened, and a little fire was grateful, though one could do very well without it. He spread his hands to the flame of the sticks, as he sat on the wooden settle by the old hearth, and he slowly gnawed his corn cake, as though a week before he had not been a great man in Paris, dining sumptuously with famous people. He was not · thinking of that. He was looking, in the flame, for a fair face that he saw continually before him, day and night. He expected to wait a long time, — some hours, perhaps.

Twenty minutes had not elapsed, however, before his man came breathless through the door, calling to him to come at once ; for the solitary rider had gone out, as was expected, and at a pace that would soon take him out of sight. Nino threw his corn bread to a hungry dog, that yelped as it hit him, and then fastened on it like a beast of prey.

In the twinkling of an eye he and his man were out of the inn. As they ran to the place where the mule was tied to an old ring in the crumbling wall of a half-ruined house near to the ascent to the castle, the man told Nino that the fine gentleman had ridden toward Trevi, down the valley. Nino mounted, and hastened in the same direction.

As he rode, he reflected that it would be wiser to meet the count on his return, and pass him after the interview, as though going away from Fillettino. It would be a little harder for the mule; but such an animal, used to bearing enormous burdens for twelve hours at a stretch, could well carry Nino only a few miles of good road before sunset, and yet be fresh again by midnight. One of those great sleek mules, if good-tempered, will tire three horses, and never feel the worse for it. He therefore let the beast go her own pace along the road to Trevi, winding by the brink of the rushing torrent: sometimes beneath great overhanging cliffs, sometimes through bits of cultivated land, where the valley widens ; and now and then passing under some beech-trees, still naked and skeleton-like in the bright March air.

But Nino rode many miles, as he thought, without meeting the count, dangling his feet out of the stirrups, and humming snatches of song to himself to pass the time. He looked at his watch, — a beautiful gold one, given him by a very great personage in Paris, — and it was half past two o'clock. Then, to avoid tiring his mule, he got off and sat by a tree, at a place where he could see far along the road. But three o'clock came, and a quarter-past, and he began to fear that the count had gone all the way to Trevi. Indeed, Trevi could not be very far off, he thought. So he mounted again, and

paced down the valley. He says that in all that
time he never thought once of what he should say
to the count when he met him, having determined
in his mind once and for all what was to be asked ;
to which the only answer must be " yes " or " no."

At last, before he reached the turn in the valley,
and just as the sun was passing down behind the
high mountains on the left, beyond the stream, he
saw the man he had come out to meet, not a hundred yards away, riding toward him on his great
horse, at a foot pace. It was the count, and he
seemed lost in thought, for his head was bent on
his breast, and the reins hung carelessly loose from
his hand. He did not raise his eyes until he was
close to Nino, who took off his hat and pulled up
short.

The old count was evidently very much surprised,
for he suddenly straightened himself in his saddle,
with a sort of jerk, and glared savagely at Nino ;
his wooden features appearing to lose color, and his
long mustache standing out and bristling. He also
reined in his horse, and the pair sat on their beasts,
not five yards apart, eying each other like a pair
of duelists. Nino was the first to speak, for he was
prepared.

" Good-day, Signor Conte," he said as calmly
as he could. " You have not forgotten me, I am
sure." Lira looked more and more amazed, as he
observed the cool courtesy with which he was ac-
costed. But his polite manner did not desert him
even then, for he raised his hat.

18

"Good-day," he said, briefly, and made his horse move on. He was too proud to put the animal to a brisker pace than a walk, lest he should seem to avoid an enemy. But Nino turned his mule at the same time.

" Pardon the liberty, sir," he said, " but I would take advantage of this opportunity to have a few words with you."

" It is a liberty, as you say, sir," replied Lira, stiffly, and looking straight before him. " But since you have met me, say what you have to say quickly." He talked in the same curious constructions as formerly, but I will spare you the grammatical vagaries.

" Some time has elapsed," continued Nino, " since our unfortunate encounter. I have been in Paris, where I have had more than common success in my profession. From being a very poor teacher of Italian to the signorina, your daughter, I am become an exceedingly prosperous artist. My character is blameless and free from all stain, in spite of the sad business in which we were both concerned, and of which you knew the truth from the dead lady's own lips."

" What then ? " growled Lira, who had listened grimly, and was fast losing his temper. " What then ? Do you suppose, Signor Cardegna, that I am still interested in your comings and goings ? "

" The sequel to what I have told you, sir," answered Nino, bowing again, and looking very grave, " is that I once more most respectfully and honestly ask you to give me the hand of your daughter, the Signorina Hedwig von Lira."

The hot blood flushed the old soldier's hard features to the roots of his gray hair, and his voice trembled as he answered : —

" Do you intend to insult me, sir ? If so, this quiet road is a favorable spot for settling the question. It shall never be said that an officer in the service of his majesty the King and Emperor refused to fight with any one, — with his tailor, if need be." He reined his horse from Nino's side, and eyed him fiercely.

" Signor Conte," answered Nino calmly, " nothing could be further from my thoughts than to insult you, or to treat you in any way with disrespect. And I will not acknowledge that anything you can say can convey an insult to myself." Lira smiled in a sardonic fashion. " But," added Nino, " if it would give you any pleasure to fight, and if you have weapons, I shall be happy to oblige you. It is a quiet spot, as you say, and it shall never be said that an Italian artist refused to fight a German soldier."

" I have two pistols in my holsters," said Lira, with a smile. " The roads are not safe, and I always carry them."

" Then, sir, be good enough to select one and to give me the other, and we will at once proceed to business."

The count's manner changed. He looked grave. " I have the pistols, Signor Cardegna, but I do

not desire to use them. Your readiness satisfies me
that you are in earnest, and we will therefore not
fight for amusement. I need not defend myself
from any charge of unwillingness, I believe," he
added proudly.

" In that case, sir," said Nino, " and since we
have convinced each other that we are serious and
desire to be courteous, let us converse calmly."

" Have you anything more to say?" asked the
count, once more allowing his horse to pace along
the dusty road, while Nino's mule walked by his
side.

" I have this to say, Signor Conte," answered
Nino : " that I shall not desist from desiring the
honor of marrying your daughter, if you refuse me
a hundred times. I wish to put it to you whether,
with youth, some talent, — I speak modestly, — and
the prospect of a plentiful income, I am not as well
qualified to aspire to the alliance as Baron Benoni,
who has old age, much talent, an enormous fortune,
and the benefit of the Jewish faith into the bargain."

The count winced palpably at the mention of
Benoni's religion. No people are more insanely
prejudiced against the Hebrew race than the Germans. They indeed maintain that they have greater
cause than others, but it always appears to me that
they are unreasonable about it. Benoni chanced to
be a Jew, but his peculiarities would have been
the same had he been a Christian or an American.
There is only one Ahasuerus Benoni in the world.

"There is no question of Baron Benoni here," said the count severely, but hurriedly. "Your observations are beside the mark. The objections to the alliance, as you call it, are that you are a man of the people, — I do not desire to offend you, — a plebeian, in fact; you are also a man of uncertain fortune, like all singers; and lastly, you are an artist. I trust you will consider these points as a sufficient reason for my declining the honor you propose."

"I will only say," returned Nino, "that I venture to consider your reasons insufficient, though I do not question your decision. Baron Benoni was ennobled for a loan made to a government in difficulties; he was, by his own account, a shoemaker by early occupation, and a strolling musician — a great artist, if you like — by the profession he adopted."

"I never heard these facts," said Lira, "and I suspect that you have been misinformed. But I do not wish to continue the discussion of the subject."

Nino says that after the incident of the pistols the interview passed without the slightest approach to ill-temper on either side. They both felt that if they disagreed they were prepared to settle their difficulties then and there, without any further ado.

"Then, sir, before we part, permit me to call your attention to a matter which must be of importance to you," said Nino. "I refer to the happiness of the Signorina di Lira. In spite of your refusal of my offer, you will understand that the welfare of that lady must always be to me of the greatest importance."

Lira bowed his head stiffly, and seemed inclined to speak, but changed his mind, and held his tongue, to see what Nino would say.

" You will comprehend, I am sure," continued the latter, " that in the course of those months, during which I was so far honored as to be of service to the contessina, I had opportunities of observing her remarkably gifted intelligence. I am now credibly informed that she is suffering from ill health. I have not seen her, nor made any attempt to see her, as you might have supposed, but I have an acquaintance in Fillettino who has seen her pass his door daily. Allow me to remark that a mind of such rare qualities must grow sick if driven to feed upon itself in solitude. I would respectfully suggest that some gayer residence than Fillettino would be a sovereign remedy for her illness."

"Your tone and manner," replied the count, "forbid my resenting your interference. I have no reason to doubt your affection for my daughter, but I must request you to abandon all idea of changing my designs. If I choose to bring my daughter to a true sense of her position by somewhat rigorous methods, it is because I am aware that the frailty of reputation surpasses the frailty of woman. I will say this to your credit, sir : that if she has not disgraced herself, it has been in some measure because you wisely forbore from pressing your suit while you were received as an instructor beneath my roof. I am only doing my duty in trying to make her understand that her good name has been seriously exposed, and that the best reparation she can make lies in following my wishes, and accepting the honorable and advantageous marriage I have provided for her. I trust that this explanation, which I am happy to say has been conducted with the strictest propriety, will be final, and that you will at once desist from any further attempts toward persuading me to consent to a union that I disapprove."

Lira once more stopped his horse in the road, and taking off his hat bowed to Nino.

"And I, sir," said Nino, no less courteously, "am obliged to you for your clearly expressed answer. I shall never cease to regret your decision, and so long as I live I shall hope that you may change your mind. Good-day, Signor Conte," and he bowed to his saddle.

"Good-day, Signor Cardegna." So they parted: the count heading homeward toward Fillettino, and Nino turning back toward Trevi.

By this manœuvre he conveyed to the count's mind the impression that he had been to Fillettino for the day, and was returning to Trevi for the evening; and in reality the success of his enterprise, since his representations had failed, must depend upon Hedwig's being comparatively free during the ensuing night. He determined to wait by the

roadside until it should be dark, allowing his mule
to crop whatever poor grass she could find at this
season, and thus giving the count time to reach
Fillettino, even at the most leisurely pace.

He sat down upon the root of a tree, and allowed
his mule to graze at liberty. It was already growing dark in the valley; for between the long
speeches of civility the two had employed and the
frequent pauses in the interview, the meeting had
lasted the greater part of an hour.

Nino says that while he waited he reviewed his
past life and his present situation.

Indeed, since he had made his first appearance
in the theatre, three months before, events had
crowded thick and fast in his life. The first sensation of a great public success is strange to one
who has long been accustomed to live unnoticed
and unhonored by the world. It is at first incomprehensible that one should have suddenly grown
to be an object of interest and curiosity to one's
fellow-creatures, after having been so long a looker-
on. At first a man does not realize that the thing
he has labored over, and studied, and worked on,
can be actually anything remarkable. The pro-
duction of the every-day task has long grown a
habit, and the details which the artist grows to
admire and love so earnestly have each brought
with them their own reward. Every difficulty van-
quished, every image of beauty embodied, every
new facility of skill acquired, has been in itself a,
real and enduring satisfaction for its own sake, and

for the sake of its fitness to the whole, — the beautiful perfect whole he has conceived.

But he must necessarily forget, if he loves his work, that those who come after, and are to see the expression of his thought, or hear the mastery of his song, see or hear it all at once; so that the assemblage of the lesser beauties, over each of which the artist has had great joy, must produce a suddenly multiplied impression upon the understanding of the outside world, which sees first the embodiment of the thought, and has then the after-pleasure of appreciating the details. The hearer is thrilled with a sense of impassioned beauty, which the singer may perhaps feel when he first conceives the interpretation of the printed notes, but which goes ever farther from him as he strives to approach it and realize it; and so his admiration for his own song is lost in dissatisfaction with the failings which others have not time to see.

Before he is aware of the change, a singer has become famous, and all men are striving for a sight of him, or a hearing. There are few like Nino, whose head was not turned at all by the flattery and the praise, being occupied with other things. As he sat by the roadside, he thought of the many nights when the house rang with cheers and cries and all manner of applause ; and he remembered how, each time he looked his audience in the face, he had searched for the one face of all faces that he cared to see, and had searched in vain.

He seemed now to understand that it was his

honest-hearted love for the fair northern girl that
had protected him from caring for the outer world,
and he now realized what the outer world was. He
fancied to himself what his first three months of
brilliant success might have been, in Rome and
Paris, if he had not been bound by some strong tie
of the heart to keep him serious and thoughtful.
He thought of the women who had smiled upon
him, and of the invitations that had besieged him,
and of the consternation that had manifested itself
when he declared his intention of retiring to Rome,
after his brilliant engagement in Paris, without
signing any further contract.

Then came the rapid journey, the excitement,
the day in Rome, the difficulties of finding Fillettino ; and at last he was here, sitting by the roadside, and waiting for it to be time to carry into
execution the bold scheme he had set before him.
His conscience was at rest, for he now felt that he
had done all that the most scrupulous honor could
exact of him. He had returned in the midst of his
success to make an honorable offer of marriage, and
he had been refused — because he was a plebeian,
forsooth. And he knew also that the woman he
loved was breaking her heart for him.

What wonder that he set his teeth, and said to
himself that she should be his, at any price ! Nino
has no absurd ideas about the ridicule that attaches
to loving a woman, and taking her if necessary.
He has not been trained up in the heart to the
wretched thing they call society, which ruined me

long ago. What he wants he asks for, like a child, and if it is refused, and his good heart tells him that he has a right to it, he takes it, like a man, or like what a man was in the old time before the Englishman discovered that he is an ape. Ah, my learned colleagues, we are not so far removed from the ancestral monkey but that there is serious danger of our shortly returning to that primitive and caudal state! And I think that my boy and the Prussian officer, as they sat on their beasts and bowed, and smiled, and offered to fight each other, or to shake hands, each desiring to oblige the other, like a couple of knights of the old ages, were a trifle further removed from our common gorilla parentage than some of us.

But it grew dark, and Nino caught his mule and rode slowly back to the town, wondering what would happen before the sun rose on the other side of the world. Now, lest you fail to understand wholly how the matter passed, I must tell you a little of what took place during the time that Nino was waiting for the count, and Hedwig was alone in the castle with Baron Benoni. The way I came to know is this: Hedwig told the whole story to Nino, and Nino told it to me; but many months after that eventful day, which I shall always consider as one of the most remarkable in my life. It was Good Friday, last year, and you may find out the day of the month for yourselves.

XVIII.

As Nino had guessed, the count was glad of a chance to leave his daughter alone with Benoni, and it was for this reason that he had ridden out so early. The baron's originality and extraordinary musical talent seemed to Lira gifts which a woman needed only to see in order to appreciate, and which might well make her forget his snowy locks. During the time of Benoni's visit the count had not yet been successful in throwing the pair together, for Hedwig's dislike for the baron made her exert her tact to the utmost in avoiding his society.

It so happened that Hedwig, rising early, and breathing the sweet, cool air from the window of her chamber, had seen Nino ride by on his mule, when he arrived in the morning. He did not see her, for the street merely passed the corner of the great pile, and it was only by stretching her head far out that Hedwig could get a glimpse of it. But it amused her to watch the country people going by, with their mules and donkeys and hampers, or loads of firewood; and she would often lean over the window-sill for half an hour at a time, gazing at the little stream of mountain life, and sometimes weaving romances about the sturdy brown women and their dark-browed shepherd lovers. Moreover, she fully expected that Nino would arrive that day, and had some faint hope of seeing him go along the road. So she was rewarded, and the sight of the man she loved was the first breath of freedom.

In a great house like the strange abode Lira had selected for the seclusion of his daughter, it constantly occurs that one person is in ignorance of the doings of the others; and so it was natural that when Hedwig heard the clatter of hoofs in the courtyard, and the echoing crash of the great doors as they opened and closed, she should think both her father and Benoni had ridden away, and would be gone for the morning. She would not look out, lest she should see them and be seen.

I cannot tell you exactly what she felt when she saw Nino from her lofty window, but she was certainly glad with her whole heart. If she had not known of his coming from my visit the previous evening, she would perhaps have given way to some passionate outburst of happiness; but as it was, the feeling of anticipation, the sweet, false dawn of freedom, together with the fact that she was prepared, took from this first pleasure all that was overwhelming. She only felt that he had come, and that she would soon be saved from Benoni; she could not tell how, but she knew it, and smiled to herself for the first time in months, as she held a bit of jewelry to her slender throat, before the glass, wondering whether she had not grown too thin and pale to please her lover, who had been courted by the beauties of the world since he had left her.

She was ill, perhaps, and tired. That was why
she looked pale; but she knew that the first day of
freedom would make her as beautiful as ever. She
spent the morning hours in her rooms; but when
she heard the gates close, she fancied herself alone
in the great house, and went down into the sunny
courtyard, to breathe the air, and to give certain
instructions to her faithful man. She sent him to
my house, to speak with me; and that was all the
message he had, for the present. However, he
knew well enough what he was to do. There was
a strong smell of bank-notes in the air, and the
man kept his nose up.

Having dispatched this important business, Hedwig set herself to walk up and down the paved
quadrangle, on the sunny side. There was a stone
bench in a warm corner, that looked inviting. She
entered the house, and brought out a book, with
which she established herself to read. She had
often longed to sit there in the afternoon and watch
the sun creeping across the flags, pursued by the
shadow, till each small bit of moss and blade of
grass had received its daily portion of warmth.
For though the place had been cleared and weeded,
the tiny green things still grew in the chinks of
the pavement. In the middle of the court was a
well, with a cover and yoke of old-fashioned twisted
iron, and a pulley to draw the water. The air was
bright and fresh outside the castle, but the rever-
berating rays of the sun made the quiet courtyard
warm and still.

Sick with her daily torture of mind, the fair, pale girl rested her at last, and, dreaming of liberty, drew strength from the soft stillness. The book fell on her lap, her head leaned back against the rough stones of the wall, and gradually, as she watched from beneath her half-closed lids the play of the stealing sunlight, she fell into a sweet sleep.

She was soon disturbed by that indescribable uneasiness that creeps through our dreams when we are asleep in the presence of danger. A weird horror possesses us, and makes the objects in the dream appear unnatural. Gradually the terror grows on us and thrills us, and we wake, with bristling hair and staring eyes, to the hideous consciousness of unexpected peril.

Hedwig started and raised her lids, following the direction of her dream. She was not mistaken. Opposite her stood her arch-horror, Benoni. He leaned carelessly against the stone well, and his bright brown eyes were riveted upon her. His tall, thin figure was clad, as usual, in all the extreme of fashion, and one of his long, bony hands toyed with his watch-chain. His animated face seemed aglow with the pleasure of contemplation, and the sunshine lent a yellow tinge to his snowy hair.

" An exquisite picture, indeed, countess," he said, without moving. " I trust your dreams were as sweet as they looked ? "

"They were sweet, sir," she answered coldly, after a moment's pause, during which she looked steadily toward him.

"I regret that I should have disturbed them," he said with a deferential bow; and he came and sat by her side, treading as lightly as a boy across the flags. Hedwig shuddered, and drew her dark skirts about her, as he sat down.

"You cannot regret it more than I do," she said, in tones of ice. She would not take refuge in the house, for it would have seemed like an ignominious flight. Benoni crossed one leg over the other, and asked permission to smoke, which she granted by an indifferent motion of her fair head.

"So we are left all alone to-day, countess," remarked Benoni, blowing rings of smoke in the quiet air.

Hedwig vouchsafed no answer.

"We are left alone," he repeated, seeing that she was silent, "and I make it hereby my business and my pleasure to amuse you."

"You are good, sir. But I thank you. I need no entertainment of your devising."

"That is eminently unfortunate," returned the baron, with his imperturbable smile, "for I am universally considered to be the most amusing of mortals, — if, indeed, I am mortal at all, which I sometimes doubt."

"Do you reckon yourself with the gods, then?" asked Hedwig scornfully. "Which of them are you? Jove? Dionysus? Apollo?"

"Nay, rather Phaethon, who soared too high" —

"Your mythology is at fault, sir, — he drove too low; and besides, he was not immortal."

"It is the same. He was wide of the mark, as I am. Tell me, countess, are your wits always so ready?"

"You, at least, will always find them so," she answered bitterly.

"You are unkind. You stab my vanity, as you have pierced my heart."

At this speech, Hedwig raised her eyebrows, and stared at him in silence. Any other man would have taken the chilling rebuke, and left her. Benoni put on a sad expression.

"You used not to hate me as you do now," he said.

"That is true. I hated you formerly because I hated you."

"And now?" asked Benoni, with a short laugh.

"I hate you now because I loathe you." She uttered this singular saying indifferently, as being part of her daily thoughts.

"You have the courage of your opinions, countess," he replied, with a very bitter smile.

"Yes? It is the only courage a woman need have." There was a pause, during which Benoni puffed much smoke and stroked his white mustache. Hedwig turned over the leaves of her book, as though hinting to him to go. But he had no idea of that. A man who will not go because a woman loathes him will certainly not leave her for a hint.

"Countess," he began again, at last, "will you listen to me?"

19

"I suppose I must. I presume my father has left you here to insult me at your noble leisure."

"Ah, countess, dear countess," — she shrank away from him, — "you should know me better than to believe me capable of anything so monstrous. I insult you? Gracious Heaven! I, who adore you; who worship the holy ground whereon you tread; who would preserve the precious air you have breathed, in vessels of virgin crystal; who would give a drop of my blood for every word you vouchsafe me, kind or cruel, — I, who look on you as the only divinity in this desolate heathen world, who reverence you and do you daily homage, who adore you " —

"You manifest your adoration in a singular manner, sir," said Hedwig, interrupting him with something of her father's severity.

"I show it as best I can," the old scoundrel pleaded, working himself into a passion of words. "My life, my fortune, my name, my honor, — I cast them at your feet. For you I will be a hermit, a saint, dwelling in solitary places and doing good works; or I will brave every danger the narrow earth holds, by sea and land, for you. What? Am I decrepit, or bent, or misshapen, that my white hair should cry out against me? Am I hideous, or doting, or half-witted, as old men are? I am young; I am strong, active, enduring. I have all the gifts, for you."

The baron was speaking French, and perhaps these wild praises of himself might pass current in a foreign language. But when Nino detailed the conversation to me in our good, simple Italian speech, it sounded so amazingly ridiculous that I nearly broke my sides with laughing.

Hedwig laughed also, and so loudly that the foolish old man was disconcerted. He had succeeded in amusing her sooner than he had expected. As I have told you, the baron is a most impulsive person, though he is poisoned with evil from his head to his heart.

"All women are alike," he said, and his manner suddenly changed.

"I fancy," said Hedwig, recovering from her merriment, "that if you address them as you have addressed me you will find them very much alike indeed."

"What good can women do in the world?" sighed Benoni, as though speaking with himself. "You do nothing but harm with your cold calculations and your bitter jests." Hedwig was silent. "Tell me," he continued presently, "if I speak soberly, by the card as it were, will you listen to me?"

"Oh, I have said that I will listen to you!" cried Hedwig, losing patience.

"Hedwig von Lira, I hereby offer you my fortune, my name, and myself. I ask you to marry me of your own good-will and pleasure." Hedwig once more raised her brows.

"Baron Benoni, I will not marry you, either for your fortune, your name, or yourself, — nor for any

other consideration under heaven. And I will ask
you not to address me by my Christian name."
There was a long silence after this speech, and
Benoni carefully lighted a second cigarette. Hedwig would have risen and entered the house, but
she felt safer in the free air of the sunny court.
As for Benoni, he had no intention of going.

" I suppose you are aware, countess," he said at
last, coldly eyeing her, " that your father has set
his heart upon our union ? "

" I am aware of it."

" But you are not aware of the consequences
of your refusal. I am your only chance of freedom. Take me, and you have the world at your
feet. Refuse me, and you will languish in this
hideous place so long as your affectionate father
pleases."

" Do you know my father so little, sir," asked
Hedwig very proudly, " as to suppose that his
daughter will ever yield to force ? "

" It is one thing to talk of not yielding, and it is
quite another to bear prolonged suffering with constancy," returned Benoni coolly, as though he were
discussing a general principle instead of expounding to a woman the fate she had to expect if she
refused to marry him. " I never knew any one
who did not talk. bravely of resisting. torture until
it was applied. Oh, you will be weak at the end,
countess, believe me. You are weak now, and
changed, though perhaps you would be better
pleased if I did not notice it. Yes, I smile now,

— I laugh. I can afford to. You can be merry over me because I love you, but I can be merry at what you must suffer if you will not love me. Do not look so proud, countess. You know what follows pride, if the proverb lies not."

During this insulting speech Hedwig had risen to her feet, and in the act to go she turned and looked at him in utter scorn. She could not comprehend the nature of a man who could so coldly threaten her. If ever any one of us can fathom Benoni's strange character, we may hope to understand that phase of it along with the rest. He seemed as indifferent to his own mistakes and follies as to the sufferings of others.

" Sir," she said, " whatever may be the will of my father, I will not permit you to discuss it, still less to hold up his anger as a threat to scare me. You need not follow me," she added, as he rose.

" I will follow you, whether you wish it or not, countess," he said fiercely ; and as she flew across the court to the door he strode swiftly by her side, hissing his words into her ear. " I will follow you to tell you that I know more of you than you think, and I know how little right you have to be so proud. I know your lover. I know of your meetings, your comings and your goings " — They reached the door, but Benoni barred the way with his long arm, and seemed about to lay a hand upon her wrist, so that she shrank back against the heavy doorpost, in an agony of horror and loathing and wounded pride. "I know Cardegna, and I

knew the poor baroness, who killed herself because
he basely abandoned her. Ah, you never heard
the truth before? I trust it is pleasant to you.
As he left her, he has left you. He will never
come back. I saw him in Paris three weeks ago.
I could tell tales not fit for your ears. And for
him you will die in this horrible place, unless you
consent. For him you have thrown away everything, — name, fame, and happiness, — unless you
will take all these from me. Oh, I know, — you
will cry out that it is untrue; but my eyes are
good, though you call me old! For this treacher-
ous boy, with his curly hair, you have lost the only
thing that makes woman human, — your reputation!" And Benoni laughed that horrid laugh of
his, till the court rang again, as though there were
devils in every corner, and beneath every eave, and
everywhere.

People who are loud in their anger are sometimes
dangerous, for it is genuine while it lasts. People
whose anger is silent are generally either incapable
of honest wrath or cowards. But there are some
in the world whose passion shows itself in few
words but strong ones, and proceeds instantly to
action.

Hedwig had stood back against the stone casing
of the entrance, at first, overcome with the intensity
of what she suffered. But as Benoni laughed she
moved slowly forwards till she was close to him,
and only his outstretched arm barred the doorway.

" Every word you have spoken is a lie, and you know it. Let me pass, or I will kill you with my hands ! "

The words came low and distinct to his excited ear, like the tolling of a 'passing bell. Her face must have been dreadful to see, and Benoni was suddenly fascinated and terrified at the concentrated anger that blazed in her blue eyes. His arm dropped to his side, and Hedwig passed proudly through the door, in all the majesty of innocence, gathering her skirts, lest they should touch his feet or any part of him. She never hastened her step as she ascended the broad stairs within and went to her own little sitting-room, made gay with books and flowers and photographs from Rome. Nor was her anger followed by any passionate outburst of tears. She sat herself down by the window and looked out, letting the cool breeze from the open casement fan her face.

Hedwig, too, had passed through a violent scene that day, and, having conquered, she sat down to think over it. She reflected that Benoni had but used the same words to her that she had daily heard from her father's lips. False as was their accusation, she submitted to hearing her father speak them, for she had no knowledge of their import, and only thought him cruelly hard with her. But that a stranger — above all, a man who aspired, or pretended to aspire, to her hand — should attempt to usurp the same authority of speech was beyond all human endurance. She felt sure that her father's anger would all be turned against Benoni when he heard her story.

As for what her tormentor had said of Nino, she could have killed him for saying it, but she knew that it was a lie ; for she loved Nino with all her heart, and no one can love wholly without trusting wholly. Therefore she put away the evil suggestion from herself, and loaded all its burden of treachery upon Benoni.

How long she sat by the window, compelling her strained thoughts into order, no one can tell. It might have been an hour, or more, for she had lost the account of the hours. She was roused by a knock at the door of her sitting-room, and at her bidding the man entered who, for the trifling consideration of about a thousand francs, first and last, made communication possible between Hedwig and myself.

This man's name is Temistocle, — Themistocles, no less. All servants are Themistocles, or Orestes, or Joseph, just as all gardeners are called Antonio. Perhaps he deserves some description. He is a type, short, wiry, and broad-shouldered, with a cunning eye, a long, hooked nose, and plentiful black whiskers, and coarse, closely cropped black hair. His motions are servile to the last degree, and he addresses every one in authority as "excellency," on the principle that it is better to give too much titular homage than too little. He is as wily as a fox, and so long as you have money in your pocket, as faithful as a hound and as silent as the grave. I perceive that these are precisely the epithets at which the baron scoffed, saying that a man can be praised only by comparing him with the higher animals, or insulted by comparison with himself and his kind. We call a man a fool, an idiot, a coward, a liar, a traitor, and many other things applicable only to man himself. However, I will let my description stand, for it is a very good one; and Temistocle could be induced, for money, to adapt himself to almost any description, and he certainly had earned, at one time or another, most of the titles I have enumerated.

He told me, months afterwards, that when he passed through the courtyard, on his way to Hedwig's apartment, he found Benoni seated on the stone bench, smoking a cigarette and gazing into space, so that he passed close before him without being noticed.

XIX.

TEMISTOCLE closed the door, then opened it
again, and looked out, after which he finally shut
it, and seemed satisfied. He advanced with cau-
tious tread to where Hedwig sat by the window.

"Well? What have you done?" she inquired,
without looking at him. It is a hard thing for a
proud and noble girl to be in the power of a servant. The man took Nino's letter from his pocket,
and handed it to her upon his open palm. Hedwig
tried hard to take it with indifference, but she ac-
knowledges that her fingers trembled and her heart
beat fast.

"I was to deliver a message to your excellency,
from the old gentleman," said Temistocle, coming
close to her and bending down.

"Ah!" said Hedwig, opening the envelope.

"Yes, excellency. He desired me to say that it
was absolutely and most indubitably necessary that
your excellency should be at the little door to-night
at twelve o'clock. Do not fear, Signora Contessina; we can manage it very well."

"I do not wish to know what you advise me to
fear, or not to fear," answered Hedwig, haughtily;
for she could not bear to feel that the man should
counsel her or encourage her.

"Pardon, excellency; I thought" — began Temistocle humbly; but Hedwig interrupted him.

"Temistocle," she said, "I have no money to give you, as I told you yesterday. But here is another stone, like the other. Take it, and arrange this matter as best you can."

Temistocle took the jewel and bowed to the ground, eying curiously the little case from which she had taken it.

"I have thought and combined everything," he said. "Your excellency will see that it is best you should go alone to the staircase; for, as we say, a mouse makes less noise than a rat. When you have descended, lock the door at the top behind you; and when you reach the foot of the staircase, keep that door open. I will have brought the old gentleman, by that time, and you will let me in. I shall go out by the great gate."

"Why not go with me?" inquired Hedwig.

"Because, your excellency, one person is less likely to be seen than two. Your excellency will let me pass you. I will mount the staircase, unlock the upper door, and change the key to the other side. Then I will watch, and if any one comes I will lock the door and slip away till he is gone."

"I do not like the plan," said Hedwig. "I would rather let myself in from the staircase."

"But suppose any one were waiting on the inside, and saw you come back?"

"That is true. Give me the keys, Temistocle, and a taper and some matches."

" Your excellency is a paragon of courage," replied the servant, obsequiously. " Since yesterday I have carried the keys in my pocket. I will bring you the taper this evening."

" Bring it now. I wish to be ready."

Temistocle departed on the errand. When he returned, Hedwig ordered him to give a message to her father.

" When the count comes home, ask him to see me," she said. Temistocle bowed once more, and was gone.

Yes, she would see her father, and tell him plainly what she had suffered from Benoni. She felt that no father, however cruel, would allow his daughter to be so treated, and she would detail the conversation to him.

She had not been able to read Nino's letter, for she feared the servant, knowing the writing to be Italian and legible to him. Now she hastened to drink in its message of love. You cannot suppose that I know exactly what he said, but he certainly set forth at some length his proposal that she should leave her father, and escape with her lover from the bondage in which she was now held. He told her modestly of his success, in so far as it was necessary that she should understand his position. It must have been a very eloquent letter, for it nearly persuaded her to a step of which she had wildly dreamed, indeed, but which in her calmer moments she regarded as impossible.

The interminable afternoon was drawing to a

close, and once more she sat by the open window, regardless of the increasing cold. Suddenly it all came over her, — the tremendous importance of the step she was about to take, if she should take Nino at his word, and really break from one life into another. The long-restrained tears, that had been bound from flowing through all Benoni's insults and her own anger, trickled silently down her cheek, no longer pale, but bright and flushed at the daring thought of freedom.

At first it seemed far off, as seen in a magician's glass. She looked, and saw herself as another person, acting a part only half known and half understood. But gradually her own individual soul entered into the figure of her imagination; her eager heart beat fast; she breathed and moved and acted in the future. She was descending the dark steps alone, listening with supernatural sense of sound for her lover's tread without. It came; the door opened, and she was in his arms, — in those strong arms that could protect her from insult and tyranny and cruel wooing; out in the night, on the road, in Rome, married, free and made blessed forever. On a sudden the artificial imagery of her laboring brain fell away, and the thought crossed her mind that henceforth she must be an orphan. Her father would never speak to her again, or ever own for his a daughter that had done such a deed. Like icy water poured upon a fevered body, the idea chilled her and woke her to reality.

Did she love her father? She had loved him, —

yes, until she crossed his will. She loved him still, when she could be so horror-struck at the thought of incurring his lasting anger. Could she bear it? Could she find in her lover all that she must renounce of a father's care and a father's affection,— stern affection, that savored of the despot,— but could she hurt him so?

The image of her father seemed to take another shape, and gradually to assume the form and features of the one man of the world whom she hated, converting itself little by little into Benoni. She hid her face in her hands, and terror staunched the tears that had flown afresh at the thought of orphanhood.

A knock at the door. She hastily concealed the crumpled letter.

"Come in!" she answered boldly; and her father, moving mechanically, with his stick in his hand, entered the room. He came as he had dismounted from his horse, in his riding boots, and his broad felt hat caught by the same fingers that held the stick.

"You wished to see me, Hedwig," he said coldly, depositing his hat upon the table. Then, when he had slowly sat himself down in an armchair, he added, "Here I am." Hedwig had risen respectfully, and stood before him in the twilight. "What do you wish to say?" he asked in German. "You do not often honor your father by requesting his society."

Hedwig stood one moment in silence. Her first

impulse was to throw herself at his feet, and implore him to let her marry Nino. The thought swept away for the time the remembrance of Benoni and of what she had to tell. But a second sufficed to give her the mastery of her tongue and memory, which women seldom lose completely, even at the most desperate moments.

"I desired to tell you," she said, "that Baron Benoni took advantage of your absence to-day to insult me beyond my endurance." She looked boldly into her father's eyes as she spoke.

"Ah!" said he, with great coolness. "Will you be good enough to light one of those candles on the table, and to close the window?"

Hedwig obeyed in silence, and once more planted herself before him, her slim figure looking ghostly between the fading light of the departing day and the yellow flame of the candle.

"You need not assume this theatrical air," said Lira calmly. "I presume you mean that Baron Benoni asked you to marry him?"

"Yes, that is one thing, and is an insult in itself," replied Hedwig, without changing her position.

"I suspect that it is the principal thing," remarked the count. "Very good; he asked you to marry him. He has my full authority to do so. What then?"

"You are my father," answered Hedwig, standing like a statue before him, "and you have the right to offer me whom you please for a husband.

But you have no authority to allow me to be wantonly insulted."

" I think that you are out of your mind," said the count, with imperturbable equanimity. " You grant that I may propose a suitor to you, and you call it a wanton insult when that suitor respectfully asks the honor of your hand, merely because he is not young enough to suit your romantic tastes, which have been fostered by this wretched southern air. It is unfortunate that my health requires me to reside in Italy. Had you enjoyed an orderly Prussian education, you would have held different views in regard to filial duty. Refuse Baron Benoni as often as you like. I will stay here, and so will he, I fancy, until you change your mind. I am not tired of this lordly mountain scenery, and my health improves daily. We can pass the summer and winter, and more summers and winters, very comfortably here. If there is anything you would like to have brought from Rome, inform me, and I will satisfy any reasonable request."

" The baron has already had the audacity to inform me that you would keep me a prisoner until I should marry him," said Hedwig; and her voice trembled as she remembered how Benoni had told her so.

" I doubt not that Benoni, who is a man of consummate tact, hinted delicately that he would not desist from pressing his suit. You, well knowing my determination, and carried away by your evil temper, have magnified into a threat what he never intended as such. Pray let me hear no more about these fancied insults." The old man smiled grimly at his keen perception.

"You shall hear me, nevertheless," said Hedwig in a low voice, coming close to the table, and resting one hand upon it as though for support.

"My daughter," said the count, "I desire you to abandon this highly theatrical and melodramatic tone. I am not to be imposed upon."

"Baron Benoni did not confine himself to the course you describe. He said many things to me that I did not understand, but I comprehended their import. He began by making absurd speeches, at which I laughed. Then he asked me to marry him, as I had long known he would do as soon as you gave him the opportunity. I refused his offer. Then he insisted, saying that you, sir, had determined on this marriage, and would keep me a close prisoner here until the torture of the situation broke down my strength. I assured him that I would never yield to force. Then he broke out angrily, telling me to my face that I had lost everything, — name, fame, and honor, — how, I cannot tell; but he said those words, adding that I could regain my reputation only by consenting to marry him."

The old count had listened at first with a sarcastic smile, then with increased attention. Finally, as Hedwig repeated the shameful insult, his brave old blood boiled up in his breast, and he sat gripping the two arms of his chair fiercely, while his gray eyes shot fire from beneath the shaggy brows.

20

"Hedwig," he cried hoarsely, "are you speaking the truth? Did he say those words?"

, "Yes, my father, and more like them. Are you surprised?" she asked bitterly. "You have said them yourself to me."

، The old man's rage rose furiously, and he struggled to his feet. He was stiff with riding and rheumatism, but he was too angry to sit still.

"I? Yes, I have tried to show you what might have happened, and to warn you and frighten you, as you should be frightened. Yes, and I was right, for you shall not drag my name in the dirt. But another man, — Benoni!" He could not speak, for his wrath, and his tall figure moved rapidly about the room, his heart seeking expression in action. He looked like some forgotten creature of harm, suddenly galvanized into destructive life. It was well that Benoni was not within reach.

Hedwig stood calmly by the table, proud in her soul that her father should be roused to such fury. The old man paused in his walk, came to her, and with his hand turned her face to the light, gazing savagely into her eyes.

"You never told me a lie," he growled out.

"Never," she said boldly, as she faced him scornfully. He knew his own temper in his child, and was satisfied. The soldier's habit of self-control was strong in him, and the sardonic humor of his nature served as a garment to the thoughts he harbored.

"It appears," he said, "that I am to spend the

remainder of an honorable life in fighting with a pack of hounds. I nearly killed your old acquaintance, the Signor Professore Cardegna, this afternoon." Hedwig staggered back, and turned pale.

"What! Is he wounded?" she gasped out, pressing her hand to her side.

"Ha! That touches you almost as closely as Benoni's insult," he said savagely. "I am glad of it. I repent me, and wish that I had killed him. We met on the road, and he had the impertinence to ask me for your hand, — I am sick of these daily proposals of marriage; and then I inquired if he meant to insult me."

Hedwig leaned heavily upon the table, in an agony of suspense.

"The fellow answered that if I were insulted he was ready to fight then and there, in the road, with my pistols. He is no coward, your lover, — I will say that. The end of it was that I came home, and he did not."

Hedwig sank into the chair that her father had left, and hid her face.

"Oh, you have killed him!" she moaned.

"No," said the count shortly; "I did not touch a hair of his head. But he rode away toward Trevi." Hedwig breathed again. "Are you satisfied?" he asked, with a hard smile, enjoying the terror he had excited.

"Oh, how cruel you are, my father!" she said, in a broken voice.

"I tell you that if I could cure you of your in-

sane passion for this singer fellow, I would be as
cruel as the Inquisition," retorted the count. "Now
listen to me. You will not be troubled any longer
with Benoni, — the beast! I will teach him a lesson of etiquette. You need not appear at dinner
to-night. But you are not to suppose that our residence here is at an end. When you have made up
your mind to act sensibly, and to forget the Signor
Cardegna, you shall return to society, where you
may select a husband of your own position and fortune, if you choose; or you may turn Romanist,
and go into a convent, and devote yourself to good
works and idolatry, or anything else. I do not pretend to care what becomes of you, so long as you
show any decent respect for your name. But if you
persist in pining and moaning and starving yourself,
because I will not allow you to turn dancer and
marry a strolling player, you will have to remain
here. I am not such pleasant company when I am
bored, I can tell you, and my enthusiasm for the
beauties of nature is probably transitory."

"I can bear anything, if you will remove Benoni," said Hedwig quietly, as she rose from her
seat. But the pressure of the iron keys that she
had hidden in her bosom gave her a strange sensation.

"Never fear," said the count, taking his hat
from the table. "You shall be amply avenged of
Benoni and his foul tongue. I may not love my
daughter, but no one shall insult her. I will have
a word with him this evening."

" I thank you for that, at least," said Hedwig, as he moved to the door.

" Do not mention it," said he, and put his hand on the lock.

A sudden impulse seized Hedwig. She ran swiftly to him, and clasped her hands upon his arm.

" Father ! " she cried, pleadingly.

" What? "

" Father, do you love me ? " He hesitated one moment.

" No," he said sternly ; " you disobey me ; " and he went out in rough haste. The door closed behind him, and she was left standing alone. What could she do, poor child ? For months he had tormented her and persecuted her, and now she had asked him plainly if she still held a place in his heart, and he had coldly denied it.

A gentle, tender maiden, love-sick and mind-sick, yearning so piteously for a little mercy, or sympathy, or kindness, and treated like a mutinous soldier, because she loved so honestly and purely, — is it any wonder that her hand went to her bosom and clasped the cold, hard keys that promised her life and freedom? I think not. I have no patience with young women who allow themselves to be carried away by an innate bad taste and love for effect, quarreling with the peaceful destiny that a kind Providence has vouchsafed them, and with an existence which they are too dull to make interesting to themselves or to any one else ; finally making a desperate and foolish dash at notoriety by a

runaway marriage with the first scamp they can
find, and repenting in poverty and social ostracism
the romance they conceived in wealth and luxury.
They deserve their fate. But when a sensitive girl
is motherless, cut off from friends and pleasures,
presented with the alternative of solitude or marriage with some detested man, or locked up to forget a dream which was half realized and very sweet,
then the case is different. If she breaks her bonds,
and flies to the only loving heart she knows, forgive
her, and pray Heaven to have mercy on her, for
she takes a fearful leap into the dark.

Hedwig felt the keys, and took them from her
dress, and pressed them to her cheek, and her mind
was made up. She glanced at the small gilt clock,
and saw that the hands pointed to seven. Five
hours were before her in which to make her preparations, such as they could be.

In accordance with her father's orders, given
when he left her, Temistocle served her dinner in
her sitting-room; and the uncertainty of the night's
enterprise demanded that she should eat something,
lest her strength should fail at the critical moment.
Temistocle volunteered the information that her
father had gone to the baron's apartment, and had
not been seen since. She heard in silence, and
bade the servant leave her as soon as he had minis-
tered to her wants. Then she wrote a short letter
to her father, telling him that she had left him,
since he had no place for her in his heart, and that
she had gone to the one man who seemed ready

both to love and to protect her. This missive she folded, sealed, and laid in a prominent place upon the table, addressed to the count.

She made a small bundle, — very neatly, for she is clever with her fingers, — and put on a dark traveling dress, in the folds of which she sewed such jewels as were small and valuable and her own. She would take nothing that her father had given her. In all this she displayed perfect coolness and foresight.

The castle became intensely quiet as the evening advanced. She sat watching the clock. At five minutes before midnight she took her bundle and her little shoes in her hand, blew out her candle, and softly left the room.

XX

I NEED not tell you how I passed all the time
from Nino's leaving me until he came back in the
evening, just as I could see from my window that
the full moon was touching the tower of the castle.
I sat looking out, expecting him, and I was the
most anxious professor that ever found himself in
a ridiculous position. Temistocle had come, and
you know what had passed between us, and how we
had arranged the plan of the night. Most heartily
did I wish myself in the little amphitheatre of my
lecture-room at the University, instead of being
pledged to this wild plot of my boy's invention.
But there was no drawing back. I had been myself to the little stable next door, where I had kept
my donkey, and visited him daily since my arrival,
and I had made sure that I could have him at a
moment's notice by putting on the cumbrous saddle.
Moreover, I had secretly made a bundle of my effects, and had succeeded in taking it unobserved to
the stall, and I tied it to the pommel. I also told
my landlady that I was going away in the morning, with the young gentleman who had visited me,
and who, I said, was the engineer who was going
to make a new road to the Serra. This was not
quite true ; but lies that hurt no one are not lies at

all, as you all know, and the curiosity of the old woman was satisfied. I also paid for my lodging, and gave her a franc for herself, which pleased her very much. I meant to steal away about ten o'clock, or as soon as I had seen Nino and communicated to him the result of my interview with Temistocle.

The hours seemed endless, in spite of my preparations, which occupied some time ; so I went out when I had eaten my supper, and visited my ass, and gave him a little bread that was left, thinking it would strengthen him for the journey. Then I came back to my room, and watched. Just as the moonlight was shooting over the hill, Nino rode up the street. I knew him in the dusk by his broad hat, and also because he was humming a little tune through his nose, as he generally does. But he rode past my door without looking up, for he meant to put his mule in the stable for a rest.

At last he came in, still humming, and apologized for the delay, saying he had stopped a few minutes at the inn to get some supper. It could not have been a very substantial meal that he ate, in that short time.

" What did the man say ? " was his first question, as he sat down.

" He said it should be managed as I desired," I answered. " Of course I did not mention you. Temistocle — that is his name — will come at midnight, and take you to the door. There you will find this inamorata, this lady-love of yours, for whom you are about to turn the world upside down."

"What will you do yourself, Sor Cornelio?" he asked, smiling.

"I will go now and get my donkey, and quietly ride up the valley to the Serra di Sant' Antonio," I said. "I am sure that the signorina will be more at her ease if I accompany you. I am a very proper person, you see."

"Yes," said Nino pensively, "you are very proper. And besides, you can be a witness of the civil marriage."

"Diavolo!" I cried, "a marriage! I had not thought of that."

"Blood of a dog!" exclaimed Nino, "what on earth did you think of?" He was angry all in a moment.

"Piano, — do not disquiet yourself, my boy. I had not realized that the wedding was so near, — that is all. Of course you will be married in Rome, as soon as ever we get there."

"We shall be married in Ceprano to-morrow night, by the Sindaco, or the mayor, or whatever civil bishop they support in that God-forsaken Neapolitan town," said Nino, with great determination.

"Oh, very well; manage it as you like. Only be careful that it is properly done, and have it registered," I added. "Meanwhile, I will start."

"You need not go yet, caro mio ; it is not nine o'clock."

"How far do you think I ought to go, Nino?" I inquired. To tell the truth, the idea of going up the Serra alone was not so attractive in the even-

ing as it had been in the morning light. I thought
it would be very dark among those trees, and I had
still a great deal of money sewn between my waistcoats.

"Oh, you need not go so very far," said Nino.
" Three or four miles from the town will be enough.
I will wait in the street below, after eleven."

We sat in silence for some time afterwards, and
if I was thinking of the gloomy ride before me, I
am sure that Nino was thinking of Hedwig. Poor
fellow! I dare say he was anxious enough to see
her, after being away for two months, and spend-
ing so many hours almost within her reach. He
sat low in his chair, and the dismal rays of the
solitary tallow candle cast deep shadows on his
thoughtful face. Weary, perhaps, with waiting and
with long travel, yet not sad, but very hopeful, he
looked. No fatigue could destroy the strong, manly
expression of his features, and even in that squalid
room, by the miserable light, dressed in his plain
gray clothes, he was still the man of success, who
could hold thousands in the suspense of listening to
his slightest utterance. Nino is a wonderful man,
and I am convinced that there is more in him than
music, which is well enough when one can be as
great as he, but is not all the world holds. I am
sure that massive head of his was not hammered so
square and broad, by the great hands that forge
the thunderbolts of nations, merely that he should
be a tenor and an actor, and give pleasure to his
fellow-men. I see there the power and the strength

of a broader mastery than that which bends the
ears of a theatre audience. One day we may see
it. It needs the fire of hot times to fuse the ele-
ments of greatness in the crucible of revolution.
There is not such another head in all Italy as
Nino's that I ever have seen, and I have seen the
best in Rome. He looked so grand, as he sat there,
thinking over the future. I am not praising his
face for its beauty; there is little enough of that,
as women might judge. And besides, you will
laugh at my ravings, and say that a singer is a
singer, and nothing more, for all his life. Well,
we shall see in twenty years; you will, — perhaps
I shall not.

"Nino," I asked irrelevantly, following my own
train of reflection, "have you ever thought of anything but music — and love?" He roused himself
from his reverie, and stared at me.

"How should you be able to guess my thoughts?"
he asked at last.

"People who have lived much together often
read each other's minds. What were you thinking
of?" Nino sighed, and hesitated a moment before
he answered.

"I was thinking," he said, "that a musician's
destiny, even the highest, is a poor return for a
woman's love."

"You see: I was thinking of you, and wondering whether, after all, you will always be a singer."

"That is singular," he answered slowly. "I
was reflecting how utterly small my success on the

stage will look to me when I have married Hedwig von Lira."

" There is a larger stage, Nino mio, than yours."

" I know it," said he, and fell back in his chair again, dreaming.

I fancy that at any other time we might have fallen into conversation and speculated on the good old-fashioned simile which likens life to a comedy, or a tragedy, or a farce. But the moment was ill chosen, and we were both silent, being much pre-occupied with the immediate future.

A little before ten I made up my mind to start. I glanced once more round the room to see if I had left anything. Nino was still sitting in his chair, his head bent, and his eyes staring at the floor.

" Nino," I said, " I am going now. Here is an-other candle, which you will need before long, for these tallow things are very short.'" Indeed, the one that burned was already guttering low in the old brass candlestick. Nino rose and shook him-self.

" My dear friend," he said, taking me by both hands, " you know that I am grateful to you. I thank you, and thank you again, with all my heart. Yes, you ought to go now, for the time is approach-ing. We shall join you, if all goes well, by one o'clock."

" But, Nino, if you do not come ? "

" I will come, alone, or with her. If — if I should not be with you by two in the morning, go on alone, and get out of the way. It will be be-

cause I am caught by that old Prussian devil.
Good-by." He embraced me affectionately, and I
went out. A quarter of an hour later I was out of
the town, picking my way, with my little donkey,
over the desolate path that leads toward the black
Serra. The clatter of the beast's hoofs over the
stones kept time with the beatings of my heart, and
I pressed my thin legs close to his thinner sides for
company.

When Nino was left alone, — and all this I know
from him, — he sat again in the chair, and meditated; and although the time of the greatest event
in his life was very near, he was so much absorbed
that he was startled when he looked at his watch
and found that it was half past eleven. He had
barely time to make his preparations. His man
was warned, but was waiting near the inn, not
knowing where he was required, as Nino himself
had not been to ascertain the position of the lower
door, fearing lest he might be seen by Benoni. He
now hastily extinguished the light, and let himself
out of the house without noise. He found his countryman ready with the mules, ordered him to come
with him, and returned to the house, instructing
him to follow and wait at a short distance from
the door he would enter. Muffled in his cloak, he
stood in the street, awaiting the messenger from
Hedwig.

The crazy old clock of the church tolled the hour,
and a man wrapped in a nondescript garment, between a cloak and an overcoat, stole along the

moonlit street to where Nino stood, in front of my lodging.

"Temistocle!" called Nino, in a low voice, as the fellow hesitated.

"Excellency" — answered the man, and then drew back. "You are not the Signor Grandi!" he cried, in alarm.

"It is the same thing," replied Nino. "Let us go."

"But how is this?" objected Temistocle, seeing a new development. "It was the Signor Grandi whom I was to conduct." Nino was silent, but there was a crisp sound in the air as he took a bank-note from his pocket-book. "Diavolo!" muttered the servant, "perhaps it may be right, after all." Nino gave him the note.

"That is my passport," said he.

"I have doubts," answered Temistocle, taking it, nevertheless, and examining it by the moonlight. "It has no *visa*," he added, with a cunning leer. Nino gave him another. Then Temistocle had no more doubts.

"I will conduct your excellency," he said. They moved away, and Temistocle was so deaf that he did not hear the mules and the tramp of the man who led them, not ten paces behind him.

Passing round the rock, they found themselves in the shadow; a fact which Nino noted with much satisfaction, for he feared lest some one might be keeping late hours in the castle. The mere noise of the mules would attract no attention in a moun-

tain town, where the country people start for their
distant work at all hours of the day and night.
They came to the door. Nino called softly to the
man with the mules to wait in the shadow, and
Temistocle knocked at the door. The key ground
in the lock from within, but the hands that held it
seemed weak. Nino's heart beat fast.

"Temistocle!" called Hedwig's trembling voice.

"What is the matter, your excellency?" asked
the servant through the keyhole, not forgetting his
manners.

"Oh, I cannot turn the key! What *shall* I
do?"

Nino heard and pushed the servant aside.

"Courage, my dear lady," he said, aloud, that
she might know his voice. Hedwig appeared to
make a frantic effort, and a little sound of pain escaped her as she hurt her hands.

"Oh, what *shall* I do!" she cried piteously. "I
locked it last night, and now I cannot turn the
key!"

Nino pressed with all his weight against the
door. Fortunately it was strong, or he would have
broken it in, and it would have fallen upon her.
But it opened outward and was heavily bound with
iron. Nino groaned.

"Has your excellency a taper?" asked Temistocle suddenly, forcing his head between Nino's body
and the door, in order to be heard.

"Yes. I put it out."

"And matches?" he asked again.

"Yes."

"Then let your excellency light the taper, and drop some of the burning wax on the end of the key. It will be like oil." There was a silence. The key was withdrawn, and a light appeared through the hole where it had been. Nino instantly fastened his eye to the aperture, hoping to catch a glimpse of Hedwig. But he could not see anything save two white hands trying to cover the key with wax. He withdrew his eye quickly, as the hands pushed the key through again.

Again the lock groaned, — a little sob of effort, another trial, and the bolts flew back to their sockets. The prudent Temistocle, who did not wish to be a witness of what followed, pretended to exert gigantic strength in pulling the door open, and Nino, seeing him, drew back a moment, to let him pass.

" Your excellency need only knock at the upper door," he said to Hedwig, " and I will open. I will watch, lest any one should enter from above."

"You may watch till the rising of the dead," thought Nino, and Hedwig stood aside on the narrow step while Temistocle went up. One instant more, and Nino was at her feet, kissing the hem of her dress, and speechless with happiness, for his tears of joy flowed fast.

Tenderly Hedwig bent to him, and laid her two hands on his bare head, pressing down the thick and curly hair with a trembling, passionate motion.

21

" Signor Cardegna, you must not kneel there, —
nay, sir, I know you love me! Would I have
come to you else? Give me your hand — now —
do not kiss it so hard — no — Oh, Nino, my own
dear Nino "—

What should have followed in her gentle speech
is lacking, for many and most sweet reasons.   I
need not tell you that the taper was extinguished,
and they stood locked in each other's arms against
the open door, with only the reflection of the moon
from the houses opposite to illuminate their meeting.

There was and is to me something divinely perfect and godlike in these two virgin hearts, each so
new to their love, and each so true and spotless of
all other.   I am old to say sweet things of loving.
But I cannot help it; for though I never was as
they are, I have loved much in my time.   Like our
own dear Leopardi, I loved not the woman, but the
angel which is the type of all women, and whom
not finding I perished miserably as to my heart.
But in my breast there is still the temple where the
angel dwelt, and the shrine is very fragrant still
with the divine scent of the heavenly roses that
were about her.   I think, also, that all those who
love in this world must have such a holy place of
worship in their hearts.   Sometimes the kingdom of
the soul and the palace of the body are all Love's,
made beautiful and rich with rare offerings of great
constancy and faith; and all the countless creations
of transcendent genius, and all the vast aspirations

of far-reaching power, go up in reverent order to do homage at Love's altar, before they come forth, like giants, to make the great world tremble and reel in its giddy grooves.

And with another it is different. The world is not his ; he is the world's, and all his petty doings have its gaudy stencil blotched upon them. Yet haply even he has a heart, and somewhere in its fruitless fallows stands a poor ruin, that never was of much dignity at its best, — poor and broken, and half choked with weeds and briers ; but even thus the weeds are fragrant herbs, and the briers are wild roses, of few and misshapen petals, but sweet nevertheless. For this ruin was once a shrine, too, that his mean hands and sterile soul did try most ineffectually to build up as a shelter for all that was ever worthy in him.

Now, therefore, I say, Love, and love truly and long, — even forever ; and if you can do other things well, do them ; but if not, at least learn to do that, for it is a very gentle thing, and sweet in the learning. Some of you laugh at me, and say, Behold this old-fashioned driveler, who does not even know that love is no longer in the fashion ! By Saint Peter, Heaven will soon be out of the fashion, too, and Messer Satanas will rake in the just and the unjust alike, so that he need no longer fast on Fridays, having a more savory larder ! And no doubt some of you will say that hell is really so antiquated that it should be put in the museum at the University of Rome, for a curious old piece of theo-

logical furniture. Truth! it is a wonder it is not
worn out with digesting the tough morsels it gets,
when people like you are finally gotten rid of from
this world! But it is made of good material, and
will last, never fear! This is not the gospel of
peace, but it is the gospel of truth.

Loving hearts and gentle souls shall rule the
world some day, for all your pestiferous fashions;
and old as I am,—I do not mean aged, but well on
in years, — I believe in love still, and I always will.
It is true it was not given to me to love as Nino
loves Hedwig, for Nino is even now a stronger,
sterner man than I. His is the nature that can
never do enough; his the hands that never tire for
her; his the art that would surpass, for her, the
stubborn bounds of possibility. He is never weary
of striving to increase her joy of him. His philosophy is but that. No quibbles of "being" and
"not being" or wretched speculations concerning
the object of existence; he has found the true uni-
ty of unities, and he holds it fast.

Meanwhile, you object that I am not proceeding
with my task, and telling you more facts, recounting
more conversations, and painting more descriptions
Believe me, this one fact, that to love well is to be
all man can be, is greater than all the things men
have ever learned and classified in the dictionaries.
It is, moreover, the only fact that has consistently
withstood the ravages of time and social revolution; it is the wisdom that has opened, as by
magic, the treasures of genius, of goodness, and of

all greatness, for every one to see ; it is the vital elixir that has made men of striplings, and giants of cripples, and heroes of the poor in heart though great in spirit. Nino is an example : for he was but a boy, yet he acted like a man ; a gifted artist in a great city, courted by the noblest, yet he kept his faith.

But when I have taken breath I will tell you what he and Hedwig said to each other at the gate, and whether at the last she went with him, or stayed in dismal Fillettino for her father's sake.

XXI

"LET us sit upon the step and talk," said Hedwig, gently disengaging herself from his arms.

"The hour is advancing, and it is damp here, my love. You will be cold," said Nino, protesting against delay as best he could.

"No; and I must talk to you." She sat down, but Nino pulled off his cloak and threw it round her. She motioned him to sit beside her, and raised the edge of the heavy mantle with her hand. "I think it is big enough," said she.

"I think so," returned Nino; and so the pair sat side by side and hand in hand, wrapped in the same garment, deep in the shadow of the rocky door-way. "You got my letter, dearest?" asked Nino, hoping to remind her of his proposal.

"Yes, it reached me safely. Tell me, Nino, have you thought of me in all this time?" she asked, in her turn; and there was the joy of the answer already in the question.

"As the earth longs for the sun, my love, through all the dark night. You have never been out of my thoughts. You know that I went away to find you in Paris, and I went to London, too; and everywhere I sang to you, hoping you might be somewhere in the great audiences. But you never went to Paris at all. When I got Professor Grandi's letter saying that he had discovered you, I had but one night more to sing, and then I flew to you."

"And now you have found me," said Hedwig, looking lovingly up to him through the shadow.

" Yes, dear one ; and I have come just in time. You are in great trouble now, and I am here to save you from it all. Tell me, what is it all about ?"

" Ah, Nino dear, it is very terrible. My father declared I must marry Baron Benoni, or end my days here, in this dismal castle." Nino ground his teeth, and drew her even closer to him, so that her head rested on his shoulder.

" Infamous wretch ! " he muttered.

" Hush, Nino," said Hedwig gently ; " he is my father."

" Oh, I mean Benoni, of course," exclaimed Nino quickly.

" Yes, dear, of course you do," Hedwig responded. "But my father has changed his mind. He no longer wishes me to marry the Jew."

" Why is that, sweetheart ?"

" Because Benoni was very rude to me to-day, and I told my father, who said he should leave the house at once."

" I hope he will kill the hound ! " cried Nino, with rising anger. "And I am glad your father has still the decency to protect you from insult."

" My father is very unkind, Nino mio, but he is an officer and a gentleman."

" Oh, I know what that means, — a gentleman !

Fie on your gentlemen! Do you love me less, Hedwig, because I am of the people?"

For all answer Hedwig threw her arms round his neck passionately.

"Tell me, love, would you think better of me if I were noble?"

"Ah, Nino, how most unkind! Oh, no: I love you, and for your sake I love the people, — the strong, brave people, whose man you are."

"God bless you, dear, for that," he answered tenderly. "But say, will your father take you back to Rome, now that he has sent away Benoni?"

"No, he will not. He swears that I shall stay here until I can forget you." The fair head rested again on his shoulder.

"It appears to me that your most high and noble father has amazingly done perjury in his oath," remarked Nino, resting his hand on her hair, from which the thick black veil that had muffled it had slipped back. "What do you think, love?"

"I do not know," replied Hedwig, in a low voice.

"Why, dear, you have only to close this door behind you, and you may laugh at your prison and your jailer!"

"Oh, I could not, Nino; and besides, I am weak, and cannot walk very far. And we should have to walk very far, you know."

"You, darling? Do you think I would not and could not bear you from here to Rome in these arms?" As he spoke he lifted her bodily from the step.

"Oh!" she cried, half frightened, half thrilled, "how strong you are, Nino!"

"Not I; it is my love. But I have beasts close by, waiting even now; good stout mules, that will think you are only a little silver butterfly that has flitted down from the moon for them to carry."

"Have you done that, dear?" she asked doubtfully, while her heart leaped at the thought. "But my father has horses," she added, on a sudden, in a very anxious voice.

"Never fear, my darling. No horse could scratch a foothold in the place where our mules are as safe as in a meadow. Come, dear heart, let us be going." But Hedwig hung her head, and did not stir. "What is it, Hedwig?" he asked, bending down to her and softly stroking her hair. "Are you afraid of me?"

"No,—oh, no! Not of you, Nino,—never of you!" She pushed her face close against him, very lovingly.

"What then, dear? Everything is ready for us. Why should we wait?"

"Is it quite right, Nino?"

"Ah, yes, love, it is right,—the rightest right that ever was! How can such love as ours be wrong? Have I not to-day implored your father to relent and let us marry? I met him in the road"—

"He told me, dear. It was brave of you. And he frightened me by making me think he had killed you. Oh, I was so frightened, you do not know!"

"Cruel"— Nino checked the rising epithet.

" He is your father, dear, and I must not speak my mind. But since he will not let you go, what will you do? Will you cease to love me, at his orders?"

"Oh, Nino, never, never, never!"

"But will you stay here, to die of solitude and slow torture?" he pleaded passionately.

"I—I suppose so, Nino," she said, in a choking sob.

"Now, by Heaven, you shall not!" He clasped her in his arms, raising her suddenly to her feet. Her head fell back upon his shoulder, and he could see her turn pale to the very lips, for his sight was softened to the gloom, and her eyes shone like stars of fire at him from beneath the half-closed lids. But the faint glory of coming happiness was already on her face, and he knew that the last fight was fought for love's mastery.

"Shall we ever part again, love?" he whispered, close to her. She shook her head, her starry eyes still fastened on his.

"Then come, my own dear one,—come," and he gently drew her with him. He glanced, naturally enough, at the step where they had sat, and something dark caught his eye just above it. Holding her hand in one of his, as though fearful lest she should escape him, he stooped quickly and snatched the thing from the stair with the other. It was Hedwig's little bundle.

"What have you here?" he asked. "Oh, Hedwig, you said you would not come!" he added, half laughing, as he discovered what it was.

" I was not sure that I should like you, Nino,"
she said, as he again put his arm about her. Hedwig started violently. " What is that? " she exclaimed, in a terrified whisper.

" What, love ? "

" The noise ! Oh, Nino, there is some one on
the staircase, coming down. Quick, — quick!
Save me, for love's sake ! "

But Nino had heard, too, the clumsy but rapid
groping of heavy feet on the stairs above, far up
in the winding stone steps, but momentarily coming
nearer. Instantly he pushed Hedwig out to the
street, tossing the bundle on the ground, withdrew
the heavy key, shut the door, and double-turned
the lock from the outside, removing the key again
at once. Nino is a man who acts suddenly and
infallibly in great emergencies. He took Hedwig
in his arms, and ran with her to where the mules
were standing, twenty yards away.

The stout countryman from Subiaco, who had
spent some years in breaking stones out of consideration for the government, as a general confession of the inaccuracy of his views regarding
foreigners, was by no means astonished when he
saw Nino appear with a woman in his arms.
Together they seated her on one of the mules,
and ran beside her, for there was no time for Nino
to mount. They had to pass the door, and through
all its oaken thickness they could hear the curses
and imprecations of some one inside, and the wood
and iron shook with repeated blows and kicks. The

quick-witted muleteer saw the bundle lying where Nino had tossed it, and he picked it up as he ran.

Both Nino and Hedwig recognized Benoni's voice, but neither spoke as they hurried up the street into the bright moonlight, she riding and Nino running as he led the other beast at a sharp trot. In five minutes they were out of the little town, and Nino, looking back, could see that the broad white way behind them was clear of all pursuers. Then he himself mounted, and the country-man trotted by his side.

Nino brought his mule close to Hedwig's. She was an accomplished horsewoman, and had no difficulty in accommodating herself to the rough country saddle. Their hands met, and the mules, long accustomed to each other's company, moved so evenly that the gentle bond was not broken. But although Hedwig's fingers twined lovingly with his, and she often turned and looked at him from beneath her hanging veil, she was silent for a long time. Nino respected her mood, half guessing what she felt, and no sound was heard save an occasional grunt from the countryman as he urged the beasts, and the regular clatter of the hoofs on the stony road.

To tell the truth, Nino was overwhelmed with anxiety; for his quick wits had told him that Benoni, infuriated by the check he had received, would lose no time in remounting the stairs, saddling a horse, and following them. If only they could reach the steeper part of the ravine, they could bid defiance to any horse that ever galloped, for Benoni must inevitably come to grief if he attempted a pursuit into the desolate Serra. He saw that Hedwig had not apprehended the danger, when once the baron was stopped by the door, conceiving in her heart the impression that he was a prisoner in his own trap. Nevertheless, they urged the beasts onward hotly, if one may use the word of the long, heavy trot of a mountain mule. The sturdy countryman never paused. or gasped for breath, keeping pace in a steady, determined fashion.

But they need not have been disturbed, for Hedwig's guess was nearer the truth than Nino's reasoning. They knew it later, when Temistocle found them in Rome, and I may as well tell you how it happened. When he reached the head of the staircase, he took the key from the one side to the other, locked the door, as agreed, and sat down to wait for Hedwig's rap. He indeed suspected that it would never come, for he had only pretended not to see the mules; but the prospect of further bribes made him anxious not to lose sight of his mistress, and certainly not to disobey her, in case she really returned. The staircase opened into the foot of the tower, a broad stone chamber, with unglazed windows.

Temistocle sat himself down to wait on an old bench that had been put there, and the light of the full moon made the place as bright as day. Now the lock on the door was rusty, like the one below, and creaked loudly every time it was turned. But

Temistocle fancied it would not be heard in the great building, and felt quite safe. Sitting there, he nodded and fell asleep, tired with the watching.

Benoni had probably passed a fiery half hour with the count. But I have no means of knowing what was said on either side; at all events, he was in the castle still, and, what is more, he was awake. When Hedwig opened the upper door and closed it behind her, the sound was distinctly audible to his quick ears, and he probably listened and speculated, and finally yielded to his curiosity.

However this may have been, he found Temistocle asleep in the tower basement, saw the key in the lock, guessed whence the noise had come, and turned it. The movement woke Temistocle, who started to his feet, and recognized the tall figure of the baron just entering the door. Too much confused for reflection, he called aloud, and the baron disappeared down the stairs. Temistocle listened at the top, heard distinctly the shutting and locking of the lower door, and a moment afterwards Benoni's voice, swearing in every language at once, came echoing up.

"They have escaped," said Temistocle to himself. "If I am not mistaken, I had better do the same." With that he locked the upper door, put the key in his pocket, and departed on tiptoe. Having his hat and his overcoat with him, and his money in his pocket, he determined to leave the baron shut up in the staircase. He softly left the castle by the front gate, of which he knew the tricks, and he was not heard of for several weeks afterwards. As for Benoni, he was completely caught, and probably spent the remainder of the night in trying to wake the inmates of the building. So you see that Nino need not have been so much disturbed, after all.

While these things were happening Nino and Hedwig got fairly away, and no one but a mountaineer of the district could possibly have overtaken them. Just as they reached the place where the valley suddenly narrows to a gorge, the countryman spoke. It was the first word that had been uttered by any of the party in an hour, so great had been their haste and anxiety.

" I see a man with a beast," he said, shortly.

" So do I," answered Nino. " I expect to meet a friend here." Then he turned to Hedwig. " Dear one," he said, " we are to have a companion now, who says he is a very proper person."

" A companion? " repeated Hedwig, anxiously.

" Yes. We are to have the society of no less a person than the Professor Cornelio Grandi, of the University of Rome. He will go with us, and be a witness."

" Yes," said Hedwig, expecting more, " a witness " —

" A witness of our marriage, dear lady; I trust to-morrow, — or to-day, since midnight is past." He leaned far over his saddle-bow, as the mules clambered up the rough place. Her hand went out to him, and he took it. They were so near that I could see them. He dropped the reins and bared

his head, and so, riding, he bent himself still further, and pressed his lips upon her hand; and that
was all the marriage contract that was sealed between them. But it was enough.

There I sat, upon a stone in the moonlight, just
below the trees, waiting for them. And there I had
been for two mortal hours and more, left to meditate upon the follies of professors in general and of
myself in particular. I was beginning to wonder
whether Nino would come at all, and I can tell you
I was glad to see the little caravan. Ugh! it is an
ugly place to be alone in!

They rode up, and I went forward to meet
them.

" Nino mio," said I, " you have made me pass a
terrible time here. Thank Heaven, you are come;
and the contessina, too! Your most humble servant, signorina." I bowed low and Hedwig bent
a little forward, but the moon was just behind her,
and I could not see her face.

" I did not think we should meet so soon, Signor Grandi. But I am very glad." There was a
sweet shyness in the little speech that touched me.
I am sure she was afraid that it was not yet quite
right, or at least that there should be some other
lady in the party.

" Courage, Messer Cornelio," said Nino. " Mount
your donkey, and let us be on our way."

" Is not the contessina tired? " I inquired. " You
might surely rest a little here."

" Caro mio," answered Nino, " we must be safe

at the top of the pass before we rest. We were so
unfortunate as to wake his excellency the Baron
Benoni out of some sweet dream or other, and perhaps he is not far behind us."

An encounter with the furious Jew was not precisely attractive to me, and I was on my donkey before you could count a score. I suggested to Nino
that it would be wiser if the countryman led the
way through the woods, and I followed him. Then
the contessina would be behind me, and Nino would
bring up the rear. It occurred to me that the
mules might outstrip my donkey, if I went last,
and so I might be left to face the attack, if any
came; whereas, if I were in front, the others could
not go any faster than I.

22

THE gorge rises steep and precipitous between the lofty mountains on both sides, and it is fortunate that we had some light from the moon, which was still high at two o'clock, being at the full.

It is a ghastly place enough. In the days of the Papal States the Serra di Sant' Antonio, as it is called, was the shortest passage to the kingdom of Naples, and the frontier line ran across its summit. To pass from one dominion to the other it would be necessary to go out of the way some forty or fifty miles, perhaps, unless one took this route; and the natural consequence was that outlaws, smugglers, political fugitives, and all such manner of men found it a great convenience. Soldiers were stationed in Fillettino and on the other side, to check illicit traffic and brigandage, and many were the fights that were fought among these giant beeches.

The trees are of primeval dimensions, for no one has yet been enterprising enough to attempt to fell the timber. The gorge is so steep, and in many places so abruptly precipitous, that the logs could never be removed; and so they have grown undisturbed for hundreds of years, rotting and falling away as they stand. The beech is a lordly tree, with its great smooth trunk and its spreading branches, and though it never reaches the size of the chestnut, it is far more beautiful and long-lived.

Here and there, at every hundred yards or so, it seemed to me, the countryman would touch his hat and cross himself as he clambered up the rocky path, and then I did likewise; for there was always some rude cross or rough attempt at the inscription of a name at such spots, which marked where a man had met his untimely end. Sometimes the moon-beams struggled through the branches, still bare of leaves, and fell on a few bold initials and a date; and sometimes we came to a broad ledge where no trees were, but only a couple of black sticks tied at right angles for a cross. It was a dismal place, and the owls hooted at us.

Besides, it grew intensely cold towards morning, so that the countryman wanted to stop and make a fire to warm ourselves. Though it was the end of March, the ground was frozen as hard as any stone wherever it was free from rocks. But Nino dismounted, and insisted upon wrapping his cloak about Hedwig; and then he walked, for fear of catching cold, and the countryman mounted his mule and clambered away in front. In this way Hedwig and Nino lagged behind, conversing in low tones that sounded very soft; and when I looked round, I could see how he held his hand on her saddle and supported her in the rough places. Poor child, who would have thought she could bear such terrible work! But she had the blood of a soldierly old race in her veins, and would have struggled on silently till she died.

I think it would be useless to describe every stone on the desolate journey, but when the morning dawned we were at the top, and we found the descent much easier. The rosy streaks came first, quite suddenly, and in a few minutes the sun was up, and the eventful night was past. I was never so glad to get rid of a night in my life. It is fortunate that I am so thin and light, for I could never have reached the high-road alive had I been as fat as De Pretis is ; and certainly the little donkey would have died by the way. He was quite as thin when I sold him again as when I bought him, a fortnight before, in spite of the bread I had given him.

Hedwig drew her veil close about her face as the daylight broke, for she would not let Nino see how pale and tired she was. But when at last we were in the broad, fertile valley which marks the beginning of the old kingdom of Naples, we reached a village where there was an inn, and Nino turned every one out of the best room with a high hand, and had a couch of some sort spread for Hedwig. He himself walked up and down outside the door for five whole hours, lest she should be disturbed in her sleep. As for me, I lay on a bench, rolled in my cloak, and slept as I have not slept since I was twenty.

Nino knew that the danger of pursuit was past now, and that the first thing necessary was to give

Hedwig rest; for she was so tired that she could not eat, though there were very good eggs to be had, of which I ate three, and drank some wine, which does not compare to that on the Roman side.

The sturdy man from Subiaco seemed like iron, for he ate sparingly and drank less, and went out into the village to secure a conveyance and to inquire the nearest way to Ceprano.

But when, as I have said, Nino had guarded Hedwig's door for five hours he woke me from my sleep, and by that time it was about two in the afternoon.

"Hi, Messer Cornelio! wake up!" he cried, pulling my arm. And I rubbed my eyes.

"What do you want, Nino?" I inquired.

"I want to be married immediately," he replied, still pulling at my elbow.

"Well, pumpkin-head," I said angrily, "marry, then, in Heaven's name, and let me sleep! I do not want to marry anybody."

"But I do," retorted Nino, sitting down on the bench and laying a hand on my shoulder. He could still see Hedwig's door from where he sat.

"In this place?" I asked. "Are you serious?"

"Perfectly. This is a town of some size, and there must be a mayor here who marries people when they take the fancy."

"Diavolo! I suppose so," I assented.

"A sindaco, — there must be one, surely."

"Very well, go and find him, good-for-nothing!" I exclaimed.

"But I cannot go away and leave that door until she wakes," he objected. "Dear Messer Cornelio, you have done so much for me, and are so kind, — will you not go out and find the sindaco, and bring him here to marry us?"

"Nino," I said, gravely, "the ass is a patient beast, and very intelligent, but there is a limit to his capabilities. So long as it is merely a question of doing things you cannot do, very well. But if it comes to this, that I must find not only the bride, but also the mayor and the priest, I say, with good Pius IX., — rest his soul, — non possumus." Nino laughed. He could afford to laugh now.

"Messer Cornelio, a child could tell you have been asleep. I never heard such a string of disconnected sentences in my life. Come, be kind, and get me a mayor that I may be married."

"I tell you I will not," I cried stubbornly. "Go yourself."

"But I cannot leave the door. If anything should happen to her" —

"Macchè! What should happen to her, pray? I will put my bench across the door, and sit there till you come back."

"I am not quite sure" — he began.

"Idiot!" I exclaimed.

"Well, let us see how it looks." And with that he ousted me from my bench, and carried it, walking on tiptoe, to the entrance of Hedwig's room. Then he placed it across the door. "Now sit down," he said authoritatively, but in a whisper; and I

took my place in the middle of the long seat. He
stood back and looked at me with an artistic squint.

"You look so proper," he said, "that I am sure
nobody will think of trying the door while you sit
there. Will you remain till I come back?"

"Like Saint Peter in his chair," I whispered,
for I wanted to get rid of him.

"Well, then, I must risk whatever may happen,
and leave you here." So he went away. Now I
ask you if this was not a ridiculous position. But
I had discovered, in the course of my fortnight's
wanderings, that I was really something of a philosopher in practice, and I am proud to say that on
this occasion I smoked in absolute indifference to
the absurdity of the thing.

People came and stood at a distance in the passage, and eyed me curiously. But they knew I
belonged to the party of foreigners, and doubtless
they supposed it was the custom of my country to
guard doors in that way.

An hour passed, and I heard Hedwig stirring in
the room. After a time she came close to the door
and put her hand on the lock, so that it began to
rattle; but he hesitated, and went away again. I
once more heard her moving about. Then I heard
her open the window, and at last she came boldly
and opened the door, which turned inward. I sat
like a rock, not knowing whether Nino would like
me to turn round and look.

"Signor Grandi!" she cried at last in laughing
tones.

"Yes, signorina!" I replied respectfully, without moving. She hesitated.

"What are you doing in that strange position?" she asked.

"I am mounting guard," I answered. "And I promised Nino that I would sit here till he came back."

She fairly laughed now, and it was the most airy, silvery laugh in the world.

"But why do you not look at me?"

"I am not sure that Nino would let me," said I. "I promised not to move, and I will keep my promise."

"Will you let me out?" she asked, struggling with her merriment.

"By no means," I answered; "any more than I would let anybody in."

"Then we must make the best of it," said she. "But I will bring a chair and sit down, while you tell me the news."

"Will you assume all responsibility toward Nino, signorina, if I turn so that I can see you?" I asked, as she sat down.

"I will say that I positively ordered you to do so," she answered, gayly. "Now look, and tell me where Signor Cardegna is gone."

I looked indeed, and it was long before I looked away. The rest, the freedom, and the happiness had done their work quickly, in spite of all the dreadful anxiety and fatigue. The fresh, transparent color was in her cheeks, and her blue eyes were clear and bright. The statue had been through the fire, and was made a living thing, beautiful, and breathing, and real.

"Tell me," she said, the light dancing in her eyes, "where is he gone?"

"He is gone to find the mayor of this imposing capital," I replied. Hedwig suddenly blushed, and turned her glistening eyes away. She was beautiful so.

"Are you very tired, signorina? I ought not to ask the question, for you look as though you had never been tired in your life."

There is no saying what foolish speeches I might have made had not Nino returned. He was radiant, and I anticipated that he must have succeeded in his errand.

"Ha! Messer Cornelio, is this the way you keep watch?" he cried.

"I found him here," said Hedwig shyly, "and he would not even glance at me until I positively insisted upon it."

Nino laughed, as he would have laughed at most things in that moment, for sheer superfluity of happiness.

"Signorina," he said, "would it be agreeable to you to walk for a few minutes after your sleep? The weather is wonderfully fine, and I am sure you owe it to the world to show the roses which rest has given you."

Hedwig blushed softly, and I rose and went away, conceiving that I had kept watch long enough. But

Nino called after me, as he moved the bench from the door.

"Messer Cornelio, will you not come with us? Surely you need a walk very much, and we can ill spare your company. My lady, let me offer you my arm."

In this manner we left the inn, a wedding procession which could not have been much smaller, and the singing of an old woman, who sat with her distaff in front of her house, was the wedding march. Nino seemed in no great haste, I thought, and I let them walk as they would, while I kept soberly in the middle of the road, a little way behind.

It was not far that we had to go, however, and soon we came to a large brick house, with an uncommonly small door, over which hung a wooden shield with the arms of Italy brightly painted in green and red and white.

Nino and Hedwig entered arm in arm, and I slunk guiltily in after them. Hedwig had drawn her veil, which was the only head-dress she had, close about her face.

In a quarter of an hour the little ceremony was over, and the registers were signed by us all. Nino also got a stamped certificate, which he put very carefully in his pocket-book. I never knew what it cost Nino to overcome the scruples of the sindaco about marrying a strange couple from Rome in that outlandish place, where the peasants stared at us as though we had been the most unnatural curiosities, and even the pigs in the street jogged sullenly out of our way, as though not recognizing that we were human.

At all events, the thing was done, and Hedwig von Lira became for the rest of her life Edvigia Cardegna. And I felt very guilty. The pair went down the steps of the house together in front of me, and stopped as they reached the street; forgetting my presence, I presume. They had not forgotten me so long as I was needed to be of use to them; but I must not complain.

"We can face the world together now, my dear lady," said Nino, as he drew her little hand through his arm. She looked up at him, and I could see her side face. I shall never forget the expression. There was in it something I really never saw before, which made me feel as though I were in church; and I knew then that there was no wrong in helping such love as that to its fulfillment.

By the activity of the man from Subiaco, a curious conveyance was ready for us, being something between a gig and a cart, and a couple of strong horses were hired for the long drive. The countryman, who had grown rich in the last three days, offered to buy the thin little ass which had carried me so far and so well. He observed that he was blind of one eye, which I had never found out, and I do not believe it was true. The way he showed it was by snapping his fingers close to the eye in question. The donkey winked, and the countryman said that if the eye were good the beast would see that the noise was made by the fingers, and would not be frightened, and would therefore not wink.

" You see," said he, " he thinks it is a whip cracking, and so he is afraid."

" Do donkeys always wink when they are frightened? " I inquired. " It is very interesting."

"Yes," said the countryman, " they mostly do." At all events, I was obliged to take the man's own price, which was little enough — not a third of what I had given.

The roads were good, and the long and the short of the matter, without any more details, is that we reached Rome very early the next morning, having caught the night train from Naples. Hedwig slept most of the time in the carriage and all the time in the train, while Nino, who seemed never to tire or to need sleep, sat watching her with wide, happy eyes. But perhaps he slept a little, too, for I did, and I cannot answer for his wakefulness through every minute of the night.

Once I asked him what he intended to do in Rome.

" We will go to the hotel Costanzi," he answered, "which is a foreigners' resort. And if she is rested enough we will come down to you, and see what we can do about being married properly in church by the old curato."

" The marriage by the sindaco is perfectly legal," I remarked.

" It is a legal contract, but it is not a marriage that pleases me," he said gravely.

" But, caro mio, without offense, your bride is a
Protestant, a Lutheran ; not to mince matters, a
heretic.   They will make objections."

" She is an angel," said Nino, with great conviction.

" But the angels neither marry nor are given in
marriage," I objected, arguing the point to pass the
time.

" What do you make of it, then, Messer Cornelio?" he asked, with a smile.

" Why, as a heretic she ought to burn, and as an
angel she ought not to marry."

" It is better to marry than to burn," retorted
Nino triumphantly.

" Diavolo!   Have you had Saint Paul for a
tutor?" I asked, for I knew the quotation, being
fond of Greek.

" I heard a preacher cite it once at the Gesù, and
I thought it a good saying."

Early in the morning we rolled into the great
station of Rome, and took an affectionate leave of
each other, with the promise that Hedwig and Nino
would visit me in the course of the day.   I saw
them into a carriage, with Nino's small portmanteau
and Hedwig's bundle, and then mounted a modest
omnibus that runs from the Termini to St. Peter's,
and goes very near my house.

All the bells were ringing gladly, as if to welcome us, for it was Easter morning ; and though it
is not so kept as it used to be, it is nevertheless a
great feast.   Besides, the spring was at hand, and

the acacia-trees in the great square were budding, though everything was still so backward in the hills. April was at hand, which the foreigners think is our best month; but I prefer June and July, when the weather is warm, and the music plays in the Piazza Colonna of an evening. For all that, April is a glad time, after the disagreeable winter.

There was with me much peace on that Easter day, for I felt that my dear boy was safe after all his troubles. At least, he was safe from anything that could be done to part him from Hedwig; for the civil laws are binding, and Hedwig was of the age when a young woman is legally free to marry whom she pleases. Of course old Lira might still make himself disagreeable, but I fancied him too much a man of the world to desire a scandal, when no good could follow. The one shadow in the future was the anger of Benoni, who would be certain to seek some kind of revenge for the repulse he had suffered. I was still ignorant of his whereabouts, not yet knowing what I knew long afterwards, and have told you, because otherwise you would have been as much in the dark as he was himself, when Temistocle cunningly turned the lock of the stair-case door and left him to his curses and his meditations. I have had much secret joy in thinking what a wretched night he must have passed there, and how his long limbs must have ached with sitting about on the stones, and how hoarse he must have been from the dampness and the swearing.

I reached home, the dear old number twenty-seven in Santa Catarina dei Funari, by half past seven, or even earlier; and I was glad when I rang the bell on the landing, and called through the keyhole in my impatience.

" Mariuccia, Mariuccia, come quickly ! It is I! " I cried.

" O Madonna mia!" I heard her exclaim, and there was a tremendous clatter, as she dropped the coffee-pot. She was doubtless brewing herself a quiet cup with my best Porto Rico, which I do not allow her to use. She thought I was never coming back, the cunning old hag!

" Dio mio, Signor Professore ! A good Easter to you! " she cried, as I heard the flat pattering of her old feet inside, running to the door. " I thought the wolves had eaten you, padrone mio! " And at last she let me in.

XXIII.

"A TALL gentleman came here late last night, Signor Professore," said Mariuccia, as I sat down in the old green armchair. " He seemed very angry about something and said he must positively see you." The idea of Benoni flashed uneasily across my brain.

" Was he the grave signore who came a few days before I left? " I asked.

" Heaven preserve us! " ejaculated Mariuccia. " This one was much older, and seemed to be lame; for when he tried to shake his stick at me, he could not stand without it. He looked like one of the old Swiss guards at Palazzo." By which she meant the Vatican, as you know.

" It must have been the count," I said, thinking aloud.

" A count! A pretty sort of count, indeed, to come waking people from their beds in the night! He had not even a high hat like the one you wear when you go to the university. A count, indeed! "

" Go and make me some good coffee, Mariuccia," I said, eying her severely to show I suspected her of having used mine ; " and be careful to make it of my best Porto Rico, if you have any left, without any chicory."

" A count, indeed ! " she muttered angrily as she hobbled away, not in the least heeding my last remark, which I believed to be withering.

I had not much time for reflection that morning. My old clothes were in tatters, and the others looked very fine by contrast, so that when I had made my toilet I felt better able to show myself to the distinguished company I expected. I had seen so much extraordinary endurance in Nino and Hedwig during the last two or three days that I was prepared to see them appear at any moment, brushed and curled and ready for anything. The visit of the count, however, had seriously disturbed me, and I hardly knew what to look for from him. As it turned out I had not long to wait.

I was resting myself in the armchair, and smoking one of those infamous cigars that nearly suffocate me, just for company, and I was composing in my mind a letter to the authorities of the university, requesting that I might begin to lecture again. I did not find out until later that I need not have written to them at all when I went away, as ten days are always allowed at Easter, in any case. It is just like my forgetfulness, to have made such a mistake. I really only missed four lectures. But my composition was interrupted by the door-bell, and my heart sank in my breast. Mariuccia opened, and I knew by the sound of the stick on the bricks that the lame count had come to wreak his vengeance.

Being much frightened, I was very polite, and

bowed a great many times as he came toward me. It was he, looking much the same as ever, wooden and grizzly.

"I am much honored, sir," I began, "by seeing you here."

"You are Signor Grandi?" he inquired with a stiff bow.

"The same, Signor Conte, and very much at your service," I answered, rubbing my hands together to give myself an air of satisfaction.

"Let us not waste time," he said severely, but not roughly. "I have come to you on business. My daughter has disappeared with your son, or whatever relation the Signor Giovanni Cardegna is to you."

"He is no relation, Signor Conte. He was an orphan, and I" —

"It is the same," he interrupted. "You are responsible for his doings."

I responsible! Good heavens, had I not done all in my power to prevent the rashness of that hot-headed boy?

"Will you not sit down, sir?" I said, moving a chair for him. He took the seat rather reluctantly.

"You do not seem much astonished at what I tell you," he remarked. "It is evident that you are in the plot."

"Unless you will inform me of what you know, Signor Conte," I replied with urbanity, "I cannot see how I can be of service to you."

"On the contrary," said he, "I am the person to

ask questions. I wake up in the morning and find my daughter gone. I naturally inquire where she is."

"Most naturally, as you say, sir. I would do the same."

"And you, also very naturally, answer my questions," he continued severely.

"In that case, sir," I replied, "I would call to your attention the fact that you have asked but one question, — whether I were Signor Grandi. I answered that in the affirmative." You see I was apprehensive of what he might do, and desired to gain time. But he began to lose his temper.

"I have no patience with you Italians," he said gruffly; "you bandy words and play with them as if you enjoyed it."

Diavolo! thought I; he is angry at my silence. What will he be if I speak?

"What do you wish to know, Signor Conte?" I inquired in suave tones.

"I wish to know where my daughter is. Where is she? Do you understand? I am asking a question now, and you cannot deny it."

I was sitting in front of him, but I rose and pretended to shut the door, thus putting the table and the end of the piano between us, before I answered.

"She is in Rome, Signor Conte," I said.

"With Cardegna?" he asked, not betraying any emotion.

"Yes."

"Very well. I will have them arrested at once.

That is all I wanted." He put his crutch stick to
the floor as though about to rise. Seeing that his
anger was not turned against me, I grew bold.

" You had better not do that," I mildly observed,
across the table.

" And why not, sir?" he asked quickly, hesitating whether to get upon his feet or to remain
seated.

" Because they are married already," I answered,
retreating toward the door. But there was no need
for flight. He sank back in the chair, and the
stick fell from his hands upon the bricks with a
loud rattle. Poor old man! I thought he was
quite overcome by the news I had communicated.
He sat staring at the window, his hands lying idly
on his knees. I moved to come toward him, but he
raised one hand and began to twirl his great gray
mustache fiercely; whereat I resumed my former
position of safety.

" How do you know this?" he demanded on a
sudden.

" I was present at the civil marriage yesterday,"
I answered, feeling very much scared. He began
to notice my manœuvre.

" You need not be so frightened," he said coldly.
" It would be of no use to kill any of you now,
though I would like to."

" I assure you that no one ever frightened me in
my own house, sir," I answered. I think my voice
must have sounded very bold, for he did not laugh
at me.

"I suppose it is irrevocable," he said, as if to himself.

"Oh, yes, — perfectly irrevocable," I answered promptly. "They are married, and have come back to Rome. They are at the hotel Costanzi. I am sure that Nino would give you every explanation."

"Who is Nino," he asked.

"Nino Cardegna, of course " —

"And do you foolishly imagine that I am going to ask him to explain why he took upon himself to carry away my daughter?" The question was scornful enough.

"Signor Conte," I protested, "you would do well to see them, for she is your daughter, after all."

"She is not my daughter any longer," growled the count. "She is married to a singer, a tenor, an Italian with curls and lies and grins, as you all have. Fie!" And he pulled his mustache again.

"A singer," said I, "if you like, but a great singer, and an honest man."

"Oh, I did not come here to listen to your praises of that scoundrel!" he exclaimed hotly. "I have seen enough of him to be sick of him."

"I wish he were in this room to hear you call him by such names," I said; for I began to grow angry, as I sometimes do, and then my fear grows small and my heart grows big.

"Ah?" said he ironically. "And pray, what would he do to me?"

"He would probably ask you again for that

pistol you refused to lend him the other day." I
thought I might as well show that I knew all about
the meeting in the road. But Lira laughed grimly,
and the idea of a fight seemed to please him.

" I would not refuse it this time. In fact, since
you mention it, I think I will go and offer it to him
now. Do you think I should be justified, Master
Censor ? "

" No," said I, coming forward and facing him.
" But if you like you can fight me. I am your own
age, and a better match." I would have fought
him then and there, with the chairs, if he had liked.

" Why should I fight you ? " he inquired, in
some astonishment. "You strike me as a very
peaceable person indeed."

" Diavolo ! do you expect me to stand quietly
and hear you call my boy a scoundrel ? What do
you take me for, signore ? Do you know that I
am the last of the Conti Grandi, and as noble as
any of you, and as fit to fight, though my hair is
gray ? "

" I knew, indeed, that one member of that illustrious family survived in Rome," he answered
gravely, " but I was not aware that you were he. I
am glad to make your acquaintance, and I sincerely
wish that you were the father of the young man
who has married my daughter. If you were, I
should be ready to arrange matters." He looked
at me searchingly.

" Unfortunately, I am not any relation of his,"
I answered. " His father and mother were peasants

on my estate of Serveti, when it still was mine. They died when he was a baby and I took care of him and educated him."

."Yes, he is well educated," reflected the count, "for I examined him myself. Let us talk no more about fighting. You are quite sure that the marriage is legal."

"Quite certain. You can do nothing, and any attempt would be a useless scandal. Besides, they are so happy, you do not know."

"So happy, are they? Do you think I am happy, too?"

"A man has every reason to be so, when his daughter marries an honest man. It is a piece of good luck that does not happen often."

"Probably from the scarcity of daughters who are willing to drive their fathers to distraction by their disobedience and contempt of authority," he said savagely.

"No, — from the scarcity of honest men," I said. "Nino is a very honest man. You may go from one end of Italy to the other, and not meet one like him."

"I sincerely hope so," growled. Lira. "Otherwise Italy would be as wholly unredeemed and unredeemable as you pretend that some parts of it are now. But I will tell you, Conte Grandi, you cannot walk across the street, in my country, without meeting a dozen men who would tremble at the idea of such depravity as an elopement."

"Our ideas of honesty differ, sir," I replied.

" When a man loves a woman, I consider it honest in him to act as though he did, and not to go and marry another for consolation, beating her with a thick stick whenever he chances to think of the first. That seems to be the northern idea of domestic felicity." Lira laughed gruffly, supposing that my picture was meant for a jest. " I am glad you are amused," I added.

" Upon my honor, sir," he replied, "you are so vastly amusing that I am half inclined to forgive my daughter's rashness, for the sake of enjoying your company. First you intrench yourself behind your furniture ; then you propose to fight me ; and now you give me the most original views upon love and marriage that I ever heard. Indeed, I have cause to be amused."

"I am happy to oblige you," I said tartly ; for I did not like his laughter. " So long as you confine your amusement to me, I am satisfied ; but pray avoid using any objectionable language about Nino."

" Then my only course is to avoid the subject ? "

" Precisely," I replied, with much dignity.

" In that case I will go," he said. I was immensely relieved, for his presence was most unpleasant, as you may readily guess. He got upon his feet, and I showed him to the door with all courtesy. I expected that he would say something about the future before leaving me, but I was mistaken. He bowed in silence, and stumped down the steps with his stick.

I sank into my armchair with a great sigh of relief, for I felt that, for me at least, the worst was over. I had faced the infuriated father, and I might now face anybody with the consciousness of power. I always feel conscious of great power when the danger is past. Once more I lit my cigar, and stretched myself out to take some rest. The constant strain on the nerves was becoming very wearing, and I knew well that on the morrow I should need bleeding and mallows tea. Hardly was I settled and comfortable when I heard that dreadful bell again.

"This is the day of the resurrection indeed," cried Mariuccia frantically from the kitchen. And she hurried to the door. But I cannot describe to you the screams of joy and the strange sounds, between laughing and crying, that her leathern throat produced when she found Nino and Hedwig on the landing, waiting for admission. And when Nino explained that he had been married, and that this beautiful lady with the bright eyes and the golden hair was his wife, the old woman fairly gave way, and sat upon a chair in an agony of amazement and admiration. But the pair came toward me, and I met them with a light heart.

"Nino," said Hedwig, "we have not been nearly grateful enough to Signor Grandi for all he has done. I have been very selfish," she said penitently, turning to me.

"Ah no, signora," I replied, — for she was married now, and no longer "signorina," — "it is never selfish of such as you to let an old man do you service. You have made me very happy." And then I embraced Nino, and Hedwig gave me her hand, which I kissed in the old fashion.

" And so this is your old home, Nino," said Hedwig presently, looking about her, and touching the things in the room, as a woman will when she makes acquaintance with a place she has often heard of. " What a dear room it is! I wish we could live here!" How very soon a woman learns that " we " that means so much! It is never forgotten, even when the love that bred it is dead and cold.

" Yes," I said, for Nino seemed so enraptured, as he watched her, that he could not speak. " And there is the old piano, with the end on the boxes, because it has no leg, as I dare say Nino has often told you."

." Nino said it was a very good piano," said she.

" And indeed it is," he cried, with enthusiasm. " It is out of tune now, perhaps; but it is the source of all my fortune." He leaned over the crazy instrument and seemed to caress it.

" Poor old thing!" said Hedwig compassionately. " I am sure there is music in it still, — the sweet music of the past."

" Yes," said he, laughing, " it must be the music of the past, for it would not stand the ' music of the future,' as they call it, for five minutes. All the strings would break." Hedwig sat down on the chair that was in front of it, and her fingers

went involuntarily to the keys, though she is no
great musician.

"I can play a little, you know, Nino," she said
shyly, and looked up to his face for a response, not
venturing to strike the chords. And it would have
done you good to see how brightly Nino smiled and
encouraged her little offer of music, — he, the great
artist, in whose life music was both sword and scep-
tre. But he knew that she had greatness also of a
different kind, and he loved the small jewels in his
crown as well as the glorious treasures of its larger
wealth.

"Play to me, my love," he said, not caring now
whether I heard the sweet words or not. She
blushed a little, nevertheless, and glanced at me;
then her fingers strayed over the keys, and drew
out music that was very soft and yet very gay.
Suddenly she ceased, and leaned forward on the
desk of the piano, looking at him.

"Do you know, Nino, it was once my dream to
be a great musician. If I had not been so rich I
should have taken the profession in earnest. But
now, you see it is different, is it not?"

"Yes, it is all different now," he answered, not
knowing exactly what she meant, but radiantly
happy, all the same.

"I mean," she said, hesitating — "I mean that
now that we are to be always together, what you do
I do, and what I do you do. Do you understand?"

"Yes, perfectly," replied Nino, rather puzzled,
but quite satisfied.

"Ah no, dear," said she, forgetting my presence, and letting her hand steal into his as he stood, "you do not understand — quite. I mean that so long as one of us can be a great musician it is enough, and I am just as great as though I did it all myself."

Thereupon Nino forgot himself altogether, and kissed her golden hair. But then he saw me looking, for it was so pretty a sight that I could not help it, and he remembered.

"Oh!". he said, in a tone of embarrassment, that I had never heard before. Then Hedwig blushed very much, too, and looked away, and Nino put himself between her and me, so that I might not see her.

"Could you play something for me to sing, Hedwig?" he asked suddenly.

"Oh, yes! I can play 'Spirto gentil,' by heart," she cried, hailing the idea with delight.

In a moment they were both lost, and indeed so was I, in the dignity and beauty of the simple melody. As he began to sing, Nino bent down to her, and almost whispered the first words into her ear. But soon he stood erect, and let the music flow from his lips, just as God made it. His voice was tired with the long watching and the dust and cold and heat of the journey; but, as De Pretis said when he began, he has an iron throat, and the weariness only made the tones soft and tender and thrilling, that would perhaps have been too strong for my little room.

Suddenly he stopped short in the middle of a note, and gazed open-mouthed at the door. And I looked, too, and was horrified; and Hedwig, looking also, screamed and sprang back to the window, overturning the chair she had sat on.

In the doorway stood Ahasuerus Benoni, the Jew.

Mariuccia had imprudently forgotten to shut the door when Hedwig and Nino came, and the baron had walked in unannounced. You may imagine the fright I was in. But, after all, it was natural enough that, after what had occurred, he as well as the count should seek an interview with me, to obtain what information I was willing to give.

There he stood in his gay clothes, tall and thin and smiling as of yore.

XXIV.

NINO is a man for great emergencies, as I have had occasion to say, and when he realized who the unwelcome visitor was, he acted as promptly as usual. With a face like marble he walked straight across the room to Benoni and faced him.

"Baron Benoni," he said in a low voice, "I warn you that you are most unwelcome here. If you attempt to say any word to my wife, or to force an entrance, I will make short work of you." Benoni eyed him with a sort of pitying curiosity as he made this speech.

"Do not fear, Signor Cardegna. I came to see Signor Grandi, and to ascertain from him precisely what you have volunteered to tell me. You cannot suppose that I have any object in interrupting the leisure of a great artist, or the privacy of his very felicitous domestic relations. I have not a great deal to say. That is, I have always a great deal to say about everything, but I shall at present confine myself to a very little."

"You will be wise," said Nino, "and you would be wiser if you confined yourself to nothing at all."

"Patience, Signor Cardegna," protested Benoni. "You will readily conceive that I am a little out of breath with the stairs, for I am a very old man."

"In that case," I said, from the other side of the room, "I may as well occupy your breathing time by telling you that any remarks you are likely to make to me have been forestalled by the Graf von Lira, who has been with me this morning." Benoni smiled, but both Hedwig and Nino looked at me in surprise.

"I only wished to say," returned Benoni, "that I consider you in the light of an interesting phenomenon. Nay, Signor Cardegna, do not look so fierce. I am an old man" —

"An old devil!" said Nino, hotly.

"An old fool!" said I.

"An old reprobate!" said Hedwig, from her corner, in deepest indignation.

"Precisely," returned Benoni, smilingly. "Many people have been good enough to tell me so before. Thanks, kind friends; I believe you with all my heart. Meanwhile, man, devil, fool, or reprobate, I am very old. I am about to leave Rome for St. Petersburg, and I will take this last opportunity of informing you that in a very singularly long life I have met with only two or three such remarkable instances as this of yours."

"Say what you wish to say, and go," said Nino roughly.

"Certainly. And whenever I have met with such an instance I have done my very utmost to reduce it to the common level, and to prove to myself that no such thing really exists. I find it a dangerous thing, however; for an old man in love is likely to

exhibit precisely the agreeable and striking peculiarities you have so aptly designated." There was
something so odd about his manner and about the
things he said that Nino was silent, and allowed
him to proceed.

" The fact is," he continued, " that love is a very
rare thing, nowadays, and is so very generally an
abominable sham that I have often amused myself
by diabolically devising plans for its destruction.
On this occasion I very nearly came to grief myself.
The same thing happened to me some time ago, —
about forty years, I should say, — and I perceive
that it has not been forgotten. It may amuse you
to look at this paper, which I chance to have with
me. Good-morning. I leave for St. Petersburg at
once."

" I believe you are really the Wandering Jew ! "
cried Nino, as Benoni left the room.

" His name was certainly Ahasuerus," Benoni
replied from the outer door. " But it may be a
coincidence, after all. Good-by." He was gone.

I was the first to take up the paper he had thrown
upon a chair. There was a passage marked with a
red pencil. I read it aloud : —

" . . . Baron Benoni, the wealthy banker of St.
Petersburg, who was many years ago an inmate of
a private lunatic asylum in Paris, is reported to be
dangerously insane in Rome." That was all. The
paper was the Paris " Figaro."

" Merciful Heaven ! " exclaimed Hedwig, " and
I was shut up with that madman in Fillettino ! "

Nino was already by her side, and in his strong arms she forgot Benoni, and Fillettino, and all her troubles. We were all silent for some time. At last Nino spoke.

" Is it true that the count was here this morning? " he asked, in a subdued voice, for the extraordinary visit and its sequel had made him grave.

" Quite true," I said. " He was here a long time. I would not spoil your pleasure by telling you of it, when you first came."

" What did he — what did my father say ? "asked Hedwig presently.

" My dear children," I answered, thinking I might well call them so, " he said a great many unpleasant things, so that I offered to fight him if he said any more." At this they both laid hold of me and began to caress me ; and one smoothed my hair, and the other embraced me, so that I was half smothered.

" Dear Signor Grandi," cried Hedwig anxiously, " how good and brave you are ! " She does not know what a coward I am, you see, and I hope she will never find out, for nothing was ever said to me that gave me half so much pleasure as to be called brave by her, the dear child ; and if she never finds out, she may say it again, some day. Besides, I really did offer to fight Lira, as I have told you.

" And what is he going to do ? " asked Nino, in some anxiety.

" I do not know. I told him it was all legal, and that he could not touch you at all. I also said you

24

were staying at the hotel Costanzi, where he might
find you, if he wished."

"Oh! Did you tell him that?" asked Hedwig.

"It was quite right," said Nino. "He ought to
know, of course. And what else did you tell him?"

"Nothing especial, Nino mio. He went away in
a sort of ill temper because I would. not let him
abuse you as much as he pleased."

"He may abuse me and be welcome," said Nino.
"He has some right to be angry with me. But he
will think differently some day." So we chatted
away for an hour, enjoying the rest and the peace
and the sweet sunshine of the Easter afternoon.
But this was the day of interruptions. There was
one more visitor to come, — one more scene for me
to tell you, and then I have done.

A carriage drove down the street and seemed to
stop at the door of my house. Nino looked idly
out of the window. Suddenly he started.

"Hedwig, Hedwig!" he cried, "here is your father coming back!" She would not look out, but
stood back from the window, turning pale. If there
were one thing she dreaded, it was a meeting with
her father. All the old doubt as to whether she
had done right seemed to come back to her face in
a moment. But Nino turned and looked at her,
and his face was so triumphant that she got back
her courage, and clasping his hand bravely awaited
what was to come.

I myself went to the door, and heard Lira's slow
tread on the stairs. Before long he appeared, and

glanced up at me from the steps, which he climbed, one at a time, with his stick.

" Is my daughter here ? " he asked as soon as he reached me; and his voice sounded subdued, just as Nino's did when Benoni had gone. I conducted him into the room. It was the strangest meeting. The proud old man bowed stiffly to Hedwig, as though he had never before seen her. Nino and Hedwig also bent their heads, and there was a silence as of death in the sunny room.

" My daughter," said Von Lira at last, and with evident effort, " I wish to have a word with you. These two gentlemen — the younger of whom is now, as I understand it, your husband — may well hear what I wish to say."

I moved a chair so that he might sit down, but he stood up to his full height, as though not deigning to be older than the rest. I watched Hedwig, and saw how with both hands she clung to Nino's arm, and her lip trembled, and her face wore the look it had when I saw her in Fillettino.

As for Nino, his stern, square jaw was set, and his brows bent, but he showed no emotion, unless the darkness in his face and the heavy shadows beneath his eyes foretold ready anger.

" I am no trained reasoner, like Signor Grandi," said Lira, looking straight at Hedwig, " but I can ‸say plainly what I mean, for all that. There was a good old law in Sparta, whereby disobedient children were put to death without mercy. Sparta was a good country, — very like Prussia, but less great.

You know what I mean. You have cruelly disobeyed me, — cruelly, I say, because you have shown
me that all my pains and kindness and discipline
have been in vain. There is nothing so sorrowful
for a good parent as to discover that he has made
a mistake."

(The canting old proser, I thought, will he never
finish!)

" The mistake I refer to is not in the way I have
dealt with you," he went on, "for on that score I
have nothing to reproach myself. But I was mistaken in supposing you loved me. You have de-
spised all I have done for you."

"Oh, father! How can you say that?" cried
poor Hedwig, clinging closer to Nino.

"At all events, you have acted as though you
did. On the very day when I promised you to
take signal action upon Baron Benoni, you left me
by stealth, saying in your miserable letter that you
had gone to a man who could both love and protect
you."

"You did neither the one nor the other, sir,"
said Nino boldly, "when you required of your
daughter to marry such a man as Benoni."

"I have just seen Benoni; I saw him also on
the night you left me, madam," — he looked severely at Hedwig, — "and I am reluctantly forced
to confess that he is not sane, according to the or-.
dinary standard of the mind."

We had all known from the paper of the suspicion that rested on Benoni's sanity, yet somehow

there was a little murmur in the room when the old
count so clearly stated his opinion.

"That does not, however, alter the position in
the least," continued Lira, "for you knew nothing
of this at the time I desired you to marry him, and
I should have found it out soon enough to prevent
mischief. Instead of trusting to my judgment, you
took the law into your own hands, like a most unnatural daughter, as you are, and disappeared in
the night with a man whom I consider totally unfit
for you, however superior," he added, glancing at
Nino, "he may have proved himself in his own
rank of life."

Nino could not hold his tongue any longer. It
seemed absurd that there should be a battle of
words when all the realities of the affair were accomplished facts; but for his life he could not help
speaking.

"Sir," he said, addressing Lira, "I rejoice that
this opportunity is given me of once more speaking
clearly to you. Months ago, when I was betrayed
into a piece of rash violence, for which I at once
apologized to you, I told you under somewhat peculiar circumstances that I would yet marry your
daughter, if she would have me. I stand here to-day
with her by my side, my wedded wife, to tell you
that I have kept my word, and that she is mine by
her own free consent. Have you any cause to show
why she is not my wedded wife? If so, show it.
But I will not let you stand there and say bitter
and undeserved things to this same wife of mine,

abusing the name of father and the terms 'authority' and 'love,' forsooth! And if you wish to take vengeance on me personally, do so if you can. I will not fight duels with you now, as I was ready to do the day before yesterday. For then — so short a time ago — I had but offered her my life, and so that I gave it for her I cared not how nor when. But now she has taken me for hers, and I have no more right to let you kill me than I have to kill myself, seeing that she and I are one. Therefore, good sir, if you have words of conciliation to speak, speak them; but if you would only tell her harsh and cruel things, I say you shall not!"

As Nino uttered these hot words in good, plain Italian, they had a bold and honest sound of strength that was glorious to hear. A weaker man than the old count would have fallen into a fury of rage, and perhaps would have done some foolish violence. But he stood silent, eying his antagonist coolly, and when the words were spoken he answered.

"Signor Cardegna," he said, "the fact that I am here ought to be to you the fullest demonstration that I acknowledge your marriage with my daughter. I have certainly no intention of prolonging a painful interview. When I have said that my child has disobeyed me, I have said all that the question holds. As for the future of you two, I have naturally nothing more to say about it. I cannot love a disobedient child, nor ever

shall again. For the present, we will part; and if
at the end of a year my daughter is happy with
you, and desires to see me, I shall make no objec-
tion to such a meeting. I need not say that if she
is unhappy with you, my house will always be open
to her if she chooses to return to it."

"No, sir, most emphatically you need not say
it!" cried Nino, with blazing eyes. Lira took no
notice of him, but turned to go.

Hedwig would try once more to soften him,
though she knew it was useless.

"Father," she said, in tones of passionate en-
treaty, "will you not say you wish me well? Will
you not forgive me?" She sprang to him, and
would have held him back.

"I wish you no ill," he answered, shortly, pushing her aside, and he marched to the door, where
he paused, bowed as stiffly as ever, and disappeared.

It was very rude of us, perhaps, but no one accompanied him to the stairs. As for me, I would
not have believed it possible that any human being
could be so hard and relentlessly virtuous; and if
I had wondered at first that Hedwig should have
so easily made up her mind to flight, I was no
longer surprised when I saw with my own eyes how
he could treat her.

I cannot, indeed, conceive how she could have
borne it so long, for the whole character of the
man came out, hard, cold, and narrow, — such a
character as must be more hideous than any de-

scription can paint it, when seen in the closeness of daily conversation. But when he was gone the sun appeared to shine again, as he had shone all day, though it had sometimes seemed so dark. The storms were in that little room.

As Lira went out, Nino, who had followed Hedwig closely, caught her in his arms, and once more her face rested on his broad breast. I sat down and pretended to be busy with a pile of old papers that lay near by on the table, but I could hear what they said. The dear children, they forgot all about me.

"I am so sorry, dear one," said Nino, soothingly.

"I know you are, Nino. But it cannot be helped."

"But are you sorry, too, Hedwig?" he asked, stroking her hair.

"That my father is angry? Yes. I wish he were not," said she, looking wistfully toward the door.

"No, not that," said Nino. "Sorry that you left him, I mean."

"Ah, no, I am not sorry for that. Oh, Nino, dear Nino, your love is best." And again she hid her face.

"We will go away at once, darling," he said, after a minute, during which I did not see what was going on. "Would you like to go away?"

Hedwig moved her head to say "Yes."

"We will go, then, sweetheart. Where shall it

be?" asked Nino, trying to distract her thoughts from what had just occurred. "London? Paris? Vienna? I can sing anywhere now, but you must always choose, love."

"Anywhere, anywhere; only always with you, Nino, till we die together."

"Always, till we die, my beloved," he repeated. The small white hands stole up and clasped about his broad throat, tenderly drawing his face to hers, and hers to his. And it will be "always," till they die together, I think.

This is the story of that Roman singer whose great genius is making such a stir in the world. I have told it to you, because he is my own dear boy, as I have often said in these pages; and because people must not think that he did wrong to carry Hedwig von Lira away from her father, nor that Hedwig was so very unfilial and heartless. I know that they were both right, and the day will come when old Lira will acknowledge it. He is a hard old man, but he must have some affection for her; and if not, he will surely have the vanity to own so famous an artist as Nino for his son-in-law.

I do not know how it was managed, for Hedwig was certainly a heretic when she left her father, though she was an angel, as Nino said. But before they left Rome for Vienna there was a little wedding, early in the morning, in our parish church, for I was there; and De Pretis, who was really responsible for the whole thing, got some of his best singers from St. Peter and St. John on the Lateran to come and sing a mass over the two. I think that our good Mother Church found room for the dear child very quickly, and that is how it happened.

They are happy and glad together, those two hearts that never knew love save for each other, and they will be happy always. For it was nothing but love with them from the very first, and so it must be to the very last. Perhaps you will say that there is nothing in this story, either, but love. And if so, it is well; for where there is naught else there can surely be no sinning, or wrong-doing, or weakness, or meanness; nor yet anything that is not quite pure and undefiled.

Just as I finish this writing, there comes a letter from Nino to say that he has taken steps about buying Serveti, and that I must go there in the spring with Mariuccia and make it ready for him. Dear Serveti, of course I will go.

www.ingramcontent.com/pod-product-compliance
Lightning Source LLC
Chambersburg PA
CBHW030905270326
41929CB00008B/577